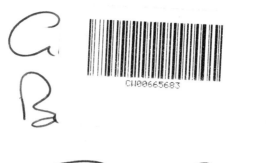

THE RISE OF
FOREST GREEN ROVERS

The Road to Wembley

Chris Gardner

To my late father, David Gardner.
He instilled the love of sport and sportsmanship
in his youngest son.
Never forgotten.

All profits from this book will go to Gloucestershire Deaf Association (GDA)
Charity No. 1015937, Company Registered by Guarantee No. 2692718
www.glosdeaf.org.uk

Published in 2016 by:

CM Cocks
Yolanda
Brewery Yard
Paganhill Lane
Stroud
Glos GL5 4JW

Typesetting & origination by Kerrin Cocks / kerrincocks@gmail.com
Cover design by iinde.com
Printed in the UK by CPI Anthony Rowe Ltd.

ISBN 978-0-9956043-0-8

British Library Cataloguing-in-Publication Data
A catalogue record for this book is available from the British Library

CONTENTS

Living confidently with
deafness and hearing loss

Gloucestershire Deaf Association (GDA)
by Jenny Hopkins (CEO)

GDA is an award-winning, Gloucestershire-based charity whose vision is of a society that actively supports ways to break down communication barriers for people who are deaf or hard of hearing.

Deafness is invisible but it marginalizes and its effect on relationships can be crippling. When a profoundly deaf child is born into a hearing family with little or no experience of how to overcome the communication challenges that deafness brings, social isolation can start at home. When an older person gradually loses their hearing, an early sign is their withdrawal from conversation.

We live in a hearing world which at best appears to lack understanding or empathy with deafness, and at worst stigmatizes it. You only have to consider how many organizations today can only be reached by telephone. As a result, deaf people are left feeling unable to access the everyday services hearing people take for granted.

GDA provides a range of services and social activities which bring deaf people back into the conversation, to enjoy greater independence and ultimately better physical and mental wellbeing.

The people whom GDA supports include adults and children who have been born deaf and whose preferred method of communication is sign language, and also those with an acquired hearing loss, who have speech but can no longer hear. Our services include deaf-awareness training, communications support (BSL interpreters), employment support, listening-aid equipment, hearing-aid clinics, lip-reading classes, and deaf children's and deaf youth clubs.

As well as being a great fan of Forest Green Rovers, this book's author, Chris Gardner, is himself severely deaf and is closely connected with GDA, initially as a beneficiary and now as a trustee of the charity. The first link between the two organizations came about when FGR directors and supporters donated and bought lots at a GDA Promises Auction. In dedicating all proceeds from the book to our cause, Chris's commitment to helping deaf and hard-of-hearing people in Gloucestershire continues. By buying a copy, you help too. We thank you.

Foreword
by Dale Vince, Chair Ecotricity & Forest Green Rovers FC

Sunday morning, not yet properly awake, eyes still closed – the first thing I'm aware of is how I feel, happy or not. It's before I have any thoughts, so I don't know why. It's just a feeling. As I start to have thoughts: I know why. It's about Saturday's result.

It's always about that – since Forest Green became part of my life.

That was summer 2010 and things weren't looking good for the club – on the verge of relegation and bankruptcy, very much in need of rescuing.

Six years later, Chris Gardner is writing about a very different club.

Different because we're pushing for promotion and financially secure. But so very different to anything that's gone before, in another way.

FGR is the first football club in the world to embed the environment into its DNA, to make sustainability its *raison d'être* – or at least its other one – after football.

Our stadium is powered by the Wind and the Sun; we have an organic pitch with inbuilt water recycling system, and a solar-powered robot lawnmower; vegan food; we drive electric cars and have the electricity pumps to charge them, for us and our visitors.

We've tackled the three big issues facing the world – Energy, Transport and Food – and we've put answers on display, showing how we can all live more sustainably. Something we think is urgently needed.

Most importantly, though, we're having fun.

Chris's book is a great insight into last season, our best yet – culminating in that trip to Wembley.

It's also an insight into one of the greatest aspects of FGR – its people.

Dale Vince
October 2016

Foreword

by Jilly Cooper OBE, journalist & author

Jilly Cooper and Aussie Stu at Wembley.

As a football ignoramus who often can't recognize offside, I feel hugely honoured to have been asked by Chris Gardner to write a foreword to his lovely book, *The Rise of Forest Green Rovers*. This is how it came about.

In April 2016 I finished a big novel on flat racing which had taken me six years. Missing my characters, I was casting about for a new subject. Two things drew me to football. The first was dining next to Sir Alex Ferguson, who was such a beguiling companion and who later made such a moving and inspiring speech about involving young people in football to reignite our national game. The second was falling in love with my local football team, Forest Green Rovers, whose chairman Dale Vince, like Sir Alex, is another visionary, a man of principle and great generosity, who passionately believes in saving the environment.

Shamefully, having lived in the Cotswolds for over 30 years, I had never visited Forest Green, although I knew they were the only vegan football club in the world. During 2015/16 however, snippets kept sifting through about their brilliant season, notching up win after win, topping the National League and trouncing superior sides in early rounds of the FA Cup.

Determined to see a game before the season ended, I was thrilled back in May to be invited to watch a semi-final play-off against Dover. Most football clubs are part of big towns, attracting large, belligerent crowds of supporters. Forest Green turned out to be ravishingly rural, surrounded by rolling hills, meadows and grazing sheep. The setting sun was casting great tree shadows over a perfect pitch, kept emerald green by rainwater alone. Forest Green played so wonderfully that as the final whistle blew, the same pitch was invaded by victorious home fans, ecstatic at victory over the two legs, at the prospect of going to Wembley and possible promotion to the League next season. I was equally excited to be invited to join them on one of Forest Green's coaches.

Our opponents were veritable Goliaths, Grimsby Town, who having failed to gain promotion on three previous play-offs at Wembley, had a huge hunger to win. They also had thrice as many supporters brandishing inflated rubber fish, to bellow them on.

Despite putting up a heroic defence, David lost out to Goliath and nothing could've been more heart-rending on the greatest day in little Forest Green's history than to see our brave players slumped in post-defeat desolation on the hallowed turf. How I wished I had been able to watch all the matches leading up to this climax.

Happily however, Chris Gardner one of the clubs most devoted and knowledgeable supporters, determined such a super season should not go unrecorded, has come up with the brilliant and unique idea of recreating it through the eyes of Forest Green fans. Holding the book together are excellent and graphic reports on each 2015/16 game written by Forest Green's press officer and pitch announcer, Rich Joyce. The Rich List is then interspersed with hilarious contributions from Chris Gardner himself, together with three more or less retired cronies including David Drew, Stroud's much loved ex-MP, and who give themselves bizarre nicknames like Foggy, Rambling Man and Deep-Throat.

Determined to liven up hundreds of miles spent driving to away games, they decided to make detours to famous castles, abbeys, stately homes and National Trust treasures. Thus poetic descriptions of passing countryside and history lessons on everything from the National Coal museum to the dissolution of the monasteries, rub shoulders with varying takes on the footie. These can be waspish. One moment 'bruisers on the pitch' are being castigated for 'bullying worse than Flashman', the next a player chided because his sole contribution is to appear on the front of the programme. Other targets are myopic refs, opposition players red-carded for spitting, sacked players who've joined the opposition returning to wreak vengeance, and ducks paddling across a deeply waterlogged pitch.

Fascinating too are Foggy's and Rambling Man's descriptions of different clubs. One stadium which must lose a lot of balls has only three sides! They also observe how the hospitality varies. Top in the hospitality stakes must certainly be Forest Green, or The New Lawn as it's known. Everyone is so welcoming and friendly here. Home games are like a wonderful party, enhanced by the delectable vegan food. Definitely Cordon Green, I defy even the most hardened carnivore not to enjoy it.

One of the most impressive aspects of Dale Vince's team is the way they interact with local schools, seeking out football talent and promoting a healthy lifestyle, with home games always full of excited, well-behaved children. Equally, one of the most charming sections of the book is the beautifully written match reports by primary school boys and a girl, bursting with pride to be chosen as club ambassadors and touchingly urging the players not to be too cast down by defeat.

The whole book also teems with statistics, witty often poignant poems and parodies and photographs, so we get to know the players. These range from the dazzling fleet-footed Keanu Marsh-Brown scorching down to score, to the stalwart Charles Clough, to drama appropriately provided by the handsome Aarran Racine, whose seventeenth-century ancestor was France's greatest playwright, to glorious gladiatorial Jon Parkin, nicknamed 'The Beast' and favourite of the fans who chant, "Feed the Beast and he will score", which Jon did ... fourteen times last season.

People continually moan that footballers are paid too much. I think they deserve every penny for the pleasure and excitement they bring to the world. A bad defeat may cast their fans into a week's black gloom but this will be transformed into a week's euphoria after a good win. Their careers can also be so fleeting with injury or age kicking in at any time and, like glorified slaves, they can be bought, sold or sacked at a manager's whim and often a manager's career is just as precarious. How resilient they have to be too to cope with blistering invective from media and fans both on the terraces and the website. While even the greatest player must rise above defeat, particularly if his missed penalty, careless finish or let-in goal deprives his teammates of promotion and untold riches. Here is the stuff of heroism.

What was particularly gratifying, after the sadness of Wembley, was last week witnessing Forest Green players, returning suntanned from a boot camp in Portugal. Radiating confidence and camaraderie, clearly inspired by Mark Cooper, their charismatic new manager, they proceeded at an environment-friendly friendly against higher division Newport County, to notch up a dazzling goal-fuelled start ahead of the season with a 4-3 victory.

I am now convinced that Dale's In-Vince-ables will go up and up, with the Premier League and sky the limit for the little club on the hill. Nor can I wait for Chris Gardner's sequel.

Jilly Cooper
August 2016

About the Author

Chris 'Rambling Man' Gardner is an addict. Self-confessed, unfortunate but true. Like most addictions, initially it was a slow-burner. He told himself he was in control and could kick it anytime. He was fooling himself. Forest Green Rovers was in his blood and the green monster called the shots.

Back in the day (well, 1953), Chris was born and bred a Bristolian. His father was a 'rugger man' and referee of 25 years though he was sympathetic to that other football played by hooligans. His three elder brothers followed both creeds but as to *soccer*, the quartet split their loyalties between the Bristol clubs: two for City, and Chris and his eldest brother for Rovers.

Until regarded as old enough to watch football with his brothers, he accompanied his father to his rugby refereeing appointments, usually at the Memorial Ground. Inevitably in calf-slapping wellington boots, worsted shorts, itchy woollen jumper and a duffel coat, he was placed in the old wooden stand, and looked after by family friends. He soon became aware of ripe language unheard at home, most of it aimed at his father.

Chris's first attendance at a football match was in the early '60s, an uninspiring 0-0 draw at Ashton Gate between City and Walsall to which he was taken by his three older siblings. Not the start he wanted. But as Chris entered teenagerdom, regular visits to Eastville began, usually watching a mid-table 'long ball' Gas slogging it out in old Division 3.

In the early 1980s, Chris had his first taste of the Nailsworth-based Rovers. Manager Steve Millard would take his squad to train at Easton Sports Centre off the M32 close in on Bristol's East Side. Chris and his work friends played 5-a-side football regularly on Thursday evenings from 8 to 9 with the Rovers squad next on, having warmed up with a run around the locality. They seemed like decent guys. Then he read about their win in the FA Vase and, from afar, kept an eye on the team from a Gloucestershire hamlet.

In 1985, Chris moved to Stroud having taken a job in Gloucester. Not yet cured of the playing bug, he turned out for Whiteshill United in the Gloucestershire Senior League Division 2, carving out a niche as a non-scoring centre forward. But they trained too hard for his liking, so he swapped back to his other autumn/winter sport, hockey with Stroud HC. He is one of few still live and kicking who played for all five of its Saturday teams, veterans and mixed XIs.

Summer meant cricket for Stinchcombe Stragglers then Stroud CC, parent club of ardent FGR fan and sometime goalkeeping coach, Jack Russell MBE.

The weekly *Stroud News & Journal* was always full of the exploits of 'The Little Club on the Hill'. Curious, and recalling the Bristol encounters, Chris took in occasional midweek and Saturday matches at The Lawn. His first fixes.

As BBC Radio Gloucestershire began to take closer interest in FGR in the Jim Harvey era (2007–9), Chris joined the inimitable Bob Hunt in the live commentary box. After two years, worsening deafness began to make this an impossible task, so Chris bowed out. His final contribution was a staggering game at Altrincham when Rovers turned a 2-0 first half deficit into a 5-2 triumph. It would have come over brilliantly on radio had not he and Bob left the commentary equipment in the BBC Radio Gloucestershire car park. Ever resourceful, Bob did what he could using his mobile phone until the battery expired.

In 2010, severe deafness forced Chris into early retirement from his development surveying career. At the invitation of long-time friend (and current FGR vice-chair) David Drew, he joined the club's new advisory board which initiates and coordinates Rovers' community activities. When asked, he chips in with media interviews and other appointments for the club and writes for the *Match Day* magazine as Rambling Man.

As a supporter, Chris prefers to stand, holding a south stand season ticket. At home games he's to be found with his friends on the 'wet' terrace, the closest thing they can find to their favoured spot at the 'Old' Lawn.

Thirty-one years after moving to the county, Chris watches all but a handful of games each season, home and away. He always looks out for the results of Bristol Rovers, but they have long since lost out in his affections to their Nailsworth rivals.

Introduction

Football is a game like no other for turning sane people into tantrum-prone teenagers. Despite the passage of years, it gets worse. For dyed-in-the wool supporters, if your team loses your mood over the next few days is darkened. The higher your team progresses up the greasy pole, *any* dropped points cause a similar funk.

Some, me being one, dissipate their worst humour by writing their thoughts on their Fans Forum. Compared to some clubs, the contributors to FGR's are relatively few. But it is strictly 'refereed' and contains a huge range of overwhelmingly witty posts and even poets.

For the 2015/16 season, editor Rich Joyce invited me to provide away match summaries for the FGR *Match Day* magazine: writing therapy given an official context as Rambling Man.

In keeping with my addiction, I attend the huge majority of home and away games, every season. I have a group of friends with whom the drive to away matches is shared. We travel together for several seasons. Initially, one factor united us – fear of coach travel, sickness and chronic back problems being chiefly to blame.

Also, we set off early to make every trip a good day out rather than just about football. In a vain attempt to save them embarrassment, the most regular are identified with strangely accurate pseudonyms: Compo, Foggy, Clegg and Deep Throat. They are season ticket holders or press and also contribute to Rovers' volunteer advisory board and supporters club. At The New Lawn, Foggy and I shun seats to stand in the Western (Wet) Terrace. Old habits and all that.

Having agreed to the *Match Day* magazine proposal, I was keen to find more rounded enjoyment in travelling to away matches, and said as much to my fellow travellers. Coincidentally, most were members of the National Trust and that proved inspirational.

Most of the National League away fixtures mean trips of 200 miles or more for FGR, Gateshead and Barrow being the longest. That involves tackling overburdened motorways, suffering the consequences of jams, and often arriving at games late and frustrated.

So, my friends and I resolved to make every away fixture a day out, so far as time and weather permitted. We began to set out half a day in advance, identifying National Trust properties (or notable castles or mansions) close to the targeted stadium as interim destinations. Whole or partial retirement affords that time luxury. A few hours of stately culture then on to the footie. Even occasional long weekends were booked.

The wider experience of a day-out helped to sweeten the bitter pill of a glum return journey when Rovers lost or dropped points. And, it persuaded me that my *Match Day* magazine ramblings should centre more on the journey, mansions and opposition club, and not get too bogged down with football.

Several friendly matches, 23 League games, 4 FA Cup & Trophy ties and 2 play-off matches later, I found myself reviewing a pile of words describing the away visits during Rovers' record-breaking 2015/16 season. Sadly, the season ended in disappointment at the final hurdle, the play-off final at Wembley v Grimsby Town. There followed eight weeks' ceasefire until the friendlies began. Not enough for effective rehabilitation nor cold turkey remedy.

My keenest feeling was that Rovers' momentous season should not pass so easily into history. So much had been achieved and that should not be coloured by one, albeit significant, defeat in the 53rd competitive match. For the record, my version of the milestones is listed below:

- Highest League finish in FGR history: 2nd place, 8 points ahead of 3rd-placed Braintree Town, 9 ahead of 4th-placed Grimsby Town. Of the 46 rounds of fixtures, FGR spent 20 in 1st place
- highest points total in National League achieved by FGR – 89
- won through to first National League play-off Wembley final
- 9 consecutive League wins from the first fixture – a record for the National League
- Rovers did not concede a League goal until 5th League game
- 9 consecutive home League wins spanning 31 October to 30 January
- most wins by FGR in a National League season – 26
- FA Cup run including a win at Wimbledon and narrow defeat at Oxford United. Both opponents went on to secure promotion to Football League Division 1
- scored in every away League game and play-off tie
- record seasonal attendance averaging more than 1,800 in League and play-off games
- won Gloucestershire Senior Cup.

In so many ways, Forest Green Rovers FC 'arrived' during 2015/16. It was a seminal season and should be celebrated. But how?

I am chair of a vibrant local charity, Gloucestershire Deaf Association. With typical generosity and warm-heartedness, FGR/Ecotricity Chair

Dale Vince and many FGR directors, members and supporters assisted in GDA's Promises Auction at Stroud Auction House in November 2015. Around £7,200 was raised. It seemed a natural progression to collate a book about FGR's season with all royalties being paid to GDA. That was the spark.

After that, it was a question of assembling contributions to obtain a rounded view of the whole season. Rambling Man aside, the Forum's Poet Laureate, The Farmcotian, came on board as did witty raconteur Jokerman. The club's own Rich Joyce threw in his match reports and loads more beside. A sprinkling of accounts provided by FGR's student ambassadors are included. Dale Vince's foreword completes the formal line-up of the FGR team.

The FGR website's Fans Forum is inspirational and brightens any day. If your addiction causes you to visit other football club's fans forums, you will become familiar with loads of knee-jerk reactions, personal jibes and more effing and blinding than you could poke a stick at.

Not at FGR. Strictly regulated (which occasionally causes friction), it abounds with acerbic wit, gallows humour, left-field reports and even poetry. You could let your mum read it and she'd pretty soon be chortling. We even get to hear from our benevolent dictator: The Electric Chair. So, respect to all posters and my gratitude to you all for allowing me to reprint your creativity.

Thus the season is retold in travellers' tales, verse, serious and not so serious eye-witness reports and summary statistics. Plus a variety of illustrations and headlines to boot, it is Rovers' season seen through the wit and angst of true supporters

May you enjoy the story of Forest Green Rovers' record-breaking 2015/16 season described by 'my team'. And sincere thanks for helping GDA to raise vital funds by buying this book

WHAT DOES A SUPPORTER GLEAN FROM PRE-SEASON FRIENDLIES? Not a lot in my opinion.

A first look at new players, relaxed football in summer sun and banter with fans from Gloucestershire's excellent lower level clubs such as Nailsworth rivals Shortwood United, Brimscombe & Thrupp, Slimbridge, Cirencester and Bishops Cleeve.

It would be fair to say that Rovers did not pull up any trees. Brimscombe & Thrupp (the 'Lilywhites') inflicted defeat while Slimbridge fought hard for a 0-0 draw.

Eye-catching home games with the assorted XIs of Aston Villa, West Bromwich Albion, Cardiff City and Plymouth Argyle brought two defeats a win (v WBA) and a draw.

Good clean fun but nothing meaningful against sides that blended youth and experience and rotated their personnel quicker than a spinning top. All in all, supporters were not expecting a flying start.

The season looks full of flipping hope
The new lads will be no flipping joke
So let us cheer them to the flipping rafters
Promo flipping beckons, these lads are flipping grafters

(Excerpt from 'Evidently Nailsworthtown' by The Farmcotian)

PRE-SEASON AWAY FRIENDLIES ROUND-UP
Rambling Man

My account dwells only on the annual encounters with local sides. A much-valued tradition that encourages amicable relationships between the clubs and renews numerous friendships among supporters.

Rovers rolled up at Brimscombe & Thrupp on Saturday 18th, the first pre-season encounter with local rivals down the pyramid. Sunshine, friendly hosts and bumper crowd did justice to The Meadow's natural amphitheatre.

A pedestrian performance by Rovers didn't. Deservedly, the Lilywhites inflicted late defeat, teaching their seniors how to cross and finish. As the football didn't last long in the memory, my attention wandered.

Fitness coach Neil told me the squad had been given training programmes for the summer – most had returned in good fettle. True of the whippets maybe, yet others look to have eaten the programme with a few side orders. They have work to do to reach desired fitness. As ever, Wedge was engaging. His fashion sense is about as developed as mine –

stillborn. During the game, he wore his strip in the old way: shirt tucked in, shorts tied somewhere near the nipple.

Newbie Aaron O'Connor was askance at Kurtis's first-half effort being disallowed. Pleading with the officials, arms outstretched as The Angel of the North. Looking forward to more of his repertoire.

And finally: how can Marcus Kelly play left back despite not owning a hairband. Answers please from Tom Bender and James Jennings.

Next up, Bishops Cleeve. A cold, suddenly autumnal, drenching Friday night, 24 July. You had to feel for the hosts. Chance of a bumper crowd dashed by the weather, school holiday getaway and the final of Celebrity Mastermind.

Even had to switch on the floodlights to illuminate the unseasonal gloom. Paul White did his best to lighten things by donning lurid dayglo yellow. It worked. Without Geiger counters and a lead-lined strip, the home forwards kept a safe distance.

Chips and tea were cheap and excellent, so in the dry of the seated stand I settled to admire an energetic Rovers' display.

Frear was buzzing down the left, and McGrory, growing in confidence by the game, was relishing the freedom of midfield. Frear was hacked down, Kelly crossed to the near post where O'Connor's sharp header made it 1-0. The boldly named West Stand was in raptures. Actually it wasn't. No one was there.

So I ignored the rain to investigate. The West Stand comprises a path and verge between the pitch advertising boards and the security fence. There is no cover. It is where spectators might stand in the west. Mystery of the name solved.

Not much to say about half 2 and I left early to dry out. Highlight was JP's quick throw to O'Connor at the near post, his cross and McGrory's sliding finish at the far post. 2-0 the final score. All in all an encouraging runabout.

So to the Swans at Slimbridge on Saturday 25th – back-to-back games to build on the squad's fitness. And summer had returned, bringing an excellent, boisterous crowd. Shazzers Snax was doing a roaring trade. Notably for Rovers, Superted Jonny Maxted had landed after the club had moved swiftly to cover injury to the luckless Steve Arnold v Aston Villa.

He was kept busy by the all-action hosts who tackled and harried with gusto, and moved the ball fast and accurately.

This was the most league-like friendly to date, evidenced by the gash in Aarran Racine's forehead. Inadequately bandaged, he did a passable

J
U
L
Y

Terry Butcher impersonation. Dale Bennett needed his turn of pace to ward off the constant threats on his side, and to counter.

It was an entertaining 0-0. Ultimately, the bouncy dry surface did for control in front of goal.

But all the players worked hard, and the second half introduction of beasts 1 to 3 (JP, Jonah and Pipey) quelled the Swans' fervour. Among several good performances, young pretenders Louis McGrory and Aidan Baldwin again took the eye.

The latter is an outstanding talent and looks to be serious competition at either right or centre back. Scotty will be dead chuffed for his protégés.

Cannot get to Cirencester* next Saturday, so my next words will be from our first league clash at Altrincham, last season's 'Tie-gate'.

* Cirencester Town 3 FGR 0

PLAYED 7, WON 7 & TOP OF THE LEAGUE! Who could possibly have expected that? All done with slick passing football, patient possession and a mean defence that did not concede a goal until 22 August.

Ady Pennock was deservedly Manager of the Month and the supporters were in dreamland, tellingly, Ady responded to media interviews confessing that he could not explain Rovers' imperious form. Disingenuous we thought at the time

Well we're not quite next to a mountain
But we stand at the top of a hill.
Yes we're not quite next to a mountain
but we stand at the top of a hill

(Excerpt in the style of Jimmi Hendrix by Voodoobluesman)

Saturday 08.08.15
Altrincham 0 FGR 1
PARKIN HEADER HANDS FGR OPENING DAY WIN
Richard Joyce

A tremendous second-half performance helped Forest Green Rovers to all three points on the opening day of the season at Altrincham's J. Davidson Stadium. Goal machine Jon Parkin began the new campaign in the same vein that had seen him lead the way last season with a superb near post header to guarantee maximum points.

The result meant Rovers have now won on the opening day for three seasons in a row – a first for the club's 18 seasons in the now newly named National League.

Ady Pennock's first team selection of the season saw him keep faith with many of last year's play-off finishing squad, although there were starting places for two debutants in the shape of Aaron O'Connor and goalkeeper Jonny Maxted.

The opening stages had all the signs of an opening day tussle, with little action until the quarter of an hour mark when Alty defender Adam Griffin advanced forward to hand Maxted his first test. And after Parkin had headed Sam Wedgbury's cross off target, Maxted denied the hosts front man Damien Reeves from finding the net with a solid stop half an hour in. Wedgbury's attempted lob over a stranded Stuart Coburn towards the end of the half was all that remained from a well contested opening 45 minutes.

The second half again began slowly with little chances of note, however

A
U
G
U
S
T

it was Forest Green who would take firm control as they took the game to Altrincham and failed to give them a sniff.

A number of corners saw Aarran Racine and Kurtis Guthrie head wide, but leading light Parkin was on hand to seal the winning goal on 74 minutes. He met Elliott Frear's pinpoint near post corner with an unstoppable header that squeezed into the back of the net. Dale Bennett's speculative effort didn't manage to further add to Rovers advantage, while an audacious effort from Wedgbury against one his former clubs also flew wide.

With little pressure to come from the hosts, Forest Green saw the game out confidently to begin the season with a win ahead of the visit of Welling United to The New Lawn on Tuesday.

DESTINATION ALTRINCHAM
Rambling Man

Compo and I agreed that our progress this season should depend on National Trust membership. I refer of course to Rovers supporters travelling to away matches and the wish to avoid the car parks that comprise the nation's motorways.

So it was that we departed Stonehouse at 8.30 a.m., before even the dawn chorus of players' tweets. Destination Tatton Park, a mere 30 minutes from Alty. An old Tudor hall, nineteenth-century mansion, deer roaming the range, gardens, woods and lakes than stretch beyond the horizon. Less a park, more a small country. The lake alone could justify its own navy.

Park visit done, we dressed to kill. Last year's Tie-gate humiliation at Alty's Boardroom still burned. Compo and I were strutting our stuff in sharply laundered smocks, fresh storks of grass clamped between our lips.

And I had raided the wardrobe for a tie I'd been saving for my funeral. We shouldn't have worried – our nemesis was not present and the Alty welcome was as warm as the weather.

Now the footie. In truth, the first half was soporific. Most interesting thing was a notice on the pitch-side hoardings: "Grass grows by the inch but dies by the foot". An argument for hoof-ball?

Arrival delayed by the M6, Chairman Dale and his party hadn't missed much.

Thankfully, Rovers awoke for the second half playing in neat, attractive style, no doubt killing whole stretches of the green stuff. Talking of grass, the *coup de* was applied by our own BFG who hovered like a Zeppelin to do justice to Elliott Frear's corner and 45 minutes of dominant play.

So, 3 points in the bag and home in time to watch Aussie Stu's mates surrendering the urn. Life is good.

Wonder what historical mansions form the gateway to Boreham Wood, our next port of call?

ROVERS CORNER: 3 POINTS
Jokerman

The National League starts today, 8 August 2015, with an away fixture at Altrincham. With temperatures heading into the twenties and nearly 40 souls on board, Kendo headed north. A weekend in August and the thick end of a hundred miles of the M5/M6 in prospect is not a good combination and so it proved. After three and a half hours the supporters coach was in Stoke-on Trent when its passengers should have been propping up the bar at Altrincham.

Last year's nightmare trip to Southport came to mind as Kendo took the National Trust route via Little Morton Hall and Biddulph Grange. It was a close-run thing and as supporters passed through the turnstiles at Moss Lane, some with serious alcohol withdrawal symptoms, the referee's whistle sounded to start the campaign.

For FGR Parkin was captain for the day and partnered up front with O'Connor and Guthrie. Jones was on the injured list so Racine was the fulcrum at the back supported by the usual suspects. An educational visit to one of the aforementioned venues would have been far more enlightening than the first 45 minutes of 'football' witnessed here. Rovers fans occupied the sun-baked open terrace behind the goal their side were attacking though I use that term loosely. In excess of 60 had nothing to cheer of note and passed the time bantering with the veteran keeper Coburn in the Altrincham goal.

For the home side Reeves shot wide under pressure and Maxted, Rovers new keeper, saved easily Griffins shot from distance as Alty started slightly the better. Parkin put a header wide on 16 minutes and Coburn slapped a Kelly cross away from the same player at the back post to concede a corner. This came to nothing as Havern and Marshall, whose hairstyle was right out of the top drawer of the Neanderthal period, coped well with any aerial attack. Taking inspiration from the cricket there was a break in play for tea and biscuits on 35 minutes. On 43 minutes Coburn livened things up a bit by rushing outside his area to head clear a through ball which eventually fell to Wedgbury, who looped it back at the unguarded goal, but unfortunately high and wide.

Half time and for the first time in Altrincham's 112-year history FGR

**A
U
G
U
S
T**

supporters were segregated. Following the first-half performance a metallic 'hand grenade' of lemonade was not the best thing to serve up at any game, but Rovers fans are a civilized bunch and accepted a day on the wagon.

The second half saw an improvement from the visitors who dominated possession and pressed Altrincham back for long periods. Having said that, the goal chances created were scarce. Corners abounded and on 58 minutes Kelly crossed one from the left which Parkin headed across goal where it was cleared only as far as O'Connor lurking at the back for just such an occurrence. He didn't just go for glory he gave the term a whole new meaning. His eyes glazed over as he swung his foot and put the ball in the 'Stretford End' two miles down the road.

Frear and Kelly were making inroads down the left and won a succession of corners but all were dealt with by a dour Alty defence. Guthrie came close, flashing a header wide from a Sinclair corner from the right. From another clearance Wedgbury from the edge of the penalty area hit a screamer into the trees behind the stand where it was no doubt relieved of its contents by an irate woodpecker.

On 73 minutes Rovers at last made the breakthrough from yet another corner. This time Frear crossed from the left and Parkin, at the near post, stepped in front of his marker and flicked a header into the roof of the net past the flailing Coburn. He had not enjoyed the best of afternoons but one cannot discount his worth to score these priceless goals.

It sparked the home side into life but they lacked the attacking edge. A couple of confident clearing punches from Maxted were sufficient while Bennett fired a shot narrowly wide for Rovers, set up by O'Connor from a Frear corner.

Five minutes of added time gave Alty a glimmer but a dangerous cross from the left was well caught high up at the back post by Maxted and the points were won.

Tuesday 11.08.15
FGR 1 Welling United 0
O'CONNOR NETS HIS FIRST IN WINGS VICTORY
Richard Joyce

Aaron O'Connor's deflected strike made it back-to-back wins at the start of the season for Forest Green Rovers. The summer signing clinched his first goal in Rovers colours on the stroke of half time to earn Ady Pennock's side another early season success after Saturday's single goal win at Altrincham.

There was also another clean sheet for young goalkeeper Jonny Maxted to saviour, as an FGR home crowd was delivered a winning performance in the team's first outing at The New Lawn this season.

O'Connor's strike on his home debut followed a first half that possessed similarities to Saturday's opening 45 minutes at Altrincham, and the away side dominated early on.

Tashan Adeyinka, Xavier Vidal and Zach Fagan all saw opportunities in the first ten minutes fail to hit the back of the net as FGR gradually began to take some control of the game.

O'Connor and Aarran Racine both saw snap shots go wide, while Jon Parkin's free kick on 24 minutes fizzed past the wall but could only hit the side netting of Tom King's relatively quiet goal.

Rovers had managed to take control of the tie, and after Kurtis Guthrie had almost steered home against his former club, O'Connor found what would prove to be the game's only goal. He smashed an effort on goal from Parkin's cushioned header, and thanks to a deflection off Harry Osbourne, the former Newport County man celebrated his first goal.

A flood of chances fell Forest Green's way in the second half, and the visitors also came close to finding an equalizer on a couple of occasions. Rob Sinclair and Guthrie almost forced the ball home early on in the half, and after Maxted had saved a Ricky Wellard effort, O'Connor was denied a goal by Ben Jefford's crucial clearance on the line and he couldn't convert a Elliott Frear cross shortly after.

Guthrie was edging ever nearer to scoring against his former club, but he was prevented from doing so on 63 minutes by a marvellous stop by King who made himself big to deny the 22-year-old. And the Wings on-loan Millwall keeper made another bright stop as the game moved towards the finish to deny the lively O'Connor when clean through.

It looked as though the points were going to be staying in Gloucestershire, but there were still two great openings for the visitors either side of a flashing Keanu Marsh-Brown shot. Vidal's strike from 20 yards drifted thankfully past the wrong side of the post, and Wellard produced a good effort from distance, only to see Maxted pluck his shot out of the air to tie up another Rovers win.

O'CONNOR – ONE NIL

Jokerman

Following a great three points taken at Altrincham on Saturday Forest Green kick off the season at home against Welling FC. Expectations are guarded, though with all due respect to Welling anything other than a victory will be regarded with doom and gloom by Rovers fans. Under ideal conditions on a perfect pitch the game kicks off as the sun sets behind the west terrace.

Welling were quickly off the mark, taking the game to Rovers through Kabba crossing from the right to the colossal Adeyinka whose shot went over when he should have scored, in only the third minute. Further efforts by Vidal and Fagan whose shot was gathered by Maxted gave notice of intent.

FGR stirred into life around the 15-minute mark when Kelly made inroads down the left, released Frear who crossed for Parkin who failed to make good contact with the ball. O'Connor and Racine both put shots wide of goal as both sides struggled to impress.

Parkin went close for Rovers on 23 minutes when he curled a free kick low round the wall but not quite enough to creep inside the right-hand post. The home side were seeing more of the ball now and Guthrie headed wide from a Pipe cross while Kelly lofted a free kick over from 20 yards.

On 37 minutes Fagan was booked for a nasty foul on O'Connor and soon after Guthrie was also carded for an innocuous brush with the Welling keeper, King, who performed an audition for a spaghetti western death scene before taking the resultant free kick. Guthrie fired a fierce shot just wide as half time approached.

In added time what transpired to be the defining moments of the game occurred. A terrific flowing move by Welling moving the ball across the park with accurate passing resulted in Kabba being presented with a free shot central inside the area which he managed to slice, for the few Welling fans that travelled, sickeningly wide. Worse was to follow.

Forest Green quickly cleared the ball down field to Parkin on the edge of the D who chested the ball to O'Connor who hit it first time into the right-hand side of the goal with King a spectator. In a half where a goal looked unlikely despite the efforts, it was a real bonus for Pennock's men.

As the sun set, the sky turned red and lit a fire under FGR. They moved up a gear and packed the midfield, pressing Welling onto the back foot from the off. Frear ripped down the left and fired a great cross into the on rushing Sinclair who miss-hit his shot and Guthrie just failed to touch the ball home. It should have been two nil.

Welling replied with a thunderbolt from Wellard that Maxted parried away only as far as Vidal who wasted a good opportunity by blazing wide. On 51 minutes Wellard, captain and the visitors' best player, again brought a save from Maxted. These were attacks on the break, however, as Rovers pressed for a decisive goal. O'Connor on the left put in a dangerous cross-cum-shot that was curling under the bar before Jefford headed it over off the line. From the resulting corner, mayhem reigned in the Welling penalty area. Sinclair with his second attempt crossed to the back post to Racine who knocked it to O'Connor who tried a 'dink' shot that King dropped under pressure. Parkin tried a back-heel to Sinclair who was finally foiled by King.

On 56 minutes Welling were again fortunate to escape when a Bennett cross from the left caught them out as O'Connor storming in connected from close range only to see the ball go agonizingly wide of the left-hand post. Another Guthrie shot went wide as did a header from Adeyinka at the other end.

Around 60 minutes Marsh-Brown replaced Parkin and quickly put in Guthrie for a shot well saved by King. Forest Green were well in control of the game but a single-goal lead is always a worry for the supporters.

More sustained pressure resulted in Frear having an effort again cleared off the line by Jefford and Sinclair, Wedgbury and Marsh-Brown combined well but the substitutes shot was wide of the mark. On 75 minutes he was again the culprit when a terrific pass from Kelly put him clear into the area where he chose to shoot across the keeper when a square pass to the closing Guthrie or O'Connor would have settled the outcome.

Maxted saved well from a good shot from Wellard and Kelly was relieved when his mistake in defence went unpunished with a flag for offside. FGR saw out the final minutes, Sam-Yorke replacing Guthrie and ensuring the points were safe. Despite the only goal it was an improved display from Rovers in the second period and with more accurate shooting they will be a force again this season.

Saturday 15.08.15
FGR 4 Barrow 0
EXCELLENT START CONTINUES WITH BARROW WIN
Richard Joyce
A third consecutive win, a third clean sheet in a row and a place at the top of the table as the only team in the league with a hundred per cent record – all as a result of Forest Green Rovers emphatic drubbing of Barrow.

An Aaron O'Connor double plus season firsts from Kurtis Guthrie and Aarran Racine helped FGR to maximum points in a notable encounter that saw the Cumbrians end the match with nine men. Danny Livesey received an early red card for the visitors, while Steve Williams's unnecessary kick out on Guthrie near the full-time whistle will condemn him to an unneeded three-match ban.

The result leaves FGR sitting pretty at the top of the National League after Tranmere, Eastleigh and Chester all dropped points, in a line-up that saw James Jennings make his first appearance of his season, and Keanu Marsh-Brown earn his first start.

Barrow had the better of the early exchanges, but the game was flipped on its head on 17 minutes when Rob Sinclair's shot was handled by Livesey. It was a definite penalty, but the red card that followed from referee Joseph Johnson could have potentially been only a yellow, however; nevertheless O'Connor swept home from the spot for his first of the afternoon. A swarm of Rovers pressure followed, and after Elliott Frear's shot had been pushed away for a corner, his corner kick landed right in the danger zone and saw Guthrie poke home from close range to double the lead.

Marsh-Brown's influence was growing on the game. His long-range strike whizzed past the post on 32 minutes, while his cross for O'Connor shortly after almost saw the latter head home. Another big opportunity to snatch a third goal presented itself at the end of the half, and it again fell to O'Connor, although he saw Barrow keeper Joel Dixon do well to spread himself.

The visitors were going to need to produce something of a memorable comeback. They struggled though to make their mark, and apart from a stinging Andy Haworth drive, well saved by Jonny Maxted, they couldn't threaten the scoreline.

It was game, set and match on 65 minutes when O'Connor extended the FGR lead with a close-range finish. It followed a fine move down the left-hand side that saw Frear and Guthrie combine to feed O'Connor who tapped in unmarked at the far post. Defender Racine picked up the sponsors' man-of-the-match award for his showing which came with a goal as he wrapped up the win. He met Frear's pin-point corner with an accurate header that left Dixon with no chance while nestling in the back of the net.

There was still time for one last piece of drama near the finish as the visitors ended the game with nine men in stoppage time. Former FC Halifax man Williams kicked out at Guthrie in an incident near the corner flag, and after expressing his views to the officials a little too forcefully, he managed to earn himself a head-start on his teammates when it came to the walk down the tunnel.

A BARROW LOAD OF GOALS FOR ROVERS
Jokerman

Two games, two goals, two wins, two clean sheets, too good to last? Hopefully not.

Today's opposition are raiders from the north in the shape of Barrow FC. They are well supported by nearly a hundred faithful followers who have made the unenviable long journey south. After Tuesday night's victory, manager Pennock has made one forced change and one of choice to the starting line-up. Marsh-Brown is in for the injured Parkin and Jennings is preferred to Kelly which raised some eyebrows.

Pipe captained the Rovers today and led the team out on a dry afternoon with broken cloud veiling the sun to the relief of spectators in the East Stand. As in their first two games FGR allowed their opponents the first sight of goal and as on Tuesday were fortunate not to go behind. Barrow split the Rovers defence and Symington set up Walker who failed to even test keeper Maxted.

After 15 minutes neither side had fired a shot on target with the visitors looking more lively. But then came the game changer on 17 minutes when Frear made a great break down the left, cut inside and played the ball back into the path of Sinclair who struck a goal-bound shot that Barrow defender Livesey desperately threw himself at, the ball striking his arm in the process. The referee immediately pointed to the spot.

The game was then effectively spoilt as a contest as he deemed it a deliberate offence and brandished the red card. O'Connor steps up and strikes the ball low to the left, Dixon the Barrow keeper guesses correctly but cannot prevent the goal. The Barrow followers who had been vociferous in support of their team were not a little incensed by the decision and went mildly hysterical.

Rovers began to press home their advantage and won a couple of free kicks in good positions, the second of which Frear fancied his chances but only succeeded in scattering the alpacas in the field the other side of the Nympsfield Road. Dixon did well to thwart Guthrie and recovered well to block away Frear's follow-up effort.

From the resulting corner Frear crossed from the left where the ball dropped to the feet of Guthrie who turned and blasted the ball into the back of the net from ten yards on 19 minutes. It was all one-way traffic up until half time. O'Connor went close with a header glancing wide from a Marsh-Brown cross and a free kick awarded for a Dixon handball from a back pass was too close to the goal line to create a chance and the ball was blocked away.

A
U
G
U
S
T

Although a chance or two went begging, FGR were well in control while the visitors' frustration at the dismissal was compounded by their lack of composure resulting in three more yellow cards.

Barrow did start the second period brightly, however, going for broke no doubt and Rovers became a little careless with their passing. Barrow won a free kick on the D which looked promising but Walker put the ball in among his own supporters behind the goal. These were led by a cheerleader fellow whose buttocks had different post codes.

During this brief spell it was left to Haworth to make the only defiant gesture when in a good position on the edge of the area his brutal shot was well saved by Maxted diving to his right. It was short-lived and on 65 minutes, Frear breaking from defence hit a slide-rule pass down the left touchline for the quick-thinking Guthrie to run onto. The striker ran into the area, reached the by-line and hit the ball hard and low across the six-yard box to O'Connor who hammered another nail into Barrow's coffin.

Soon after, on 70 minutes, he was replaced by Sam-Yorke and received a standing ovation as he left the field. Two minutes later a Frear corner on the left was taken with precision and Racine on the charge powered his header into the top left-hand corner of the net and Barrow's miserable day was nearly complete.

Kelly replaced Sinclair on 83 minutes and his defence-splitting pass to Frear nearly added a fifth but the cross just evaded Guthrie. Kamdjo also put in an appearance and put a difficult chance wide.

An eye-catching run from Marsh-Brown ended with a shot well saved by Dixon. The yellow peril hanging over Barrow took its toll at the death when Williams was shown a second and dismissed following an altercation with Guthrie, which triggered his trademark arm waving and muttering when hard done by.

Mercifully for Barrow the game ended but ahead was a long painful journey home with too much time to contemplate. Forest Green Rovers did the job well, kept another clean sheet and are at the top of The National League. The side travel to Boreham Wood on Tuesday and should not lack confidence.

Tuesday 18.08.15
GUTHRIE HEADER EXTENDS MARVELLOUS START
Richard Joyce
Kurtis Guthrie's pinpoint second-half header continued Forest Green Rovers' fantastic start to the new season as Rovers made it four wins

from four at new boys Boreham Wood. The 22-year-old rose highest to nod in a terrific Rob Sinclair free kick, as FGR held on at last season's Conference South play-off winners to also clinch an impressive fourth consecutive clean sheet. It maintains the club's hundred per cent record this season as Ady Pennock's charges tasted success against a team who lost only four times at home last season.

Boreham Wood had the stand-out Billy Clifford sent off for a second bookable offence in the second half, but despite a late flurry of attacking substitutions, they couldn't find a way past Jonny Maxted in the FGR goal – despite hitting the woodwork three times.

The Hertfordshire club looked more than capable of providing a threat at this level, and from as early as the fifth minute they rattled Rovers' crossbar for the first time on the night.

Clifford picked the ball up just outside the box but saw his chipped attempt clip the bar. The frame of Maxted's goal was shaken once again only seven minutes later when the Wood's on-loan Bristol Rovers forward Jamie Lucas tried his luck with a header from a Ricky Shakes cross. Former Chelsea man Clifford demonstrated his pedigree throughout the evening, and he produced two shots that slipped wide at the end of the half.

The rhythm of the second half mirrored the opening 45 minutes, and Forest Green's best opportunity yet fell to Keanu Marsh-Brown on 55 minutes from a free kick on the edge of the box, but it failed to threaten James Russell's goal.

Both teams continued to struggle to force the goalkeepers into action, although Wood keeper Russell was picking the ball out of his net when Guthrie claimed the tie's only goal.

Luke Howell's handball offence on the edge of the Boreham Wood area offered Sinclair the opportunity to ship a ball into the danger zone. And the former Salisbury City man did so to brilliant effect as he picked out Guthrie, whose header was terrifically directed into the bottom corner. The hosts' challenge was made even harder only minutes later, when key man Clifford saw red for a second bookable offence after he brought down Guthrie.

It didn't stop them from threatening to level the affair though. Junior Morais, on as a substitute, saw his looping header connect with the FGR woodwork for a third time.

It looked like Boreham Wood were out of luck on the night, and after Guthrie had seen another header go close, the full-time whistle was blown on another Rovers victory.

A
U
G
U
S
T

Boreham Wood 0 FGR 1
DESTINATION BOREHAM WOOD
Rambling Man
Conveniently Baron Rothschild invited Compo and me for tea at Waddesdon Manor, Tuesday 18th. In your dreams! Anyhow, we planned Waddesdon as the next stop in our National Trust FGR away day tour, being 40 miles up the A41 from Borehamwood

If you are into a no-fortune-spared nineteenth-century recreation of the definitive French chateau, you'll like Waddesdon: majestic, more turrets and finials that you could shake a linesman's flag at. Shame we hadn't noticed the website pronounced it closed on Mondays and Tuesdays.

We regrouped in the Five Arrows map in hand. Ah, Verulamium! (St Albans to Britons). As tempus was fugiting, we set the chariot's Satnav and hit Watling Street. Good decision. Excellent touchy-feely Roman museum though the Mosaic and Amphitheatre shut at 4.30 and 5.00 p.m. respectively, too early for us. We opted to circumnavigate St Albans Cathedral. High in the post-Roman town, it dominates Verulamium below. A stately hotch-potch of honey stone, red brick and flint, mixing Medieval, Tudor and Georgian designs.

Culture done, off to Boreham Wood. Surprising trip inside the M25 across rolling countryside – could have been rural Gloucestershire. Meadow Stadium is a compact, smart, new ground with properly welcoming locals. They reminded me of us in the 1990s, rubbing our eyes in disbelief that multi-promotions had brought Conference Premier to Nailsworth.

The match was tight as a drum. Sides evenly matched fought for dominance. Crisp, fast passing, but few chances: Wood scraped our crossbar early on. Second half saw the hosts up the ante and push Rovers harder than in any of our previous matches. But the storm was weathered, and with 15 minutes remaining, FGR broke local hearts. Sincs' swirling free kick and three Rovers players rose, perpetual-motion Kurtis fittingly the match winner. Tough on Boreham, a hard lesson about life in the fifth tier.

Saturday 22.08.15
FGR 3 Lincoln City 1
FINE START KEEPS GOING AGAINST LINCOLN CITY
Richard Joyce
The National League table is a handsome sight for Forest Green Rovers fans at the moment after a fifth consecutive win was recorded over

Lincoln City at The New Lawn. Ady Pennock's team made it five from five to brush aside former Football League outfit Lincoln who threatened to derail Rovers' quest for victory in the second half. Alex Simmons' close-range finish had offered the Imps a route back into the tie in the second half after a missed FGR penalty; however, a third goal late on settled any potential nerves that Rovers would be denied three points for the first time this season.

It was a positive start in hot conditions and front man Aaron O'Connor headed narrowly wide only six minutes in after Elliott Frear had worked a good opportunity. Keanu Marsh-Brown was looking lively and his neat footwork offered him the chance to shoot on goal on the quarter-of-an-hour mark but his driven effort was scooped wide.

James Jennings was the man responsible for breaking the deadlock when the left back claimed his first goal in an FGR shirt. The former Manchester City youngster drove home inside the Lincoln box midway through the half after Frear's dangerous free kick had caused the away side problems in front of their own goal.

And with five minutes to go till the interval, the lead was increased courtesy of an O'Connor strike. Kurtis Guthrie battled his way through a number of Lincoln challenges to offer O'Connor the chance to shoot inside the penalty area – and he did so lethally despite goalkeeper Paul Farman's best efforts to block his low attempt.

Frear and Jennings both saw efforts early in the second half fail to find the back of the net, while Jonny Maxted was called into action shortly after the hour mark when he kept out Conner Robinson's deft header. Forest Green were handed the perfect opportunity to put the game to bed three minutes later when Guthrie was brought down in the box. O'Connor couldn't take advantage though as Farman did well to save his effort from 12 yards, and it was a save that installed some confidence in the Lincoln attack.

It eventually told when on 70 minutes they drew a goal back via Simmons – the first goal FGR have conceded this season. Apart from another Simmons' attempt that whistled past the post, the away side struggled to create any openings against a resolute Forest Green defence.

The game, and the points, were made safe late on when Rovers two-goal lead was restored with two different players claiming the goal. Delano Sam-Yorke teed up Marsh-Brown whose goal-bound effort was brilliantly executed. It was helped over the line by the on-rushing Jon Parkin who also claimed the goal – for what would be his second strike of the season.

A
U
G
U
S
T

That one may need to be decided by the FGR dubious goals committee, but for another match day at least the points belonged to Rovers, who are in no mood to give up their fantastic start to the season.

LINCOLN IMPS FALL TO ROVERS
Jokerman

Forest Green Rovers bring their one hundred per cent record into today's game following, by some reports, a fortuitous victory at Boreham Wood on Tuesday evening. Today's visitors, Lincoln City, will be on recent form their sternest test to date. As the Budding ale is sunk it is generally agreed that Lincoln will probably score and Rovers need to improve markedly from Tuesday to keep their unbeaten tag.

The temperature is in the high twenties as Pipe leads the team out. It is the same line-up that started on Tuesday. Parkin returns to the bench following injury. Kelly still tweaked one supposes.

Lincoln are first out of the blocks winning a free kick in a central position 30 yards out. Bush strikes the ball low through the wall where it takes a deflection but Maxted is alert and saves well diving to his right. On six minutes Bush again tests Maxted from a free kick. This time the Rovers custodian quickly throws the ball to Pipe who sets Rovers on attack. The ball is worked across the park to Frear on the left who 'skins' Bush and crosses from the by-line to the unmarked O'Connor who puts his header wide from a great position. Good work from Marsh-Brown gave Guthrie a chance but his shot went wide.

Lincoln were conceding possession to the home side in midfield and Guthrie took advantage, taking the ball from defence right to the edge of the Lincoln penalty area where he was brought down, only to see Jennings put the kick over the bar.

On 24 minutes Rovers took a deserved lead from a free kick, again won by Guthrie on the right. Frear crossed and as the heads went up the ball ran loose across goal, struck central defender Waterfall and rolled to Jennings. To his dismay and nearly 200 Red Imps fans behind the goal the Rovers full back slotted the ball inside the right-hand post.

Lincoln endeavoured to hit back immediately and only a terrific block by Bennett denied one chance, the ball breaking to veteran striker Rhead who curled his effort wide.

Marsh-Brown and Guthrie are working well together and on 40 minutes an exchange of passes on the edge of the area ended with Guthrie's run being blocked, the ball spinning to O'Connor who repeated Jennings finish inside the right-hand post. Lincoln were reeling as half time approached but forced a succession of corners before the whistle, all comfortably dealt with by Maxted and his defence.

Only half way but FGR fans are well pleased and somewhat surprised by Lincoln's performance. The Brazil strip appears a bit wasted on them. On 52 minutes a Marsh-Brown free kick from the right presents Jennings with another goal-scoring chance but his header is wide. Soon after, a quick break from defence sees Marsh-Brown bearing down on the retreating Lincoln defenders with O'Connor screaming for the pass to seal the game. Instead M-B takes on one more and the cross goes astray.

Lincoln are showing a bit more effort and a cross from the left sees Robinson flick wide from close range. Guthrie, the proverbial thorn in the visitors' defence, is making inroads in the penalty area but is facing away from goal as Waterfall makes unnecessary contact, and the referee points to the spot. O'Connor steps up and, to be fair, his penalties are not convincing. Farman, the Lincoln keeper, only had to watch last week's effort against Barrow. He must have and fell to his right to save.

Twenty-five minutes remaining, regrets pending. A minute later Rhead has a clear sight of goal from 15 yards and blasts the ball over the bar. What can one say about this journeyman only that he has become the block that everyone goes around these days; he certainly got no change from Racine this afternoon.

Forest Green finally conceded a goal on 70 minutes, engineered by two Lincoln substitutes. A free kick from the left corner of the penalty area was taken by Power, the ball fell in a ruck and Simmons pounced and beat Maxted from close range. Pennock made a change: Sam-Yorke on for O'Connor. He was soon in the thick of it and tangled with Wood which led to a lot of handbags. He must have transgressed, receiving a yellow card for his trouble.

With only a single-goal advantage it got a bit nervy for home fans especially when the overworked Pipe misjudged and allowed the ball to be crossed to Robinson who was again wasteful and put his effort wide.

Parkin replaced Frear on 86 minutes. A minute later Rovers made the game safe with the best moment of the afternoon. Sam-Yorke on the run threaded the ball through to Marsh-Brown who took it into the area and coolly lifted the ball over Farman as he went to ground. Parkin followed the ball in but it was Marsh-Brown's goal. Sublime. Look and learn Hernandez v Newcastle just over two hours ago.

Rovers ran the clock down and on the whistle Marsh-Brown flashed a shot narrowly wide.

Five straight wins, each one becoming more significant. The club

**A
U
G
U
S
T**

and supporters are in a great position just now. Manager Ady Pennock bemoans the lack of credit for achievement and the 'so-called moneybags tag' but the club is no longer being run on a shoestring. The financial 'them and us' mentality has always existed. The transition from non-league to league cannot occur without bags of money. While FGR strive to cross this line, the stigma will always be applied by those less fortunate and those naturally cynical. Promotion for the club would readjust the values. He has assembled a team very capable of doing this. The question remains: Are he and his coaching staff capable of managing this? Pressure, what pressure?

Saturday 29.08.15
Kidderminster Harriers 0 FGR 2
SECOND HALF STRIKES FIRE FGR TO KIDDY WIN
Richard Joyce
Kidderminster Harriers became the latest club to end up on the wrong side of a fine Forest Green Rovers showing as FGR made it six wins from six at Aggborough. Ady Pennock's side kick-started the bank holiday weekend in style with a convincing victory, sealed with a fifth clean sheet this season. Keanu Marsh-Brown's rocket finish and Jon Parkin's delightful header clinched a comfortable win in front of a large Forest Green following who have fully embraced the club's marvellous start to the season.

Former Football League side Kiddy never really looked like threatening to ruin Rovers' sunny visit to Worcestershire with a return to Nailsworth due on Monday for the visit of division new boys, Bromley.

Starting with the same team for a fourth consecutive game, the hosts were finding Forest Green's early movement in attacking areas hard to deal with. Aarran Racine couldn't find the target with a header in the tie's first major chance after he had drifted round the back to find space at a set piece.

Meanwhile Kurtis Guthrie, James Jennings and Aaron O'Connor all tried their best to break the deadlock from balls that had been driven into the area. Forest Green would have been disappointed to go into the break without a goal. The home side had struggled to threaten, although Adam Dawson's powerful shot flew just over early in the second period to serve as a warning to what had previously been a watertight FGR defence.

Guthrie looked to find the net with a fine solo effort on 57 minutes; however, the opening goal did eventually come shortly after, with Marsh-Brown the man to snatch it. Frear's intelligent cross was driven to the edge of the area after the wide man had done well to make space, and Marsh-Brown was on hand to emphatically drive home in front of the 286 travelling supporters.

The Rovers faithful were in raptures once again minutes later when Parkin, shortly after coming on as a substitute, got in on the goal scoring act. His deft header was brilliantly directed past Harriers keeper Alex Palmer from a deep David Pipe free kick to essentially tie up the points.

The wind was truly blown out of the Kidderminster sails, and apart from an Andrew Fox shot that was driven wide, they struggled to muster a comeback. In fact it was Forest Green who pushed for a third, and were it not for a good stop by Palmer, O'Connor would have been celebrating another goal to add to his tally this season.

Guthrie also had a couple of chances, while Kiddy's Andre Wright had the final say in the game when his header from a Dawson free kick was drilled just wide of Jonny Maxted's right-hand post.

DESTINATION KIDDERMINSTER
Rambling Man

So far a perfect record away from home. Played two, no traffic jams conceded, early arrival at stadia. Clearly the Compo–Rambling Man National Trust strategy works, so why change a winning formula?

Today, an appointment with Harriers and Aggborough's famous pie

As it was his turn, Compo revved the Beamer and engaged warp speed. Initial destination was the Brockhampton Estate near Bromyard. The main building is half-timbered Red and White Rose dynasty job built in the 1430s. It is surrounded by a moat and entered past a tiny, matching timber-framed gatehouse, built in Tudor times 100 years later – for all the world looking like a big dolls' house. The experience is completed by a ruined Norman chapel, craft barns, 40 acres of leafy grounds and bands of locals recreating all manner of period stuff.

Yet there is a dark side. For decades, residents of Hereford and Worcestershire have asserted that Ambridge in Borsetshire (fictitious home of the *appalling Archers radio soap)* is none other than their own. Why would you claim that? As Tony Hancock had spoofed, it is "an everyday story of simple people". Rural drivel complete with ooh-arr accents, inbreeding and bestiality. Or so I am told. Was Brockhampton the stage set?

Lovely as the estate was, I could not help glancing over my shoulder. Wary of any over-friendly peasant or hawkish lord of the manor, and listening for strains of that infernal rumpty-tumpy tune.

**A
U
G
U
S
T**

"Let's be away, Compo, I want my pie!"

I've always liked Aggborough. Ever since Marc McGregor led us back from 3-0 down with 20 minutes to go. That draw went some way to rescuing our second Conference season in 2000.

And I was looking forward to seeing Jared Hodgkiss and Reece Styche, popular FGR old boys.

The match itself was bittersweet. We dominated in style with Keanu M-B and JP enhancing their goal tallies. Harriers were given nothing and looked low on confidence and ability.

Even Reece couldn't get convincingly angry. Good to see affable Chris Stokes come to support us, his Coventry City playing on Monday. Unexpectedly, I did not enjoy or finish my Aggborough pie – maybe I was missing Quorn?

HARRIERS ON THE WING DON'T HAVE A PRAYER
Jokerman

It is with increasing regularity one sees examples of how the tides of fortune turn in the world of football. Today's fixture again illustrates this phenomenon. Kidderminster Harriers won league status following a sustained campaign only to fall back into the non-league abyss. Today they seek their first win in five attempts.

Their opponents Forest Green Rovers, so long the whipping boys of this league, are chasing a sixth straight victory. It is astonishing to think this all came about for the Rovers when a man to whom football was remote, left a lay-by near you with an idea.

Pacesetters this season under Ady Pennock, FGR supporters making the journey up the M5 to their near neighbours will be hoping the nosebleed eases without falling back to earth. Always a popular fixture with Rovers fans if for no other reason than the food kitchen, which is legendary.

The Harriers bar was off limits to away fans following trouble with recent visitors Grimsby. The social club barn did enable one to stretch out and the ale was excellent. Observing the queue for the kitchen, very few fans were relinquishing the opportunity to partake of the meals on offer.

The team remained unchanged from the Lincoln game with Kelly returning to the bench after injury. Nearly 200 Rovers fans were behind the goal at the away end as the game kicked off.

Forest Green pressed early in the shape of Frear on the left. The winger crossed into the box and with O'Connor and Guthrie both trying to make contact Kidderminster custodian Palmer made the save.

It was a low-key start from both sides but Rovers looked the more accomplished. The home side were not posing much threat apart from a corner on 15 minutes punched well clear by Maxted in the Rovers goal. A Frear free kick to the back post saw Racine head wide while a Guthrie header from a Sinclair flicked cross was well saved by Palmer, conceding a corner that Jennings headed wide.

Rovers were creating the chances, limiting Kiddy to efforts from distance. On 39 minutes Kelly replaced Sinclair who was obviously injured as he limped off. The half ended with Rovers fans confident their side would step up the pace in the second period.

The game did indeed pick up and Kelly and Frear created a good chance for O'Connor early on but the striker could not make contact with the useful cross. At the other end Dawson from the edge of the area brought the only real save Maxted had to make all afternoon.

A tremendous run from halfway by Guthrie ended with him striking a fierce shot narrowly wide of the left-hand post. Around the hour mark Styche, the ex-FGR striker, replaced Verma in the Kidderminster attack. He certainly livened things up for the home side.

His first contact was a collision with Racine that threatened to realign his jaw and he was not pleased to see the referee wave play on. He did however win several free kicks for his side that saw them have their best spell of the game.

Ironically it was a break from defence during this period on 64 minutes that Forest Green took the lead. O'Connor slipped a pass down the left to Frear who raced to the by-line and pulled a low cross into the path of Marsh-Brown coming in on the edge of the area.

The striker hit a superb shot with controlled power into the roof of the net with Palmer helpless. The goal changed the complexion of the match and Rovers were now showing their superiority. Parkin replaced Frear on 70 minutes to add weight (ahem) to the attack.

Pipe just inside his own half near the touchline hoisted a free kick high into the Kiddy penalty area where the defence left it to Palmer. Parkin had other ideas and glanced the ball past the exposed keeper into the net with his first touch of the game on 72 minutes.

It was game over and following a flowing move from left to right between Wedgbury, Parkin and O'Connor, Rovers' top scorer was only denied by a good save by Palmer. Guthrie fired a powerful drive over the bar and at the death; substitute Wright perhaps came closest for Kidderminster when his header from a free kick found the side netting.

This was another clean sheet for Forest Green and Maxted would be the first to concede how well his defence protected him. Pipe was superb,

A
U
G
U
S
T

ably supported by the consistent Racine, Bennett and Jennings. The forwards are improving with every game. There are bigger tests ahead but success builds confidence and this team of players should fear no one in this league.

Monday 31.08.15
FGR 2 Bromley 1
JENNINGS AT THE DOUBLE IN LATEST VICTORY
Richard Joyce

A brace from the most unlikely of goalscorers helped Forest Green Rovers to make it a bank holiday weekend double against Bromley at The New Lawn, and extended the team's outstanding start to the season. Left back James Jennings has been known to pop up with one or two goals over his career, but his two goals ensured Rovers made it seven wins from seven to continue their stunning start at the top of the table.

Bromley will rank highly in terms of Forest Green's opponents so far. Last season's Conference South champions provided a tough test; however, the confidence streaming through Ady Pennock's side led to another three points. Jennings two goals were both scrappy, but Pennock won't care how they find their way in as his charges kept up the pace at the summit.

It was a hectic start that saw FGR push in front after only six minutes via an unorthodox Jennings touch. Elliott Frear's corner was met in the air by Aarran Racine, whose header was guided into Jennings's path at the back post, with the ball left to dart in. Within 60 seconds though, the away side hit back. Ali Fuseini's free kick from the left was met by the towering Alex Wall, and the former Luton Town man's looping header dropped in. Bromley's power was demonstrated when they took a stranglehold of the tie, and Rovers keeper Jonny Maxted produced a truly stunning save from Moses Emmanuel's to keep the scores level on 17 minutes, diving high and to his left.

Alan Julian is an experienced goalkeeper at this level, and he too was forced into action when he kept out Delano Sam-Yorke's effort in a frantic first half. He couldn't deny FGR from retaking the lead just before half time though when Jennings was on hand to snatch his second. Sam-Yorke had done well to power an effort through a sea of bodies toward goal, where the ball was picked up by Jennings on the line and shifted into the net, although there was a hint of offside surrounding the incident.

Rovers' fans wouldn't have cared how the ball had gone in though, but they would have been relieved to see Maxted in fine second-half form.

Firstly, he denied Bradley Goldberg with a brilliant save with his legs, and then produced an even better double-save minutes later from the same player. Not to be undone by his opposite number, Julian then kept the away side just about in the tie with two terrific saves. Jon Parkin was the first to be denied and then substitute Charlie Clough saw his header saved. There was still time for Keanu Marsh-Brown and Sam-Yorke to try and extend Rovers' lead, but Jennings's two goals were enough for another victory and another crucial three points.

GROTESQUE BUT ROVERS WIN AGAIN
Jokerman

Pennock has no qualms about changing a winning side and today sees Parkin and Sam-Yorke make the starting line-up, Guthrie and Marsh-Brown alongside Jones and Clough on the bench for the visit of Bromley FC. Newly promoted, the visitors are an unknown quantity apart from the goalkeeper Julian who has opposed Rovers for numerous clubs.

The rain had passed but the game was played under a cover of dark cloud. Forest Green started brightly for once and from a second-minute corner a shot from O'Connor brought a good save from Julian diving to his left.

On six minutes Rovers took the lead following a corner from the left taken by Frear. Racine 12 yards out mistimed his header but the ball dropped into the bottom right-hand corner of the goal.

A great start for Rovers that lasted all of a minute. A free kick to Bromley just inside Rovers' half on the left saw Fuseini put a high cross into the penalty area where a seven-foot Wall looped a header over Maxted caught in no-man's land. It knocked the home side out of their stride and fired Bromley who stormed into contention.

On 17 minutes they broke down the centre where Ademola created space for a shot struck viciously from the edge of the box for the top right-hand corner, denied only by Maxted's fingertips. Racine was then called upon to make a terrific block to deny Cook. Rovers replied when Yorke tested Julian after good link-up play between Pipe and Parkin. Bennett had to be replaced by Clough on 35 minutes with what turned out to be a broken nose.

Bromley then enjoyed better possession for a ten-minute spell with no end product which they came to regret on 43 minutes. A corner on the left by Kelly to the near post ended with the ball flashing across goal where a scramble ensued. Sam-Yorke stabbed the ball goalward and Jennings near the line forced it home. Julian was incensed, probably claiming an

**A
U
G
U
S
T**

offside but the referee waved him away. He was still protesting as the teams left the field for the half-time break.

Bromley felt short-changed for their first half endeavour and following a Frear shot early on that was caught by Julian at his near post, set about seeking an equalizer. They pressed Rovers back and a corner from the right found Wall challenged by Maxted who miss-hit his punch and the ball was hooked away.

Soon after Jennings was injured after some desperate defending and replaced by Jones. Tempers were getting a little heated and when O'Connor was tackled in the Bromley area screaming for a penalty, not given, it kicked off a 12-player conference. Pipe and Fuseini seemed to be the main subjects. The referee just let them all sort it out which, to be fair, they did so with no bloodshed.

Rovers were attacking mainly on the break now and Frear was wasteful blazing over a pass from Sam-Yorke.

Bromley substitute, Goldberg, made room on the edge of Rovers' penalty area and slipped the ball into the path of Ademola to his right. Maxted did brilliantly to save with his foot.

Around 65 minutes the Rovers keeper did even better when Cook played in Goldberg in the same position ten yards out. Again saving with his legs, the ball came back to Goldberg who smashed another shot that Maxted blocked away with Cook screaming for the simple pass when Maxted was on the floor.

Bromley lost a bit of heart after that and Rovers created a couple of chances at the other end. Frear and Parkin combined well ending with Julian making a good save to concede a corner and deny Parkins's clever flick. From the kick Clough powered a header goal-ward into the ground only to see Julian tip the bouncing ball over the bar.

Marsh-Brown replaced O'Connor for the final 20 minutes which saw Rovers defending their narrow advantage which took both them and the Forest Green supporters a long way out of their comfort zone.

They did, however, see the game out and will have learnt a great deal about the task ahead.

Bromley will feel gutted to have nothing to show but pleased with their performance.

Injuries pending, it will be interesting to see how Pennock manages the team on Saturday at Chester.

Lucky seven going on eight for Forest Green Rovers.

PERHAPS WE FLEW TOO CLOSE TO THE SUN? Two further victories saw the 100% streak reach a League record start of nine consecutive wins, leaving Rovers a yawning eight points ahead of second-placed county rivals, Cheltenham. Three defeats and a draw (at home to Cheltenham Town in the first of two thrilling El Glosicos) brought Rovers supporters down to earth and narrowed the lead at top place over the improving Robins.

there are Llamas in a field beside the entrance
and they're posing for the passing crowd who stare
there's a big red bus that's serving drinks and nibbles
and a festival-like feeling in the air

(Excerpt from 'No More The Little Team Upon The Hill' by Crispin Thomas)

Saturday 05.09.15
Chester 1 FGR 2
ROVERS SET LEAGUE RECORD WITH CHESTER WIN
Richard Joyce

Forest Green Rovers are National League record-breakers as victory at Chester saw the club become the first in the 36-year history of the league to earn eight consecutive victories at the start of a season. Rovers' unstoppable start to the campaign continued at the Lookers' Vauxhall Stadium as Elliott Frear and Aaron O'Connor fired home the goals that sealed another win. The contest was by far Ady Pennock side's toughest yet, but the strength and character of this group of players can never be doubted, and they passed the test posed by the opposition with flying colours.

Forest Green were on it from the start, and Chester goalkeeper Jon Worsnop was kept busy early on, with the 32-year-old made to produce a good save to deny Keanu Marsh-Brown's powerfully struck effort. Worsnop was required to make another crucial stop minutes later, when he denied FGR the chance to open the scoring from the penalty spot. After Kurtis Guthrie had been brought down in the box, Worsnop prevented Jon Parkin from firing home from 12 yards with a solid stop when diving to his left.

Jonny Maxted had remained untested in the opening half hour. The former Hartlepool keeper executed a fabulous save though to keep Chester at bay when it looked like they could have snatched a goal from a free

**S
E
P
T
E
M
B
E
R**

kick. The breakthrough came from Frear five minutes before the break when he netted for the first time this season. He latched onto Parkin's superb header to race clear on the left-hand side before dispatching a fine finish. It should have been two just before the interval when a similar situation led to Parkin trying his luck from 20 yards; however, Worsnop was equal to his low attempt.

Forest Green had dominated the opening 45 minutes, but the home side threw more into the game in the second period and offered a much bigger threat. Maxted tipped over Tom Shaw's strong hit but couldn't stop the hosts from finding an equalizer. John Rooney's fierce free kick, aimed towards the back post, was met by Luke George who nodded home emphatically to level the scores.

FGR's spirit remained unaffected, and it was O'Connor, stepping off the bench, who scored the afternoon's final goal to clinch the three points. The former Newport County man seized upon Marsh-Brown's excellent assist and fired in with a brilliant finish in front of the travelling Rovers supporters.

Forest Green have become something of experts of seeing out games this season, and they did just that despite the home side's best attempts to try and steal something. Maxted was equal to Ryan Higgins's low strike and the final opening fell to George Thomson who couldn't direct a header on target when he looked like he could head home.

DESTINATION CHESTER
Rambling Man
Man down! Compo failed a fitness test on his back which had succumbed to a return drive from Devon. So, it was Foggy and I who headed t'north to Cheshire, home of pristine, pimped 4-wheel drives.

Inspired by last week's rummage through fifteenth-century merrie England, we added a century and alighted at Little Moreton Hall, the famed black and white Tudor mansion. With admirable foresight, the wealthy Moreton family had sited their family seat conveniently close to M6 junctions 15 and 16. If you have but a spark of interest in how our Tudor ancestors lived, Little Moreton Hall is a must. Improbably built on marshland, the structure sits on a plinth of rosy stone, overbalanced and distorted as a Dismaland castle. Believe me, none of the rooms would suit Ikea square furniture even if you could erect the pesky things. The house is a wonder of pegged and carved ancient oak, lovingly maintained by the National Trust. Outside is a beautifully restored period garden and all is surrounded by a moat, the only access a stumpy stone bridge. Inside,

Tudor estate agents would no doubt have boasted about the two en-suite garde-robe facilities – small panelled rooms with stout wooden benches, holed to provide vertical drop to the moat. Who'd be a fish?

Unhappily for the Moretons, they backed the wrong side during the Civil War, and the Roundheads were quick to exact financial penalty. As their fortunes waned, the beneficiaries were the Dales (really!). Originally carpenters, the Dales retained the property all the way through to the 1950s, when it was donated to the National Trust. Older readers may ponder whether Mrs Dale kept a diary?

But hey, footie was on the menu at Chester's Lookers' Vauxhall Stadium. Good name, eh? Some indifferent welcomes in recent years were supplanted by a warm reception, and a good crowd including 60–70 of Gloucestershire's finest.

The well-oiled FGR machine produced another compelling performance to make it eight out of eight, with well-taken goals from Elliott Frear and Aaron O'Connor, and despite the unlikely sight of The Beast's saved spot kick. Yet the highlight for me was the nearly goal. At 2-1 up, we were deep in defence. Wedge snaffled the ball and passed forward to Keanu M-B who ignited the afterburners. From nowhere, he was overtaken by – was it a bird, was it Superman? – no, it was Dale Bennett! Scorching the ground behind him, he took Keanu's pass, left the full back for dead and centred. Chester cleared with difficulty as Aaron O'Connor and Kurtis threatened. When your team is burned off by the opposition's centre half, you know you are in trouble!

Saturday 12.09.15
FGR 2 Southport 1
SOUTHPORT LATEST SIDE WHO CAN'T STOP FGR
Richard Joyce
A couple of late scares did little to disrupt Forest Green Rovers' unbelievable start to the National League season that continued at pace with victory over Southport. Aaron O'Connor's and Keanu Marsh-Brown's first-half goals helped Rovers make it nine wins in a row and extended the club's fifth-tier record for consecutive league opening wins.

Liam Nolan's goal came as part of a resurgent Southport second-half performance, and although the Sandgrounders pushed hard for what would have been a terrific point, Ady Pennock's side hung on to claim all three points yet again.

A calm opening burst into life on 11 minutes when O'Connor slotted with a cool finish. The former Newport County man broke behind the

**S
E
P
T
E
M
B
E
R**

Southport line inside the box and applied an accurate effort that handed FGR the lead. It was two only ten minutes later when Marsh-Brown continued his goal-scoring habit with a fine goal. Kurtis Guthrie's pass to the wide man was met with a fierce strike that left Southport goalkeeper Andy Coughlin helpless.

Guthrie himself looked to get in on the goal scoring act midway through the half; however, his stinging drive was pushed away brilliantly by Coughlin. The former Wrexham keeper was busy in the opening stages of the second period as FGR looked to tie up a third goal to settle the tie early on. They struggled to get past Coughlin though who was equal to two good strikes from Marsh-Brown and O'Connor.

From that moment onward it was the opponents who claimed a grasp on the tie, and they almost drew a goal back on 55 minutes, as Connor McCarthy's deft header clipped the top of the bar. After Aarran Racine had headed powerfully over from an Elliott Frear corner, the visitors managed to edge back into the tie when they scored their first away goal of the season. Nolan was the man who had the final touch as the ball found its way in after Andrew Wright's initial header had been fantastically blocked on the line by Rob Sinclair. Southport sensed the opportunity to steal what would be a valuable point to take back to Merseyside, and they launched a late crusade on the FGR goal, but were almost nearly pegged back by a stunning effort from Sam Wedgbury. Wedgbury, yet to score in a Rovers shirt, was inches away though from adding what would have been a very useful match-winning goal, but his marvellous long-range effort smashed against the crossbar.

The visitors pushed on with substitute Jamie Allen denied brilliantly by David Pipe's block, and Jonny Maxted produced a stunning save at the near post from the threatening Mike Phenix.

They were crucial interventions in the closing stages of another key win that sees Pennock's side leading the way firmly at the top of the table.

Tuesday 15.09.15
Woking 2 FGR 1
WOKING MANAGE TO HALT FINE WINNING RUN
Richard Joyce
Woking became the first club this season to inflict defeat on Forest Green Rovers as Ady Pennock side's incredible winning run was brought to an end at Kingfield. John Goddard's and Jimmy Keohane's goals helped the Cardinals to all three points and ended Rovers' run of nine consecutive victories. An inspired late rally did see FGR almost pick up a point, and

after Kurtis Guthrie had found the back of the net, there was a big shout for a penalty late on. There was another unfortunate first for the season as Marcus Kelly was shown a second yellow card deep into stoppage time to become the first Rovers player sent off this season.

Woking's intentions were demonstrated right from the start in a first half they dominated. Jonny Maxted was forced into a good stop to deny Dan Holman's fierce strike, while Harry Cardwell's header fell only inches past the post. After Holman had again come close, Sam Wedgbury's vital clearance off the line kept the scorelines level.

A number of Forest Green half chances tripped up the Woking momentum, and Aaron O'Connor did have the ball in the back of the net on 41 minutes. However, the linesman had his flag up for offside after the striker had expertly headed in Rob Sinclair's neat ball. With the scores level heading for the break, a late Woking surge ensured they would score the game's first goal. Goddard broke free on the left, and after Maxted had saved his original strike, the ball looped up in the air and allowed the wide man to head into an empty net. Garry Hill's side pushed on in an attempt to clinch a quick second, but Maxted got his body behind the dangerous Bruno Andrade's well-struck effort.

If the first half had belonged to the hosts, the second was most definitely Forest Green's, and Aaron Racine, of all people, forced Jake Cole into his first meaningful save two minutes into the new half. Guthrie forced Cole into a simple save with a header, when, against the run of play, the Cardinals extended their lead. Former Exeter City man Keohane stroked home at the back post after the ball had eventually fallen to him, and Rovers' challenge became even greater.

The FGR response was swift, courtesy of a disastrous goalkeeping error from Cole, who couldn't stop Guthrie's hit from the right-hand side, and the ball trickled into the back of the net. A strong Rovers attack was launched for the clashe's final quarter of an hour, and Keanu Marsh-Brown went close with a header, while Delano Sam-Yorke, lining up against his former club, was even closer to nodding in an inch-perfect Marsh-Brown cross.

Two major incidents dominated the five minutes of stoppage time indicated by the fourth official. The first saw a major shout for a FGR penalty as Woking's on-loan Charlton Athletic defender, Terrell Thomas, looked to have awkwardly handled the ball in his own area. But after referee Chris Powell had ignored any Rovers appeals, he brandished a second yellow card to substitute Kelly right near the end of the game, to send him off for the first time in his career.

S E P T E M B E R

DESTINATION WOKING
Rambling Man

Not to put too fine a point on it, Woking is a bit of a cultural desert. Now, before Cards supporters put a contract out on me, I mean that is when you are looking for conveniently situated National Trust mansions. Eighteenth-century Clandon Park would be a good candidate had it not been torched in April. I blame the Jihadist acolytes of Norman Foster and Richard Rodgers. Why have the police taken so long to throw them into the clink and demolish some of their absurd cucumbers that litter the capital's skyline? I digress. So it was that Clegg, Compo and I set off for Kingfield (catchily renamed The Laithwaite Community Stadium), a destination short of a full trip. We were bereft of the culture hit that our giant intellects demanded.

But what this part of Surrey lacks in historical interest, it makes up for in the welcome their club affords to all supporters. Always a joy to see them even if they keep sending us away with bloodied noses. Also, I have to commend the giant, tasty sausages I consumed which I told myself were 100% Quorn.

Rovers had better get used to being Goliaths, strange though that may seem. If our form continues, along with the TV exposure, we will always be facing Davids on testosterone, even if they come in the form of bigger clubs. And a young, injury-hit Woking side were up for this one. Slick and fast-moving, and in our faces in midfield: a typical Gary Hill unit. The match was a compelling, high-quality spectacle. Woking deservedly led at half time but Rovers had carved out several good chances, all spurned. Second half belonged to Nailsworth, but the 2-1 reverse reflected Woking's sharper cutting edge and poor finishing by the away side, who laid siege to the home goal. First points dropped and Marcus Kelly dismissed for two un-Marcus like fouls.

As it happened, the rambling side of our trip took place after the match. With the M4 closed between Reading and Hungerford, we headed back through Abingdon, Farringdon, Fairford and Cirencester. Would have been nice if we could have seen anything. May Macclesfield bring country mansions aplenty and a return to winning ways

Saturday 19.09.15
Macclesfield Town 4 FGR 1
FOREST GREEN SLIP UP AT THE MOSS ROSE
Richard Joyce

Forest Green Rovers have very rarely suffered off-days in the past 12 months, so defeat at Macclesfield Town will be very quickly forgotten, especially in light of the team's continued leadership of the National League table.

Jon Parkin's early goal looked to set Rovers on their way to what would have been an incredible tenth win in eleven matches this season. However, a Kristian Dennis double, coupled with further strikes from Paul Lewis and Danny Whitaker, clinched a huge three points for their former Football League hosts. Looking to bounce back from a first defeat this season on Tuesday at Woking, the occasion started perfectly when Parkin rammed home against his former club. The experienced front man profited from a fine run by Keanu Marsh-Brown down the left, who drew the ball back for him to give Ady Pennock's side an early advantage.

Macclesfield's response was immediate, and Jonny Maxted was called upon to make a stunning diving save to deny Lewis from heading in an equalizer. Rovers' young goalkeeper was involved in a rare error on the quarter of an hour mark though that saw the Silkmen draw the tie level. A difficult back pass saw him robbed of the ball by the pressuring Dennis, and the opposition's top goalscorer this season profited by snatching the ball to roll into an empty net. The hosts looked to threaten without ever really testing the FGR goal, and were it not for a vital Neill Byrne tackle on 31 minutes, then Rob Sinclair would surely have raced through to restore Forest Green's lead.

Instead the midfielder was sent off for the first time in his career on the stroke of half time as Macclesfield were awarded a penalty. The former Stevenage midfielder was adjudged to have handled Lewis's header on goal in an unexpected incident that saw none of the home side's players appeal, who themselves appeared shocked to profit by the official's decision. They took full advantage though from the spot as Dennis rolled the ball in to hand Macclesfield a half-time lead and leave Rovers with an uphill battle, while down to ten men.

Rovers set up for the second half with three at the back, as the hosts resumed control of the affair, claiming their third goal on 64 minutes. Lewis found a gap in the FGR box and nodded home terrifically for his second goal of the season. Maxted made a crucial save minutes later from Danny Whitehead in an attempt to try and keep his side in the game. It would take a massive push for Rovers to prevent a second consecutive defeat, and only a Delano Sam-Yorke header, saved comfortably by Shwan Jalal, ever really threatened. So much so that Macclesfield rubbed salt into the wounds late on when they sealed a fourth. Whitaker was the beneficiary as the midfielder swept home past the outstretched Maxted's

S
E
P
T
E
M
B
E
R

glove. It was a rare bad day at the office for a Forest Green side whose unbelievable start to the season still sees them reign supreme at the top of the National League table – with back-to-back home games to follow next.

DESTINATION MACCLESFIELD
Rambling Man

Hungry for another taste of northern architecture, Compo, Foggy and I met bright and early at Stonehouse Court and whizzed up the M6. At Compo's request our first stop was a period estate whose popularity could easily be gauged by the hordes of parked cars. There we met some Grecian fans and compared notes on our respective fixtures that day. Unfortunately, we lost track of time, and ended up leaving Keele Services rather hurriedly, still an hour from our intermediate destination, Lyme Park House at Disley, near Stockport.

Not sure Jeremy Corbyn would take to this impressive pile, owned by the same filthy capitalist dogs for some 600 years. Only kidding prime minister elect; hope that doesn't affect my knighthood.

Ramrod straight, the grey-buff elevations are classical, tall and austere and hark back to the mid-1500s, with major modifications in the eighteenth and nineteenth centuries. It is a world away from the bent, half-timbered manors we have seen in recent weeks. No doubt its architects would have been overjoyed to know that Lyme Park House's status has been assured for posterity – by its use for TV costume soaps such as *Pride and Prejudice*, and inevitably featuring Colin Firth. Does he ever wear jeans – don't think I have ever seen him in anything other than breeches and hunting boots? I appear to be digressing again. The undulating 400-acre estate also contains a turreted Elizabethan hunting tower, not that we had chance to take a peak. To our shame, three quarters of an hour supping Costas at Keele meant a quick 20-minute march around Lyme Park House. Oops, the Philistines are upon us.

Regrettably, 20 minutes at Lyme was a whole lot better than 90 at The Moss Rose. It pains me to recall all but the first minute when Keanu strolled through most of the Silkmen before crossing to the unmarked Beast. So alone was he that he syringed his ears and buffed his nails before tapping in. The following 89 was a disjointed mess which left me needing counselling by the soothsayers on our Forum. In the scheme of things, maybe it was a clever ruse by Ady to lull The Robins ahead of Tuesday's Gloucestershire derby (Part 1). I sure hope so.

THE SILKMEN APPLY THE FEATHERS AS ROVERS ROLL OVER
Jokerman

The fog was still down as Forest Green fans headed north on the Kendo Flyer. There was time to reflect on Tuesday's first defeat at Woking. According to witness accounts, it was a continuation of the second-half showing against Southport the previous Saturday. It is disconcerting that the result was no great surprise and shadowed by Ady Pennock's team selection, particularly the Marcus Kelly issue.

Be that as it may, events transpired that would give Tom Bender his chance this afternoon. Macclesfield is one of the most welcoming clubs in non-league and Moss Rose has a scenic backdrop to match TNL. Unfortunately the local proper ale was absent today but no matter: the sun had broken through and the playing surface looked immaculate. The team news broke and it was clear that Bender had been marginalized by only making the bench. Pennock played Jones and moved Bennett to left back. He also trod on Guthrie's ego by forcing him wide in place of Frear and instated Parkin as main striker with O'Connor.

The new white strip clearly dazzled Macclesfield as, after only two minutes' play, Marsh-Brown danced down the left wing, turned two defenders inside out, cut inside and picked out Parkin who, from close range, crashed the ball into the net via a couple of desperate attempts to block. A dream start which stung the home side into action and a pinpoint cross from the right saw Lewis power a header that Maxted palmed away with a flying save to his left. For Rovers Sinclair floated in a good free kick that was nodded down but Parkin missed the ball completely when he could have doubled the score.

It proved costly as on 15 minutes a long clearance down field from Macclesfield resulted in Dennis, the liveliest striker on the park, chasing a forlorn hope. Maxted failed to deal with the back pass from Pipe. Dennis arrived and prodded the ball past him and with both players on the floor the ball spun in slow motion over the goal line. It was agony for Rovers and encouraged the home side who won two quick corners. Rovers hit back when Parkin threaded a pass through to Sinclair running into the area only to be thwarted by a goal-saving tackle by Byrne. Jones hesitated on a clearance which gave Sampson a sight of goal but fortunately his shot fizzed wide of Maxted's left-hand post. The impressive Dennis again went close from an acute angle.

After 40 minutes with neither side dominating proceedings it was all about to change. A corner from the right by Fitzpatrick to the back post was met with a downward header from Sampson. The ball bounced

**S
E
P
T
E
M
B
E
R**

dangerously towards the far corner and the defence went up and in the melee the unfortunate Sinclair was challenged as he jumped for the ball which struck his arm and went over the bar. The lino started waving his flag in a demented fashion which indicated a foul (a penalty is a flag across the chest). Whatever, the referee gave a penalty and sent Sinclair off, a decision that surprised even the Macclesfield players. Dennis stepped up and hit the ball into the bottom left-hand corner as Maxted moved right.

The half time whistle blew. As the emergency services flew in Sherpas from Nepal and Pennock issued ice axes and clamp-ons, the 56 FGR fans were left to ponder. Surely it wasn't just weight of money that racked up nine wins against the also-rans.

No changes at half time and Pennock's answer to start was to move Pipe to midfield (is Lionel Messi a goalkeeper?) and Bennett to full back. Macclesfield were on top from the off, pushing Rovers back. The danger was down the flanks and full back Halls raided on the right and crossed superbly for Lewis whose powerful header skimmed narrowly over. After an hour with the defence struggling Pennock changed the attack, replacing Marsh-Brown and Guthrie with Sam-Yorke and Frear which had fans puzzled. It made no difference as Macclesfield continued in the ascendency with Whitehead testing Maxted from distance and soon after on 64 minutes it was effectively game over. Another telling cross, this time from the left saw the unmarked Lewis put an unstoppable header past the exposed Maxted. The Rovers keeper was more than making up for his howler and was at his best to palm away a blistering shot from Whitehead and Sampson also had an effort frantically blocked away.

On 70 minutes Rovers should have reduced the deficit when in a rare attack Bennett broke through on the left and squared the ball to Sam-Yorke who failed to make proper contact and put the ball wide from close range. To compound Rovers' misery Wedgbury was booked for a foul which triggered a one-match ban. From the free kick Maxted beat away a good effort from Dennis. On 75 minutes Pennock finally replaced Parkin with Kamdjo relieving Pipe in midfield. Rovers were finally laid to rest on 84 minutes when a neat ball over the top of the back line found Holroyd who picked out Whitaker with a square pass and he duly buried the ball and any recovery hopes. As the game ended O'Connor did set up Sam-Yorke in a good position but the striker blazed hopelessly over the bar which summed up the afternoon for FGR fans.

The importance of Tuesday's game cannot be underestimated. The quicker Ady Pennock makes the author eat his words and changes the perception that FGR have the players but Cheltenham have the manager, the happier everyone will be. As FGR fans headed into the sunset the red sky reflected the embarrassment of today's performance and one envied Bob Hunt, John Light and co who no doubt enjoyed a glorious day for Gloucestershire at Lords.

Tuesday 22.09.15
FGR 2 Cheltenham Town 2 (El Glosico 1)
ROVERS RESPOND TWICE TO EARN DERBY DRAW
Richard Joyce

The first Forest Green Rovers and Cheltenham Town derby for 16 years lived up to the hype at The New Lawn as Forest Green twice came from behind to earn a point. David Pipe's first goal for the club, and Kurtis Guthrie's fourth of the season, helped Rovers continue their reign at the top of the National League table against a Cheltenham side who stay second. Amari Morgan-Smith's opener on the stroke of half time had given the Robins the lead, and after Pipe had got FGR back in the game, Harry Pell stroked home to restore Gary Johnson's side's lead. However, Guthrie continued to illustrate his outstanding aerial prowess by getting up well to head home an equalizer eight minutes from time.

Injuries and suspensions led to a new look central midfield with Pipe joined by new arrival Darren Carter whose signing was only revealed just before kick-off. Meanwhile, another new arrival was also featured on the team sheet with goalkeeper Dale Eve named among the substitutes following his loan move from Premier League Stoke.

Good early pressure from Rovers put Cheltenham on the back foot. Elliott Frear tried his luck from distance, while Keanu Marsh-Brown's fierce strike was brilliantly tipped round the post by Dillon Phillips. Another fine Phillips save denied Aaron O'Connor who looked like he was about to burst the back of the net, with the match's opening goal falling the way of the visitors only minutes later. Morgan-Smith's guided finish from a low George McLennan cross was finely tucked away by the former Luton Town forward only seconds before the interval.

Forest Green were again the better side after the break, and Aaron Downes almost put the ball through his own net for Cheltenham ten minutes into the second half, only to see his deflection from Pipe's cross fly onto the post. Pipe, a former Cheltenham player, then levelled the affair. He nodded home Marsh-Brown's pinpoint free kick to put his current side on level terms. Frear then tried completing an FGR reverse, but Phillips was equal to his low thump after the tricky winger had engineered a snapshot in the away side's box. A crucial Jonny Maxted

**S
E
P
T
E
M
B
E
R**

double-save denied the away side on 74 minutes. The young keeper first denied Morgan-Smith and then got up quickly to superbly block Jack Barthram's follow-up. He couldn't stop Pell from putting Cheltenham back in front though, as minutes later the former AFC Wimbledon midfielder fired home from Jack Munn's intelligent over-the-top ball.

The former Football League outfit's lead was short-lived though, and Guthrie drew the tie level once again with the evening's final goal. Frear's cross towards the back post from the left saw Guthrie unchallenged by defender Danny Parslow, and the 22-year-old produced an unstoppable header that maintained Forest Green's leadership of the National League for yet another week.

ROBINS' WINGS CLIPPED TWICE AS ROVERS STAY TOP
Jokerman

Going in to this much-anticipated local derby visitors Cheltenham Town were by far the form side having recently beaten both Macclesfield and Woking who each in turn floored the Rovers. Understandably there was much trepidation among FGR supporters and only the most optimistic were expecting a home win. Pennock's team selections were coming under scrutiny following the two defeats and the loaning out of Kamdjo to Boreham Wood caused some consternation. Tonight's team sheet indicated that Darren Carter had been signed and was in the line-up which saw the return of Kelly and Frear, with Pipe remaining in midfield and Parkin warming the bench.There was a good atmosphere in the stadium as 3,000- plus fans warmed up as the air temperature dropped on a fine but cool evening.

From the kick-off Forest Green took the game to Cheltenham and with little exaggeration camped in their half for 45 minutes. The visitors played Wright up front as a lone striker and were content to play deep and absorb Rovers' efforts on goal. Added to this was some very robust tackling with defenders diving in and making the FGR attack aware they were in for a no-quarter game. For all their territorial advantage and several corners it was only in the 34th minute that Rovers came close when a deflected shot from Marsh-Brown went narrowly wide.

The referee was keeping his notebook in his pocket despite Cheltenham's aggression conceding free kicks for fun, so it was ironic that Carter was booked for Rovers especially as the chopsy Cheltenham defender Storer had a lot to say about it. To the delight of the FGR fans he himself was booked soon after.

On 40 minutes new signing Carter, who was impressing, picked out

O'Connor in the right corner of the area. The striker took a touch but his low shot was too close to Phillips the Cheltenham keeper who was down well to make the save. Soon after Marsh-Brown made a great run on the left along the by-line and crossed invitingly for Guthrie or O'Connor to apply the finish, but the ball somehow evaded both and the chance was gone.

A minute later Rovers were behind. The ball was cleared down field and in the first meaningful Cheltenham attack they took the lead. Wright knocked the ball wide to McLennan; overlapping on the left he cut into the box and squared the ball to Morgan-Smith who, under pressure, slipped the ball wide of Maxted into the net on 45+1 minutes. It was greeted with a stunned silence by the home fans and some amazement by the visitors. One of those cruel-game moments. It would alter Pennock's team talk but Rovers had done little wrong and were playing well.

The second half started with Cheltenham indicating they would not be sitting on their lead and immediately went on the offensive. The game opened up and following a corner to the visitors their fans were screaming for a penalty when Wright went down but the referee was having none of it. Rovers stepped up their own game and began to apply some real pressure on the Cheltenham defence. Pipe who was putting this column straight on a few points, was having a storming game in midfield and was inspirational on the night.

Around 55 minutes he found himself put through into the area and despite the 'nosebleed', he hit a cross that Downes in blocking came close to an OG but for the ball striking the post. This lifted Rovers and they won a succession of corners which gave good voice to their fans behind the goal.

On 64 minutes the pressure paid off when they won a free kick 35 yards out to the left of goal. Marsh-Brown stepped up and delivered a mighty cross over the penalty spot. Pipe, now acclimatized, his head shining like a homing beacon and the ball wired correctly, flicked it goal-wards beyond Phillips and inside the right-hand post. The crowd were up and it was game on. Frear tested Phillips with a low shot as Rovers went after a second goal. Cheltenham were by no means subdued and on 73 minutes Maxted had to be at his very best with a tremendous double-save. Morgan-Smith, with a clear sight of goal, hit a ferocious shot that had the keeper at full stretch to parry away only as far as Barthram who wasted no time in smashing a shot that Maxted, on his knees, again blocked away.

This in turn inspired the visitors and on 77 minutes they regained their

SEPTEMBER

advantage with a goal from Pell. Munns, the diminutive Cheltenham winger who would be vertically challenged by a corner flag, put in a splendid cross that found Pell in space in the centre; the striker took the ball brilliantly, turned in one movement and placed a controlled shot wide of Maxted into the right side of the goal.

It was a goal to savour for Cheltenham fans but just when they thought they were top of the league five minutes later they weren't any more. A Rovers raid down the right flank saw a dangerous cross punched away by Phillips. The ball fell to Frear lurking on the left edge of the area; he quickly cut to the by-line and crossed accurately to Guthrie at the back post who powered his header past Phillips. RJ went into South American commentary mode to acclaim the goal and it was no more than Forest Green deserved.

The final minutes of the game were played out with both sides wary of losing and Rovers fans could take solace from the fact the team had put in a really good shift in all departments after recent reversals. A win against another strong side in Gateshead on Saturday and Ady Pennock will have his troops back on track for the formidable trip to Grimsby.

Saturday 26.09.15
FGR 0 Gateshead 1
GATESHEAD LOSS LEAVES ROVERS FRUSTRATED
Richard Joyce

A single Jimmy Phillips goal condemned Forest Green Rovers to a first home loss of the season, although Rovers will be left to wonder how they didn't at least come away with a point. Phillips's early strike stunned The New Lawn crowd early on, but despite a dominant display that led to a series of openings in front of goal, the returning Sam Russell failed to see the back of his net breached. Results elsewhere mean FGR stay top of the National League table for another week, although the three points for the travelling Tynesiders means they've closed the gap at the summit.

There were encouraging signs in the opening couple of minutes. Aaron O'Connor managed to break free near the start but was foiled by Russell. While at the other end, Gateshead clinched an all-important early goal when Phillips, who played under Ady Pennock in the youth set-up at Stoke City, scored with a fine finish into the bottom corner, having been teed up by another former FGR face in the shape of James Marwood.

Rovers seemed hardly rattled by Gateshead's quick lead, and they set about looking to find a quick equalizer. Great work by Elliott Frear down the left saw him find O'Connor twice, but the former Newport

County man couldn't level the scores. The lively forward then had his best chance yet just past the half-hour mark. He couldn't take it though as he slammed an effort inside the box onto the crossbar. A scramble in front of the Gateshead goal five minutes before the break somehow saw the visitors left unscathed in the opening half's final major moment.

New life was needed if FGR were to find a fresh way to break down a sturdy Gateshead defence, and Jon Parkin's introduction as a substitute saw the experienced striker force two openings. After Kurtis Guthrie had fired wide, Rovers biggest second-half chance fell the way of Frear, whose low strike was blocked on the line at the last moment when it looked as though the tricky winger was all but set to level the tie. Time was running out, but there was still time and still chances for Ady Pennock's charges to find a way through. Keanu Marsh-Brown's strongly hit drive was deflected inches past the post, while Russell saved well from Darren Jones's strike from distance. Late substitute Charlie Clough produced the match's final effort deep into stoppage time, although his header from a Frear cross couldn't provide the home support with the last-gasp moment of glory they craved.

GATES CLOSED ON ROVERS' POINTLESS EXERCISE
Jokerman

On a beautiful spring afternoon Forest Green Rovers went in search of a result that would strengthen their position at the top of the National League. A tally of one point from nine in the three previous encounters was sowing seeds of doubt among the pessimists. The optimists, however, were encouraged by an improved display against Cheltenham Town on Tuesday, Rovers twice coming from behind to gain a point. The revolving door on suspensions was in operation as Sinclair replaced Pipe in midfield. O'Connor and Guthrie led the attack.

There was a minute's applause to mark the passing of Paul Kirby, a true gentleman and loyal Rovers supporter, prior to kick-off. Rovers pressed and as early as the second minute Gateshead keeper Russell saved low down from O'Connor who was to have a major influence on the game's outcome. Gateshead's only meaningful attack of the afternoon occurred on five minutes when Marwood on the right slipped a short pass inside to Phillips. From the corner of the area he struck a low shot across Maxted into the bottom left-hand corner of the net. The 30 travelling Heed supporters thought that was a decent start. The atmosphere inside the stadium went into tumbleweed mode.

Rovers replied when Frear gave O'Connor a pass that saw Russell block away the striker's shot. Twenty minutes and Frear again did well down the left and put in O'Connor with his back to goal six yards out and who chose not to turn but back-heeled the ball wide. All Rover's meaningful attempts on goal were coming through Frear. On 27 minutes he switched to the right flank and resisted two fierce tackles to set up O'Connor with a clear sight of goal. Rovers' top marksman lashed the ball into the space between the top of the stand and the moon. Five minutes later another Frear cross was deflected into O'Connor who then from point-blank range and with no composure whatsoever, but hey! this is non-league, smashed his shot against the crossbar. Marsh-Brown also fired over from distance and as the half ended no one could put the finishing touch to a goalmouth scramble.

At half time fans seemed resigned to one-of-those-days scenarios. The second half began as the first ended with Rovers chasing the game. The Gateshead defence was coping well, with skipper Clark marshalling his troops well. He himself was dominating the aerial battle and Russell was determined to remain unbeaten on his return to TNL. Pennock replaced the luckless O'Connor with Parkin on 54 minutes and things did improve albeit only by a small margin. The big man came close with an overhead kick as the ball bounced high inside the area. With Russell helpless the ball went narrowly wide of the left-hand post. Parkin then put in Marsh-Brown down the right and his cross fell to Frear in front of goal, but his goal-bound shot was cleared away off the line via Russell and full back Baxter.

As the clock ticked away desperate minutes, Frear again did well to pass inside to Marsh-Brown, who cut in to the Gateshead defence and unleashed a terrific shot that was heading for the right-hand corner, only to skim the wrong side of the post with the slightest of deflections. With time running out Jones fired the ball into the arms of Russell from distance and late sub Clough looped a header wide to bring down the curtain on a day of frustration for Forest Green.

As O'Connor headed towards the cowshed with his banjo for extra training, Rovers fans were left to reflect on missed opportunities. They can take solace from the results in the division. Overall it is taking on a picture of mediocrity. There are form upsets every week. Forest Green will be fishing for points at Grimsby on Saturday who are on an unbeaten run of six, so that's due to end. With such inconsistencies, who knows? Even O'Connor may play a decent tune assuming he is on board the trawler, of course.

A DRAW AT GRIMSBY, two defeats, and four wins served to stabilize Rovers' season and kept them at the top of the pile, stalked as ever by Cheltenham Town

Farmcotian's shorts are magic
They brings us such great luck
But when Guiseleys goalie wore them
They looked like they'd got stuck

(Excerpt from 'The Farmcotian's Shorts' by The Operator)

Saturday 03.10.15
Grimsby Town 1 FGR 1
PARKIN STRIKES TO EARN GRIMSBY POINT
Richard Joyce

Jon Parkin's stunning first-half goal earned Forest Green Rovers a very useful point in a clash between two entertaining sides at Blundell Park. The big striker popped up with a magnificent strike to cancel out Jon-Paul Pittman's goal from only a couple of minutes before. An eye-catching contest was well fought between the two outfits, who will both be targeting a finish at the top end of the National League this year.

Looking to recover from a frustrating afternoon last time out against Gateshead, Rovers started this encounter strongly in front of a vociferous home crowd. Pinball in the hosts' box saw the former Football League survive an early scare, while Parkin saw a header from close range blocked well by Josh Gowling. Grimsby themselves offered a real threat going forward. Ben Tomlinson spurned a couple of openings, but Pittman's tidy finish just past the half-hour mark saw them gain the upper hand. He latched onto Craig Disley's header from a throw-in, and on the turn produced a powerful shot that couldn't be kept out by Jonny Maxted.

The Rovers response was remarkably swift. Despite suffering from a calf problem that came close to ruling him out, Parkin scored a fine equalizer. He received the ball on the right, tucked inside away from a defender, and fired beautifully past the outstretched James McKeown with a brilliant left-footed effort.

From that point onwards both sides took their turn to battle for what would have proved to be a winner. Disley volleyed narrowly over for Grimsby just before the break, while Tomlinson struggled in his attempts to guide the ball home after Jack Mackreth's cross from the right had found the on-loan Barnet man. After Tomlinson had headed narrowly

O
C
T
O
B
E
R

over on 59 minutes, Darren Jones proved the unlikely provider of two good chances for FGR as they looked to take on the task of applying attacking pressure on the home outfit. The Welsh defender had a low shot saved by McKeown, and last-ditch defending prevented him from forcing the ball home after it had found its way through to him from a set piece. Grimsby boss Paul Hurst threw on a number of dangerous substitutes in an attempt to steal all three points. Marcus Marshall provided a real threat when introduced, and his low cross for the energetic Disley was very nearly headed in by the former Bristol Rovers midfielder, only for Maxted to snatch the ball out of the air. Marshall again delivered a good ball into the box for Shaun Pearson to meet late on, but the towering defender couldn't hit the target with a header, and the contest was brought to an end with Rovers returning to Gloucestershire with a very useful point in tow.

DESTINATION GRIMSBY
Rambling Man

Man down! Compo had rung to rasp his defeat by triple pneumonia. So it was just Foggy (at the wheel) for the journey to Cleethorpes with me managing the Satnav.

The immediate target was Tattershall Castle, yet another homage to Tudor England, right next door to RAF Conningsby, home of the Battle of Britain Flight. Just 45 minutes' drive from the Theatre of Fish, Tattershall is the definitive Tudor castle, looking for all the world like a brick-built Tower of London. Still wonderfully complete, inside and out, it dates from 1231. But much of what is now on show is a state of the art castle/palace commissioned for Ralph, Lord Cromwell, Treasurer of England. It was erected over a period of 20 years from 1430, mostly during the reign of Henry VIII.

Tattershall has a deep-walled moat (as any self-respecting castle should) and no less than five storeys. The view from the dizzying 40-metre-high battlements is astonishing and likely to daunt anyone who suffers vertigo. Cheek by jowl is the Guardhouse (now National Trust ticket office and Café), a drunkenly settled brick outhouse, and the contrasting grey Ancaster stone Collegiate Church of the Holy Trinity, all built about the same time as the castle.

Now if that was not enough pre-match entertainment, the sky filled with the throb of Merlin engines as a Hurricane and Spitfire swooped and climbed around the castle grounds. It was mesmerising, an unforgettable experience, unlike the afternoon's game. Looking on the bright side, in my five visits to Blundell Park, the mistake-littered 1-1 draw was an improvement on four straight defeats. But the 5,000-strong crowd saw little to enthuse, and many started the trek home with ten minutes or more to go.

Highlights were few – Pittman's control swivel and shot for Grimsby's opener, and The Beast's shrugging off of rugby tackle and sublime finish soon after. As usual, Elliott teased and scampered past his markers but his spot-on crosses had no takers. The second half produced nought but amnesia.

Tuesday may see Rovers demoted from top position from the first time in two months. May we show our better side on TV v Aldershot on Wednesday 7th, to ensure any such aberration is temporary.

Tuesday 06.10.15
Aldershot Town 0 FGR 3
ROVERS TURN ON THE STYLE FOR ALDERSHOT WIN
Richard Joyce

A stunning first-half performance saw Forest Green Rovers reclaim top spot in the National League with an impressive televised win at Aldershot. Temporarily knocked off the division's top perch for the first time since mid-August by Cheltenham on goal difference on Tuesday, a superb showing at the EBB Stadium restored Rovers' position at the top of the non-league pyramid. A first goal for Darren Carter, as well as goals from striking duo Kurtis Guthrie and Aaron O'Connor, helped Ady Pennock's side move three points clear at the summit.

Keen to get back to winning ways in front of the BT Sport cameras, FGR dominated the opening 45 minutes with a stylish display, although it was very much end to end from the first whistle early on.

The lively Rhys Browne provided an early threat for the hosts, while Keanu Marsh-Brown forced ex-Swindon Town goalkeeper Phil Smith into a smart stop in one of the opening quarter of an hour's most notable chances. From the midpoint of the half Forest Green took control. Jon Parkin came agonizingly close to finding the net from a Dale Bennett cross, and the front man was again denied by a crucial block on the line just minutes later. Aarran Racine's headed effort from a Marcus Kelly free kick was well stopped by Smith, but he couldn't prevent Carter from deservedly breaking the deadlock. Fine play in the attacking third saw the ball reach Elliott Frear on the left-hand side, and the winger teed up Carter for a well-placed strike from distance that nestled in the bottom corner. It was two just before half time when Guthrie's classy finish

OCTOBER

extended the Rovers advantage – and there could be no complaints from the Aldershot faithful in the crowd. Marsh-Brown slipped a perfect pass into Guthrie's path, and with Smith coming out to narrow the angle, the young striker produced a wonderful, dinked finish over the 35-year-old to seal a superb first-half showing.

The first 45 minutes had been breathless, and rather inevitably the second half began gradually. The Shots's Damon Lathrope generated the first opening when his low shot was well stopped by Jonny Maxted. And the young FGR keeper was on hand to pull off a terrific reaction save minutes later as he denied Jim Stevenson who looked set to head his team back into the tie. Carter was playing a leading role in the Rovers midfield, and he almost bagged himself a second goal when on 74 minutes his header from a corner smashed onto the crossbar. Forest Green's attacking qualities had impressed, and at the other end Aldershot couldn't break down a resolute defensive performance, while substitute O'Connor put the cherry on the top of the cake late on. He latched onto a marvellous knock-down header from Parkin and dispatched a well-driven finish past Smith to clinch the evening's final goal.

There was still time in stoppage time for both teams to share some big chances. Maxted pushed Cheye Alexander's long-range shot over the bar, while Parkin could have scored his team's fourth with a strike on goal that trickled just wide of the post, in what was the final opportunity in an excellent Rovers performance.

DESTINATION ALDERSHOT
Rambling Man

No cultural destinations ahead of the Aldershot match. Clegg and Compo joined me early evening at Stroud for the 'Shots' trip, having earlier attended Paul Kirby's funeral at Westerleigh Crematorium.

I did not know Paul other than as a face in the Carole Embrey. But I was touched by the many tributes paid to him on the Forum and best wishes passed to his loved ones. Much was said about his dry-stone walling around the county and how it represents an enduring tribute to a much-loved person. It put me in mind of the epitaph for Christopher Wren in St Paul's Cathedral: "Reader, if you seek his monument, look around you."

So, we reached the EBB Stadium in a more reflective mood than usual. Not least because Rovers had gone five games since a win and our bogey team was in town – BT Sport Live. Yet by the end of the evening we were fizzing! The EBB is an old stadium in genteel decay. But it is characterful and a reminder of the football experience of many decades ago. More to the point, it is a welcoming and friendly place. I like it and still recall Beesley's first-minute goal, in Jim Harvey's best season, 2007/08, that gave Rovers a one nil win. Yet, Aldershot had the last laugh as they were promoted.

In habitual fashion, Rovers started slowly. So slowly in fact that diminutive rocket Rys Browne ran from the kick-off through the entire team. He would have scored the quickest individual goal in history had Superted not been awake.

It took a while for Rovers to come to terms with Browne, but they did soon enough, and then set about their task in style. As at Woking and v Cheltenham and Gateshead, they fashioned and spurned heaps of glorious chances.

But two goals at the end of the half were worth the tease. Frear set up Carter for his first goal for the club, then Keanu and The Beast worked a thing of beauty for Kurtis. Rovers rather sat back in half two. But Kurtis had a second disallowed, for what turned out to be an ill-judged offside flag. Then Carter's header rattled the bar.

Finally, Aaron O'Connor played supersub again to complete the impressive 3-0 scoreline. And just to show strength in depth, Cloughie replaced Jonah for the last eight minutes in a dominating cameo. So, our smile returned. Bring on Yorkshire's finest, namely Guiseley.

Saturday 10.10.15
FGR 3 Guiseley 0
THERE'S NO STOPPING HIGH-FLYING ROVERS
Richard Joyce
Another three goals, another clean sheet and another three points helped Forest Green extend their stay at the top of the National League table. Rovers' lead at the summit of the fifth tier is now five points over closest rivals Cheltenham. Elliott Frear's terrific finish started the scoring midway through the first half, while second-half goals from Jon Parkin and Aaron O'Connor wrapped up a fine home win.

FGR will now face a tough trip to Eastleigh on Tuesday, after overcoming a Guiseley side who started brightly when Wayne Brooksby's third-minute shot came close to finding the net. Kurtis Guthrie couldn't find the target with his low effort on 15 minutes, and Keanu Marsh-Brown was foiled by a great Steven Drench stop shortly after. The visitors, facing Rovers for the first time in a league fixture, threatened through on-loan wide man George Maris, but they were pegged back when Frear got Forest Green's first. Parkin's delightful cross found the left winger in

O C T O B E R

acres of space inside the box, and he cannoned an emphatic half-volley into the back of the net.

Former Morecambe 'keeper Drench was determined to not be beaten again before half time, and he saved well from efforts powered towards goal by Parkin and Darren Carter. Parkin had the ball in the back of the net five minutes into the second half, but it was ruled out for a foul after he had headed in Frear's corner. Jonny Maxted made a good stop to secure Rovers' lead from Maris shortly after, while Guthrie's thunderbolt was pushed away well by Drench at the other end. The Guiseley glove-man was picking the ball out of his own net again only a minute later though when Parkin made no mistake from the spot after Guthrie had been brought down just inside the area.

O'Connor came off the bench in Wednesday's televised win at Aldershot and scored with virtually his first touch. And last season's top goal scorer for Newport County in League Two did just that once again when he was introduced as a substitute in the 77th minute. He latched on to a through ball and finished spectacularly to round up a terrific win ahead of two tough tests against Eastleigh and Tranmere in the next few days.

O'CONNOR CONTINUES TO SPLINTER THE 'BARN DOOR'
Jokerman

Forest Green Rovers have weathered a spell of indifferent results in recent weeks. The performance at Grimsby once again underlined they should fear no one at this level and will be strong contenders for the National League title. Now back on the winning trail following a 'bloodless' victory at Aldershot, today's visitors Guiseley, with all due respect, should give Rovers a chance to maintain their position at the top. Anything less will see the long knives drawn on this forum. Fans in The Green Man prior to kick-off witnessed the demise of Kidderminster Harriers losing at Macclesfield with their new manager Mr Hockaday at the helm. Rovers' supporters fell to their knees and offered up prayers of thanks. Ady Pennock is unsurprisingly keeping faith with the side selected on Tuesday.

Guiseley had not read the script and started by far the better, moving the ball around confidently. As early as the third minute Brooksby fired a shot across Maxted in Rovers' goal which went narrowly wide. It was more than 15 minutes before the home side mounted a serious effort, with Bennett crossing from the right to Guthrie whose volley was blocked away. Despite appearing to handle the ball, Marsh-Brown was allowed to continue into the area but was foiled by keeper Drench who saved low down. The Guiseley contingent were not enamoured with the officials from here on.

Guiseley could well have taken the lead when Maris reached the by-line and pulled the ball back beyond Maxted but found no strikers to take advantage of the empty net.

Two minutes later they were behind when a thumping cross from Parkin on the right found Frear in acres of space on the corner of the six-yard box. Enjoying a rich vein of form the Rovers winger controlled well and struck the ball high into the net on 25minutes. It took the wind out of Guiseley who were no doubt feeling hard done by. Conversely Rovers picked up the pace and took a grip on proceedings. Sinclair was working hard in midfield and created a good chance for Carter whose shot was weak and Parkin was unlucky to see his effort deflected wide after a terrific cross from Frear. Rovers finished the half much improved.

Jones had picked up an injury in the first half and was replaced by Clough at the break. One goal is never comfortable and this was underlined when Guiseley built a flowing move from the back to get behind Rovers defence on the right. A cross to the back post found Maris who was only denied by a terrific block by Maxted near the goal line. Guthrie replied with a pile driver from distance that Drench, diving low to his right, tipped round for a corner. From Frears's cross Guthrie spun his marker and went to ground. Sometimes you get the decision; he did. The referee pointed to the spot and Parkin stepped up and hit the ball with immense power high to the left and on 57 minutes Rovers had daylight on the scoreboard.

In control now Marsh-Brown set up Carter who blazed over from a good position. Wedgbury replaced Sinclair, fresh legs to stifle any chance of recovery by the visitors. On 77 minutes O'Connor came on for Guthrie. At the change Guiseley matched the power supply to the stadium by switching off completely. The ball was quickly played down the centre where O'Connor and Marsh-Brown arrowed through a static back line and closed in towards goal. It was a case of 'after you' so from 15 yards O'Connor rifled the ball high into the net past the hopelessly exposed Drench. It was game over and Guiseley knew it was not their day when substitute Dickinson struck a shot that beat Maxted only to hit the post. The ball came out to Lockwood who hit it firmly only for Wedgbury to prevent the goal by blocking superbly.

It was a workmanlike performance by Forest Green who move five points clear at the top of the league table and reduce Cheltenham's goal difference advantage to a single goal. Pennock needs to keep his troops focused. A trip to Eastleigh on Tuesday but, with the Constable not on

OCTOBER

duty, maybe Rovers can smash, grab and pillage the points. Followed by Tranmere on Saturday where a win, never mind six-, will feel like a 12-pointer. Against the odds but onward my friends for Rovers, Victory, Glory … and The Plot is gone. Or has it?

Tuesday 13.10.15
Eastleigh 3 FGR 2
LATE GOAL DENIES ROVERS EASTLEIGH POINT
Richard Joyce
Ross Lafayette's stoppage-time goal at the Silverlake Stadium helped Eastleigh inflict a gut-wrenching late defeat on Forest Green Rovers. The former Welling United striker had only been introduced as a substitute just a couple of minutes before his last-gasp strike, which saw Rovers suffer their fourth defeat of the season against an Eastleigh side under the caretaker management of former FGR man, Chris Todd.

Having gone behind early on, Forest Green fought back and held the lead at half time thanks to goals from Aaron O'Connor and Elliott Frear. However, Eastleigh hit back in the opening minutes of a second half they dominated, and they denied FGR the chance to claim a point by poking home at the death. Another former Forest Green face, Yemi Odubade, was the Spitfires' two-goal scoring hero, and he put them in front after only two minutes. Lee Cook's well-struck free kick was saved by Jonny Maxted, although Odubade was on hand to drive home the rebound for the match's opening goal.

It was an early setback for Ady Pennock's troops, although they steadily set about the task of finding an equalizer, which they did in the 21st minute. O'Connor found himself free behind the home defence, and with only Ross Flitney to beat, he rounded the goalkeeper to slot calmly. Things got even better for Forest Green minutes after Flitney had saved from Rob Sinclair's stabbed effort. Frear found the back of the net with his third goal this season when the ball fell to him on the edge of the box, and he drove in sweepingly to complete a first-half turnaround on the stroke of half time.

The lead didn't last long though. Eastleigh drew level five minutes into the second half with a controversial goal that saw Odubade slam home. It appeared the attacker was offside when he fired in on goal, but the decision went against Rovers and the ex-Oxford United front man was awarded his second of the night. The goal gave the hosts the momentum they needed to try and push for a third goal that they would have hoped would see them reclaim the advantage. Maxted was called upon to make some important stops from Jai Reason, and then Cook's dangerous long-range strike. Eastleigh edged closer, and on 73 minutes a cleverly produced, chipped effort from Reason struck the woodwork. Odubade was denied his hat-trick by a good stop from Maxted late on, but the Rovers keeper couldn't stop Lafayette from snatching maximum points for his side. He knocked in a fierce cross from the left past a helpless Maxted, leaving FGR with an almighty battle to try and earn something from the game in the final minutes of stoppage time. Darren Carter and Kurtis Guthrie both had tame efforts late on, but they couldn't influence the scoreline, which sat in Eastleigh's favour, along with the three points.

DESTINATION EASTLEIGH
Rambling Man

Tonight's fixture in Hampshire is the last on page one of our fixture booklet. The season is whistling by and amazingly FGR has been top since the incongruous mid-summer start.

As the nights draw in, no time for cultural stops. Just the rush hour joust with M4/A34 and M3 after which I lost track and the will to live. Clegg was pilot with occasional friend Norah up front, while Foggy and I gripped our seats in the back.

This was my second visit to the Silverlake Stadium, on both occasions the crowd inflated by a generous free-admission night. Like so many in the National League, the club is friendly and well run.

However, I confess I am not keen on the stadium. Silverlake conjures images of a gleaming waterside location. Maybe South Cerney? Not an isolated spot, surrounded by the coils of the M27.

The car park is miles from humanity and refreshments exist only in caravan burger vans beyond the turnstiles. Bring your partner if you are trying to dissuade him/her from cramping your style at away games – he/she will not come again! FGR was allocated half of the new end stand which was just a patch of grass the previous season.

Clad in silvery galvanized sheet, only the lake bit was missing. It contains an astonishing 2,400 seats. They rise so gradually that you need to be far back to get a clear view the length of the pitch, by which time you are closer to Southampton than Eastleigh. There is a wide footway between the seats and pitch-side hoardings to allow for wheelchair bays as well as circulation. Yet the bays are proud of the roof overhang and so suffer the elements in poor weather. Two massive metal pillars obstruct your view and the whole structure clangs endlessly, the seats being mounted on reverberating metal staging.

O
C
T
O
B
E
R

Nope, it does not float my boat. I can honestly say that it was hard to tell how the game was played out in the half furthest from view.

As to the match, bewilderingly Rovers reverted to the Macclesfield tactic with similar 'success'. Three specialist left backs were discarded as Pipey switched to left from right. It all ended in tears as Eastleigh exploited the weakness from the get-go, deservedly overturning their disjointed opponents 3-2. Much grumpiness and head-scratching by 200 travelling Gumps. And that left us to negotiate a chaotic evacuation of the car park and dismal return to the M27. Oh joy!

Saturday 17.10.15
FGR 0 Tranmere Rovers 2
FGR CAN'T GET GOING IN TRANMERE DEFEAT
Richard Joyce

Tranmere Rovers front line duo of Gary Taylor-Fletcher and James Norwood inflicted a second defeat in a week on Forest Green Rovers, although results elsewhere mean Ady Pennock's side remain top of the National League table. Handed his debut by Tranmere boss Gary Brabin, having been announced as a new signing an hour before kick-off, experienced forward Taylor-Fletcher was in and among the goals in the first half. As was the returning FGR favourite Norwood, as he lined up in a Tranmere side who hit the net twice in a dominant opening 45 minutes against a Forest Green team who couldn't find a way to break through.

Injury problems saw Keanu Marsh-Brown line up as part of the attack alongside Kurtis Guthrie, while Sam Wedgbury returned to the side in an unfamiliar right midfield role. Looking to bounce back from Tuesday's loss at Eastleigh, Tranmere's opening goal after only five minutes was a real blow for Pennock's charges' ambitions in front of a healthy home crowd. It involved the Merseyside outfit's two goalscorers. Norwood squared the ball for Taylor-Fletcher, and the former Premier League hitman made no mistake, rolling an accurate finish into the back of the net from the edge of the box.

The momentum was with the visitors, and after Jonny Maxted had comfortably saved Adam Mekki's shot, they found themselves two up. Norwood, who left The New Lawn at the end of last season, found the net with a looping header, silencing the home crowd with his fourth goal of the season. Tranmere's fizz continued with Mekki and Norwood both trying their luck, while Elliott Frear came closest to clawing a goal back for FGR. His shot from the left-hand side of the box was however well saved by Scott Davies.

It was much of the same in the second half as Forest Green struggled to apply pressure on an energetic Tranmere display. Maxted saved well from Mekki early on in the half, and Frear tried his luck again, only to flash a shot wide across the face of goal, having met a superb long-distance, diagonal pass. Taylor-Fletcher continued to provide a threat for the visitors. FGR though were the side who came nearest to scoring the game's next goal. Good work by Frear led to him delivering a good corner into the box, where substitute Charlie Clough was on hand to head at goal, only to see his effort well cleared by the defender on the post. Dale Bennett and Norwood both spurned late openings for either side in the closing stages of a clash that saw Tranmere move back into the play-off places, and Forest Green's lead at the top of the summit narrowly continue.

FOREST GREEN ROVERS TOP OF THE FLOPS LEAGUE
Jokerman
Reading the post mortem following Tuesday's defeat at Eastleigh, manager Ady Pennock's team selection came under close scrutiny. Aficionados on the forum as always are keen to point out the error of his ways and give heaps of helpful advice. Most managers, if not all, treat forums as explicit and probably 'lock on' Google safe search. Generally they stand or fall by the 'Old Blue Eyes' method. Today's visitors, Tranmere Rovers, are also on a losing run of two home defeats. Talking to some 'wackers' from south of the Mersey in The Green Man, and there were many, they said their team was playing kite or a word similar. The eagerly awaited team news announced that some advisers had their wish with Kelly and Wedgbury returned to the starting line-up. O'Connor, however, was missing through injury along with Parkin so it was Marsh-Brown and Guthrie up the sharp end.

Tranmere brought Norwood back to TNL and their ghostly white strip was very apt. In front of a good crowd of over 2,000, including 400 from Merseyside the game kicked off. It took only five minutes for Norwood's gaily coloured pink boots to show a clean pair of heels to Rovers' defence. Showing good control on the left-hand side of the penalty area, he cut the ball back to the edge of the box. Bennett slipped on the recently sodden turf and was on the floor as Tranmere striker Fletcher swept the ball home first time low inside the right-hand post. This goal had a startling effect on the home side akin to an ingestion of the notorious dating drug. They were conscious but didn't have a clue what they were doing. On 22 minutes a cross from the right was met by Norwood in oceans of space

O
C
T
O
B
E
R

and facing away from goal but, equally aware, he looped his header over Maxted and under the bar. Forest Green were dead in the water.

It took 35 minutes for Rovers to make an attempt on the Tranmere goal when a Frear corner was headed over by Racine. An excellent interchange of passes between Fletcher and Norwood inside the Rovers area gave the ex-FGR striker the opportunity to kill the game but he blazed the ball wildly over the bar. In first-half time added on Frear had Rovers' first shot on target which saw Davies in the Tranmere goal save well, diving to his left to concede a corner followed by two more which were ably defended as the half-time whistle blew.

Things were desperate in the Forest Green dressing room but there was no cow pie and the spinach was limper than Mr Humphries' wrist. Pennock was speechless so the players wandered back out. Tranmere were enjoying hot Bovril and studying Google Maps wondering if they were at the correct venue. Before the hour was up Pennock knew things were not improving and replaced Sinclair with Sam-Yorke. It made no difference and ten minutes later Pipe limped off to be replaced by Clough. He at least made some impact and put a header just over from a Kelly free kick. However, the game was being played mainly in the Forest Green half and Fletcher twice and Ridehalgh really should have increased Tranmere's advantage. To be fair to Rovers they had a spell around 85 minutes which may have resuscitated this abject display. Sam-Yorke sent Frear down the left who cut the ball back to Carter whose wild shot was deflected for a corner. Frear crossed to the back post and Clough's header was cleared from under the bar by Harris. Racine headed the resulting corner into the net but the referee had already penalized Guthrie for pushing. That's as good as it got for Forest Green and Tranmere ended up comfortable winners.

A look at recent results in the National League gives strong indications that it is a weak affair. Forest Green are quite capable of winning the title along with probably 16 other contenders if results continue in this vein. This in turn will bring much angst and 'blood on the carpet'.

Saturday 24.10.15
Margate 1 FGR 2 (FA Cup 4th qualifying round)
ROVERS IN THE HAT AFTER MARGATE TRIUMPH
Richard Joyce
Monday's FA Cup first round proper draw will feature Forest Green Rovers for a third consecutive season after goals from Keanu Marsh-Brown and Kurtis Guthrie clinched a fourth qualifying round win at

Margate. Live in front of the BT Sport cameras for the second time in three weeks, Rovers did enough to seal their progress against their National League South opponents, who provided a scare in the second half when Luke Moore levelled for the Kent side.

In control for much of the tie, an assured start settled an injury-depleted FGR side who were forced to change their set-up, using Guthrie as a solo front man with support from the flanks provided by Elliott Frear and Marsh-Brown. Frear and Darren Carter both forced early opportunities, while experienced goalkeeper Nikki Bull saved comfortably from Guthrie's header on 20 minutes. Forest Green's regular delivery from wide areas allowed Aarran Racine and James Jennings to produce efforts on goal, and the breakthrough eventually came, five minutes before the break. Good work by Frear on the left saw the former Exeter City man draw the ball back to Marsh-Brown who was ready and waiting to guide a right-footed shot in off the post.

It was a great way to end the half, although the hosts did begin to threaten in the second 45 minutes, as a lack of tempo allowed the home side to find their way back into it. Former Lincoln City striker Jamie Taylor produced a fizzing shot that flew just over, and after Charlie Clough had forced Bull into a fine reactive stop down the other end, the home side equalized. Moore was the man who scored their leveller. He latched onto a ball played down the middle and dispatched a well-judged lobbed finish that left Rovers' goalkeeping debutant Dale Eve helpless. Margate were back in the game, although if anything Moore's strike did more to reignite Forest Green's performance than their own, and the lead was restored three minutes later. A bullet header from close range by Guthrie slammed into the net after Clough's excellent aerial pull-back from a Carter cross had set up the front man.

FGR were now back to being well on top, and further daylight was nearly installed between the two sides when a sensational long-distance strike from Jennings rocketed onto the crossbar. Terry Brown's Margate did little to put Rovers under pressure in the closing stages, and what could have been a difficult Cup trip on the road proved to be a success, and attentions now turn to who the club's opponents will be at the next stage in November.

DESTINATION MARGATE
Rambling Man
Frustratingly inconsistent League performances were put aside for the 4th qualifying round of the FA Cup. For Rovers that meant a long eastward

O
C
T
O
B
E
R

trip to Margate, last landfall before Belgium and Holland. And as BT Sport was doing live, early coverage, that meant a 12.30 kick-off.

Unaccountably, our usual travelling companions were busy with other things. Hair washing, nail cutting – you get the picture. Thus only Foggy and I met at the Glider Café, with the sun barely out of its pyjamas, and birds summoning their first coughs.

A fast but dull drive across England saw us alight at The Theatre of Portakabins in time for elevenses: Hartsdown Park, a celebration of temporary buildings down the ages; some old, some new, they comprise the changing rooms, several burger bars, Board and hospitality rooms and a generous scattering of toilets. If you had a low loader, you could steal the stadium in an hour. That said, the locals were a funny lot and good company. Fancy dress, mime artists, a herd of dragon mascots, tons of club scarves and rosettes.

The match passed without too many alarms for an injury-hit Rovers. A classy finish from KMB and a header by Kurtis settled the tie despite a sloppily conceded goal in between.

The return journey was from Hell. As the M20 gave way to the M25, warnings flashed about long delays between Junction 9 (Leatherhead) and all the way round to M40 Oxford So we headed anticlockwise around the top of the London Orbital. That meant plunging down the Dartford Tunnel, where there are no toll booths, just warnings of penalties of up to £70 if you do not pay. How do you pay? Unsurprisingly, as most drivers are not telepathic, it has become the most penalty-producing section of road in the UK. Or so Foggy found out as he grappled to pay the toll on his internet phone, cursed by unhelpful bandits posing as Highway Agency sites. Boy done good though. Thirty miles later, he was £2.50 poorer but had freed us of the threat of bailiffs.

Then, the monsoon struck. Just as we were breaking down on the M40 near Oxford. By breakdown, I have to 'fess up to my failure to notice the trusted Passat was running out of diesel. Green Flag eventually saw us on our way and we crossed Stroud City Limits at 8 p.m. An exhausting day. Thanks be for the extra hour in bed.

Saturday 31.10.15
FGR 2 Chester 1
FIRST HALF GOALS CLINCH CHESTER VICTORY
Richard Joyce
Two goals in three first-half minutes helped Forest Green Rovers back to the top of the National League with a sixth straight win over Chester.

The returning Jon Parkin, and dynamic Keanu Marsh-Brown, both struck in quick succession to deny the visitors any opportunity to hang onto an early first-half lead, which they had richly deserved.

Out of the blocks quickly, Ross Hannah's header after just 12 minutes put them in front. They were pegged back by a resurgent FGR performance though, as Ady Pennock's charges reclaimed top spot after Cheltenham Town's temporary stay at the top following their win over Grimsby on Friday. Chester's early pressure saw James Roberts and Tom Shaw foiled by Jonny Maxted, although they did find a way through in a dominant early showing. Hannah was the beneficiary as the former Grimsby Town forward flicked home at the near post from a corner for his fourth goal of the season.

After another Roberts effort had slammed into the side netting, Rovers burst into life, and Elliott Frear worked Jon Worsnop into a good save having been set by Parkin.

The duo combined again for what would eventually be the equalizer. After Frear had picked up a ball down the left from James Jennings, the wide man pushed a dangerous low cross into the Chester area, where Parkin was on hand to stab home from close range. Only two minutes later and the score line was fully reversed. Marsh-Brown took advantage of a major error in the Chester defence, and kept his head to classily slot when one-on-one with the goalkeeper. Rovers' aerial threat from set pieces was clear to see, and both Charlie Clough and Jennings spurned good chances in the box at the end of the first half and start of the second.

FGR were looking comfortable after the break, although a mistake at the back very nearly allowed Shaw the opportunity to level, only to be prevented from doing so by a fine Maxted stop. Gradually Rovers edged toward the finish with the belief that despite the one-goal scoreline, victory was theirs. And Frear very nearly capped the result when he broke clear on 78 minutes, only to see his strike clip the crossbar, having been set free by Darren Carter's terrific through ball. The visitors were still left with two good chances though. Shaw should have done better with a header in the box that slipped a yard wide, and debutant James McDonagh saw his low strike from distance well stopped by Maxted, as victory belonged to Rovers.

HALLOWEEN HOWLER PUTS ROVERS OVER THE MOON
Jokerman
The TV all stars are back at TNL this week. Last weekend was spent at the seaside where they expelled water on BT's hopes of an FA Cup home

O
C
T
O
B
E
R

win that focused on a bloke who ended up as sick as his parrot. The reward is to follow the circus to the next venue which is Wimbledon who won the competition once with a bunch of ball-grabbing clowns. Book your ringside seats for 7/11 now.

All eyes and minds today turn to league football with the visit of Chester. Forest Green's league form has been sorely tested recently. Today they will be without the services of Kurtis Guthrie who has suffered an attack of yellow fever. It leaves manager Ady Pennock with limited options up front with leading scorer O'Connor still injured. Fortuitously Jon Parkin returns to lead the line.

The teams are led out under clear blue skies on a gloriously mild autumnal afternoon. Chester's skipper won the toss and invited Forest Green to play into the blinding sun. He may have noticed Maxted, like most goalkeepers, thinks a cap is neck protection for idiot car drivers.

The first 15 minutes of the game were dominated by the visitors as once again Rovers were slow to find any cohesion in their play. Roberts in particular gave Jennings a torrid time of it. As early as the third minute he seized on a mistake and brought a save from Maxted. He then turned the defender inside out to win a corner from which Shaw from the edge of the area saw his shot well saved by Maxted diving low to his left.

Rovers could not retain possession and the pressure on the defence told on 12 minutes when yet another corner by Chappell from the left dropped into a ruck in the centre of the six-yard area, where Hannah headed the ball firmly past Maxted who was doing seal impressions. The 200 travelling fans behind the goal got a little excited at how well the game was going.

On 15 minutes another Chester attack saw the ball crossed from left to right where Roberts met it on the volley, but fortunately for Rovers his spectacular effort only found the side netting.

Then after 20 minutes the complexion of the game changed. Chester gave the ball away in midfield to Parkin who drove into the area and scrambled the ball left to Frear who forced a good save from keeper Worsnop at his near post. From the resulting corner Jennings saw his header deflected wide.

Rovers had found their game and Carter shooting from distance saw his low shot pushed round the post by a diving save from Worsnop. Clough had a header deflected wide and from the corner Racine headed back across goal to Carter who headed over when perhaps he should have scored.

It was all Forest Green now and in a breath the game was turned on its head. Carter charging down the left slipped the ball inside to Frear, who raced into the area and unselfishly squared the ball to Parkin, who swept in the equalizer on 31 minutes.

Two minutes later Chester defender Higgins afternoon turned into nightmare. Midway in his own half he back passed to nobody. Marsh-Brown was lurking on the off-chance; perhaps he called for it but he finished with class, and similar to last week at Margate, he steered the ball low inside the left-hand post. Chester were a bit upset and Carter and visiting defender George had a difference of opinion which took some calming down as tackles became robust.

In time added on in the first half Clough went close with a header from a Carter free kick. To put the old cliché to slightly better use it was a half of two halves and certainly sobered up the visiting contingent.

The Dale Vince culinary delights, however, do invite the aforesaid supporters to cast aspersions. This week it was eye-watering suggestions on what to do with runner beans.

The second half began with Hannah shooting low across Maxted and narrowly wide of the right-hand post. Rovers replied through Jennings, who having recovered from his shaky start joined the attack and twice went close with headed efforts from corners. Chester then applied more pressure and forced Rovers' defence back much to the angst of their manager. Chester's Shaw drove forward and hit a terrific shot from 20 yards that Maxted saved brilliantly with his legs. From the resulting corner George directed a free header the wrong side of the post, a let-off for Rovers. Chappell then saw his cross-shot land on the top netting with Maxted scrambling.

Rovers then had their chance to finish the contest on 78 minutes when Carter sent Frear one on one with Worsnop. His shot beat the keeper but skimmed the bar which meant a tense final few minutes for the home fans. None more so than when raiding full back Hunt cut into the area on the left and chipped the ball perfectly for Shaw unmarked ten yards out. His header beat Maxted but went inches wide of the right-hand post.

At the death Chester sub McDonagh hit a cracking shot from distance that thankfully for Rovers, Maxted was equal to.

Forest Green are back at the top of the table even though their performances are not always convincing, which says a lot about this league.

If they can improve, and they should with the return of O'Connor and Guthrie, there is no reason they cannot stay there.

A DRAW AT WELLING ON 10 NOVEMBER saw Rovers surrender top spot to Cheltenham, after heading the National League Table for two and a half months. November saw the second El Glosico, at Cheltenham. Another draw that was poor reward for a dominant performance. Yet Rovers' form was picking up again, being undefeated in the month and scalping Wimbledon away from home in the FA Cup 1st round proper

When old red red robin comes sob, sob, sobbing along along
He'll be regretting his decision to support the Robins all nightlong
Wake up, wake up you dunderhead get promotion out of 'yer head
Cheer up Cheer up the league is dead, pray, lose, cry be unhappy

(Premature celebration: excerpt from 'When the Red Red Robin Comes Sob Sob Sobbing Along' by The Farmcotian as a repost to our CTFC guest forum-poster RedRobin)

Saturday 07.11.15
Wimbledon 1 FGR 2 (FA Cup 1st round)
FREAR'S LATE STRIKE SECURES GIANT-KILLING
Richard Joyce
Elliott Frear's stunning stoppage-time winner booked Forest Green Rovers a place in the FA Cup second round with a giant-killing victory at League Two side, AFC Wimbledon. The tricky winger's bottom corner finish was a late reward for a testing outing at the Cherry Red Records Stadium, as Rovers overcame Football League opposition in the world-famous competition for only the third time in their history.

Darren Carter's early goal set FGR on their way to what looked like a possible upset, but after Callum Kennedy had equalized for Wimbledon, it was going to take an almighty effort to try and regain the advantage. That moment came when deep into second half stoppage time, Frear stepped up to execute a superb finish.

Ady Pennock's side were ahead from as early as the sixth minute when Keanu Marsh-Brown nicked the ball off a Wimbledon defender in the box, and teed up Carter, who slammed home a key early goal. The hosts' slow start had been punished, although they responded well, and Tom Elliott forced Steve Arnold, making his first appearance of the season, into a good save when shooting on the turn. Kennedy's excellent strike drew the Football League outfit level. He received the ball on the left of the area and placed a well-struck effort into the top corner, out of Arnold's reach.

Jon Parkin fired off target in a rare FGR chance towards half time, while Lyle Taylor's effort for the hosts was slammed wide after Forest Green youth team product Sean Rigg had edged the ball towards the former Partick Thistle attacker.

The start of the second half almost mirrored the first for Rovers, as they almost took the lead again. Marsh-Brown's delivery from a wide area into the box was inch perfect, and Charlie Clough's well-connected header slammed onto the crossbar. AFC Wimbledon were dominant, and they forced Arnold into two good stops in quick succession, when he kept out strikes on goal from Taylor and Rigg. The latter was through again on the hour mark, only to poke wide, and Carter looked to make an impact at the other end; however, his shot from distance skittled past the post.

Belief gradually grew in the FGR ranks as the home side continued to falter in front of goal, and Marsh-Brown had a great opportunity to score, only to be denied by Ben Wilson when the ball fell to him in the area. As the clock ticked towards the 90-minute mark, Rovers had the ball in Wimbledon's final third, and the chance to snatch a last-gasp giant-killing presented itself. Frear was the man who provided the magical moment. He picked the ball up on the right-hand side and slammed home brilliantly into the bottom corner. It sent both players and the 229 travelling supporters alike into raptures, and leaves everyone connected with Forest Green eager to find out what comes next when the second round draw takes place on Monday.

DESTINATION WIMBLEDON
Rambling Man
The right result v Chester meant the fragile health of we FGR supporters was in steady recovery. And the stress-free prospect of the FA Cup always helps. Foggy was on a short break and Compo a longer one – Dubai then India. Have a nasty feeling that I might have told a mutual friend he'd gone to Libya. Hope that GCHQ were not listening or else on return he might be slapped into an orange jump suit. So I was joined by a new character: old friend Woody. He is not a typical FGR fan. Lives near Worcester, hails from (and supports) Rochdale ('The Dale') but has surrendered to my continuous FGR propaganda – a sort of verbal water-boarding. Thus he and his wife are now season ticket holders at TNL.

We met at idyllic Burford, just over the Oxon border. Every American's view of what a Cotswold town should be, and with more half-timbered pubs and antique shops than you can shake a walking stick at. Had the metre-thick stone walls of Huffkins Tea Shop allowed a mobile signal,

I'd have been checking whether the monsoon outside was threatening the match. Fortunately it did not.

Woody does not hang around in his German spaceship. So, I'd no sooner hidden in terror behind the front seats than we'd arrived at Womble HQ. Lots of friendly folk apparently pleased to renew acquaintance with a team from below level 4 of the pyramid. To my regret I'd not been to the stadium, even when we used to play Kingstonian here. Maybe the memories of the FA Trophy defeat at Wemberlee were too raw?

These days, Kingsmeadow is a tightly enclosed little ground with pitch dimensions that are on the small side of what is allowed. Good atmosphere though and full of cheerful folk who wish you well. It got my seal of approval. And it did not take long for my smile to broaden – six minutes when Darren Carter opened our account. Callum Kennedy notched a classy equalizer, but Rovers finished the stronger, and Elliott Frear's cut-in and shot from the right wing in the 93rd minute was a deserved winner. Cue 230+ from the Five Valleys (and one from the North West) in raptures. Thus we will travel in hope to Welling in Erith. Time for Ady (and Jamie) to break their virginity at an old stamping ground with a win? My next account will reveal the good, the bad or the ugly!

FREAR SMASHES WIMBLEDON TIE-BREAKER
Jokerman

November 7th, FA Cup 1st round. A storm was raging and the winds were blowing gales as the FGR supporters coaches steadfastly clawed their way out of the valley. Destination Kingston, the home of displaced AFC Wimbledon. The M4 corridor is mile after mile of 'kickback' spray. Kendo presses on M3 into Sunbury where we hit the buffers. Over two miles at walking pace. Time to ponder. Through Richmond towards Hampton Court Palace, the area steeped in Tudor history, a time when football was played long before this dainty tippy tappy stuff. Arms, legs necks and backs were broken on a frequent basis. The yokels skived off archery practice to play to such an extent that Henry's government banned the game in 1540. Ah, the good old days, eh.

Eventually we passed the hole in the road where thousands of illegal Wombles were pouring out and setting up camp in Richmond Park across the way from the Housing Association. One woke to find ale time completely evaporated and Kendo flooring it through Kingston High Street and across the river bridge. Road restrictions prevented a hand-brake-turn parking manoeuvre which would have tested the underwear but impressed Clarkson.

Supporters disembarked and entered the Kingsmeadow Stadium under tight security, probably the rodent scare back at Richmond. Frisking guards. Why does one have to cough? The Remembrance Day silence is just ending. The storm clouds are clearing as the game kicks off. As many predicted Arnold has replaced Maxted in goal for FGR. Parkin leads the line with Marsh-Brown while Guthrie, Kelly and Pipe are on the bench. Forest Green are up and running from the first whistle and stun the 2,000-plus home fans with a goal after six minutes. Marsh-Brown chases down Wimbledon defender Bulman inside the area and muscles him out of possession, to set up Carter who thumps the ball past keeper Wilson via a desperate blocking attempt. The 200 Rovers fans are in good voice after that.

It took the home side a good 15 minutes to find their feet but having done so began to threaten the Rovers back line. Main striker Elliott was winning all the aerial battles and his side began to show more composure in possession. On 20 minutes Elliott forced a good save from Arnold diving low to his right; on 24 minutes and Rovers failed to cut out a move on the right wing as Taylor crossed to the edge of the area, picking out Kennedy in acres of space. He struck a controlled shot high past Arnold whose right hand could not prevent the goal. A minute later Elliott was denied and penalty appeals waved away. Parkin shot wide from a Bennett cross but the big man was beginning to look isolated up front. Just before the half-time whistle Kennedy raided down the right, passing inside to Taylor who, with a clear sight of goal, screwed his shot across Arnold and wide of the post when perhaps he should have done better. Rovers had worked hard and overall the half time scoreline was a fair reflection.

Again Forest Green started the half in attack mode. Frear won a soft corner on the left and crossed to Parkin whose header skimmed out to Marsh-Brown, who exchanged passes with Sinclair before crossing to the back post, where Clough cannoned a free header off the crossbar which was scrambled away for another corner. An impressive start for the visitors but once again the league side began to assert and Arnold became the busier keeper. He was equal to shots from both Taylor and Rigg, who as an ex-FGR player missed the opportunity to put his side in front when shooting wide, when well placed to score on the hour. Carter had a shot saved by Wilson but Rovers attack was blunt.

Wimbledon were first with the substitutes and amazingly replaced Elliott, by far their most dangerous striker, on 70 minutes, a decision met with boos from home fans unsurprisingly. Pennock waited until 75 minutes before replacing Parkin with Guthrie. Wimbledon lost Kennedy

The newspaper clipping:

THE TIMES | Saturday November 7 2015 — 3

Who ate all the pies? Not Vegans United

Simon de Bruxelles, David Sanderson

In 2010 Forest Green Rovers were facing oblivion. They were 20th in their league, verging on bankruptcy and could not shift many pies and Bovrils.

Then along came the football club's saviour: a new age traveller with a hemp bag of quorn nuggets.

Dale Vince bought the club, threw out the pies, introduced soya milk, laid an organic pitch and then signed a solar-powered robot to mow it.

The club, based in Nailsworth, Gloucestershire, is now top of the league, planning a new stadium complete with a sports science hub and preparing for an FA Cup match against AFC Wimbledon. They are the "green" club going for gold.

Mr Vince, who founded Ecotricity, Britain's largest green power company, in 1995 and whose wealth has been valued at £110 million, made some simple rules when he agreed to save the club from bankruptcy.

His insistence on an environmentally friendly ethos, including a meat-free regime, was initially greeted with a squirt of Deep Freeze. He said this week that football was thirty years behind the rest of the country in terms of its "environmental awareness".

"It is a challenging place to take the message," he said, "but things that would have been unthinkable a few years ago are getting closer to the mainstream, like solar panels, water harvesting and using electric vehicles.

"It is the same with the food. I was planning to make the club vegan from the start but decided to do it in stages. I was going to wait until we got in the Football League but then I thought 'Why wait?'"

So out went the hot dogs and burgers; in came quorn nuggets, vegetarian fajitas, panzanella salads, vegan beers and meat-free pie and mash. Soya milk cools down the half-time cuppas.

The solar-powered "mobot" tends the playing surface, and the players' kit is free of vinyl. Their new 5,000-seater stadium will, naturally, be known as Eco Park. Mr Vince believes that the ethos can fire the club, which is top of the National League, into the fully professional Football League. Supporters, instilled with the pie'n'Bovril attitude of clubs across Britain, have been won over, according to Richard Joyce, the club spokesman. He said that it did not take them long to realise that a well-made veggie burger could be a lot tastier than a meat pattie made from "lips and bums".

"The burgers they used to sell here cost 4p each to buy in, so you can imagine the quality of the meat," he said. "What we realised early on was that in order to get people to eat the vegetarian food it needed to be really, really good, so although the profit margins may be smaller there are always queues in the restaurant."

David Pipe, who arrived at the club in 2014, said that his team-mates "hardly notice that the food here is vegan because it is so good". He added: "I am very careful about what I eat during the week. I monitor my energy levels and eat five small meals a day."

Not every day, though, as he happily conceded. "I do have a binge one day a week after the match, from 7pm on Saturday to 7pm on Sunday, when I'll eat whatever is going."

Mr Vince, who employs about 600 staff at Ecotricity's head office in Stroud, has employed a vegan café, Star Anise, in the town to handle the club's catering. "Many people think the dairy industry is harmless but they have no idea how milk is produced or the suffering it causes to cows," he said.

Chris Gardner, a member of the club's supporters advisory committee, said "Dale is dedicated and has a very good moral compass. I don't think there's a supporter who doesn't think he's the best chairman in the league."

But maybe not everyone is completely convinced. Skulking at the back of the player's fridge was a carton of semi-skimmed milk.

Dale Vince, the chairman of Forest Green Rovers, says that football is decades behind the rest of society in green awareness

Behind the story

At first glance the matchday menu on offer at Forest Green Rovers' Devil's Kitchen is little different to that at any other football ground in the country (Simon de Bruxelles writes).

There is burger and chips or pie and mash at £6.95, nuggets and beans for £5.50 or soup and salad.

It is only in the small print that the vegan truth is revealed. The "Q-Pie" is quorn mince, the burgers are bean and the hot chocolate is made with soya rather than cow's milk.

Dale Vince, the club's chairman, believes that it is better to let customers discover the delights of vegan food for themselves. That is why they are described as burgers and nuggets rather than "bean burgers" or "quorn nuggets".

Other items on the menu are less ambiguous: chips with curry or chilli sauce; panzanella salad with croutons, olives, tomatoes, spinach, basil and balsamic vinegar; and "delicious vegan cake".

The queues for food at the Devil's Kitchen are evidence that given no choice even the most dedicated meat eater will swallow a vegetable.

Rovers players endorse the food at the Devil's Kitchen

Dale Vince was once again in the media spotlight in the week preceding Rovers' FA Cup tie at Division 2's AFC Wimbledon, on 7 November 2015. It had become an increasingly regular occurrence for news media, including national and local TV, to seek audiences at The New Lawn Stadium, attracted by his ground-breaking energy, and his ecological and dietary stances. Often, the interviewers sought wider opinion, for example from among the club's supporters. I was asked to attend to expound on personally held views as a long-time supporter.

That week, 'The Thunderer' (the London *Times*) came to call. As requested by the club's press officer, Richard Joyce, I rolled up at the stadium to speak to their journalist David Sanderson on Wednesday, 4 November, just as the late-afternoon autumn gloom was setting in. Earlier, he and his photographer had been speaking to Dale and his management team as well as Rovers players. My views as a supporter would complete their picture.

Seeking warmth, light and shelter, David and I retreated to the small office in the stadium's changing-room complex. It serves as a manager's retreat when needed and, among other things, contains a drinks' fridge. The interview did not take long and centred mainly on how supporters viewed the club's vegan policies, a question I know he'd put to the players too. My responses were pretty positive, not least as I have strong opinions on healthy lifestyle and diet, albeit I am neither vegan nor vegetarian. Just as we were packing up, one of the players, Delano Sam-Yorke, breezed in, reached into the fridge and took out a carton of full-cream milk, guzzling it with some gusto. I gulped myself as I saw David lapping up the spectacle. Oh dear! Rovers won a famous victory at Wimbledon. During the return journey, a friend rang me. Had I seen *The Times* article? It covered the first half of page 3 that day. I stopped at a garage at Cirencester to pick up a copy and, sure enough, Delano's thirst had provoked a contrast with all things vegan. On getting home, I banged off an apologetic email to Dale. Typically, he replied quickly and reassuringly. 'The Electric Chair' is a benevolent dictator. He does not object to people bringing their choice of food to the club, simply that the only goods the club will sell are vegan. I was off the hook!

who had failed to run off a muscle pull and with ten minutes left Kelly came on for Marsh-Brown for Rovers. Forest Green benefited most from the changes, with Kelly playing on the left and Frear switching wings. As the clock ran down the final minutes, it was Rovers applying the pressure, their fans much the noisier anticipating at least a replay. The board goes up: four minutes. Tick tock, tick tock, tick tock.

Bennett raids down the right with Frear in close attendance. With defenders snapping, Bennett plays a one-two with Frear, only he doesn't get the two. Frear cuts inside to the corner of the area, and pressured, he cuts again, sees the gap and hits a solid left footer low past a startled Wilson who is on the wrong foot. Pandemonium breaks out on the away end terrace and Frear is suitably mobbed on the pitch. The celebrations mean the referee extends the added time and Wimbledon give it a right go to retrieve the situation but it is all in vain. Rovers' defence stands firm and the circus moves on.

The FA Cup: don't ya just love it.

Tuesday 10.11.15
Welling United 1 FGR 1
GUTHRIE STRIKES LATE ON TO EARN A POINT
Richard Joyce
Kurtis Guthrie's late header on his return to his former club rescued a point for Forest Green Rovers at Park View Road. The striker, who won promotion into the fifth tier with Welling back in 2013, rose to nod home a superb Elliott Frear cross in the 83rd minute, to earn Rovers a deserved point.

Cheltenham's high-scoring win over Guiseley back home in Gloucestershire meant, despite the point, that FGR were knocked off top spot. Although a point in south-east London turned out to be a good result for Rovers after Michael Bakare had earlier found the net for the home side in the second half.

A rugged start saw Forest Green produce the first opportunities. Darren Carter's fabulous effort was tipped over well by Tom King, while Charlie Clough was only inches away from whipping the ball home from Jon Parkin's clever through ball. Jonny Maxted was forced into his only meaningful save of the night when he punched away Xavier Vidal's fiercely struck free kick on 25 minutes. The attempts on the Welling goal continued to come, although they were all from distance, as Sam Wedgbury and Parkin both tried their luck with strikes from outside the area.

It was the home side who drew first blood in the second half, when

N
O
V
E
M
B
E
R

they seized upon a mistake in the middle of the park. A loss of possession allowed Bakare to snatch hold of the ball, and he drove forward and dispatched an unstoppable finish to break the deadlock. The goal sparked FGR into life, and King made a tremendous stop from a Parkin header that looked sure to hit the back of the net on 71 minutes, after he had met the ball from a corner. A mazy run from Frear followed, which ended with a shot dragged wide, and Carter's low attempt from the edge of the area was comfortably held by King. The pressure was all on the Welling goal, and Rovers' dominance eventually told when Guthrie netted with a finely taken header. Frear's terrific cross from the right was met by the attacker whose header couldn't be stopped. The ascendancy was with Rovers, but only a Clough effort that was blazed over the bar late on represented any possibility of sealing what would have been a dramatic winner.

DESTINATION WELLING
Rambling Man

For the third successive away game, we summoned the horsepowers for a journey due east. We being Foggy, Clegg and Norah, with me piloting the VW (on whose pollutive output we can but speculate). Dark autumn evenings meant no cultural visits to lighten the gloom. Just a clogged M25 and zombie driving. 2015 represents my fourth visit to Welling, which I like more each year. For Park View Road is unlike any other National League venue. Moreover, the small crowds that the home side attracts bristle with East End characters. They shun more famous neighbours like The Hammers, Addicks and Os, preferring their duels with Old Kent rivals Bromley. Good for them, say I.

The stadium is a funny old place. The home stand is a museum piece fronted with dozens of rusting stanchions. Opposite is a more modern affair, base to Erith and Belvedere who share the stadium. To its left, the dull, corrugated roof of a non-stadium building is a discordant backdrop. An open terrace backs onto Park View Road itself, while the facing end boasts a unique feature: a natural stone retaining wall some two metres high. The stone has a reddish hue, clumps of fern and Aubrietia protruding between some nailed-on advertising banners. It is barely a stride beyond the goal line and encourages speedy wingers to apply the brakes rather early for fear of eating masonry sandwich. Because there is no segregation, opposing fans take it in turns to take up lemming positions atop the wall. What is not to like?

The match was good and competitive. Welling parked the bus, defended a high line and tried to catch FGR on the break. For their part, Rovers attacked from the get-go with patience and variety but missed the chances they carved out. Half time and stalemate.

In the stand, the main amusement was provided by the machine-gun-mouthed and very loud assistant coach for the home team: MM, one Matthew McEntegart. His most insistent command is "High! High! High! High!" (I think you get the drift). Think he may have written the 'Boom went the Guns' poem that Baldrick recited in the trenches. No wonder one of the biggest hoardings was Bexley Tinnitus Support Group – they must get new clients after every match.

The second half saw Welling's only chance. Wedge slipped in taking a routine sideways pass on the halfway line and the Wings pounced, three on two. A combination of poor finishing and acrobatic saves looked like preserving the lead, until old Wing Kurtis Guthrie headed parity with ten minutes left. One point only meant that Rovers surrendered top place for the first time since August, and to local rivals Cheltenham. The next two Saturdays will be pivotal – Dover at home, Robins away. The season is really hotting up.

Saturday 14.11.15
FGR 3 Dover Athletic 1
ROVERS FIGHT BACK TO EARN FINE DOVER WIN
Richard Joyce
A second-half comeback in the most testing of conditions saw Forest Green Rovers claim all three points in a second against third place clash at The New Lawn. Heavy winds and rain made Dover Athletic's visit to Nailsworth a challenging occasion for both sides, and it was ultimately Ady Pennock's outfit who came out on top, to set up a teasing week of preparation before next weekend's trip to Cheltenham Town.

Nicky Deverdics's excellent free kick gifted Dover a first-half lead, but with the wind in their favour, FGR produced an effective second-half performance as James Jennings, Darren Carter and then Elliott Frear helped seal a superb three points. The stormy weather across the country certainly did not miss out on The New Lawn, and both sides set about trying to make the most of a tough encounter in tricky conditions.

Carter saw two good opportunities fall wide as his late runs from a midfield position offered a threat to the visitors in the opening stages. Although it was a key figure in Dover's midfield who gave the Kent side the lead, seven minutes before the interval: a well-worked free kick saw former Gateshead man Deverdics guide a fantastic dead-ball effort

**N
O
V
E
M
B
E
R**

past Steve Arnold, who was making his first league appearance of the campaign.

Rovers' heads did not drop, and a response to Dover's opener was secured early in the second half, when Jennings notched with a neat finish from a corner. The left back was left with room in the box, and he directed a corner from the right expertly into the back of the net to draw the tie level.

It was the lift FGR needed, and four minutes later they took the lead when Carter produced a moment of class with a wonderful finish. He picked up the ball from Sam Wedgbury's accurate pass, and notched with a right-footed attempt that left Dover goalkeeper Andy Rafferty helpless.

A significant moment was to follow, as Arnold produced a stop that denied what looked to set to be an equalizing goal from Dover's leading talisman, Stefan Payne. The former Gillingham attacker's fierce right-footed shot was outstandingly tipped over the bar. It was a key moment, although Frear's addition to the tally proved to be even more important, as the left winger netted straight from a corner. With the help of the elements, his in-swinging corner was too much for Rafferty to handle, and it dropped in near to the back post. The two-goal margin looked to have killed off the clash in Forest Green's favour, although there was nearly a reward for Kurtis Guthrie's moment of brilliance ten minutes from time. His neat footwork and shot with his left foot curled dramatically, only to slam against Dover's crossbar, in what would have been an excellent way to crown the victory. An emphatic second half comeback was complete though, and now Rovers can look forward to a short trip to the World of Smile Stadium, next weekend.

ANSWER BLOWING IN THE WIND FOR ROVERS
Jokerman

Forest Green Rovers, disappointed at losing top spot in mid-week at Welling, a game they feel they should have won, were facing a tough task at home to close rivals Dover Athletic today. Shelter was sought in The Green Man escaping the driving wind and rain. Team news filtered through the alewaves that Jones had kept his place and Arnold again replaced Maxted in goal. With almost a full-strength squad to choose from, the bench was made of oak with Clough, Pipe and O'Connor included. Guthrie and Parkin would lead up front. Storm clouds continued to roll in over the eesi stand as the teams paraded. The immaculately observed Armistice silence was shrouded in irony today, with France having made a declaration of war and peace on earth nought but a dream. In reply

Mother Nature orchestrated and conducted the backdrop to the events about to unfold.

Dover chose the wind at their backs leaving Rovers to confront the teeth of the gale. It was soon obvious the elements were going to be decisive.

The visitors laid in to Rovers and Jones twice had to make timely clearances from threatening attacks. Under the conditions back passes were not the best option on the wet surface and Dover blocked two Arnold clearing kicks which could have been costly. Modeste, the Dover winger, was looking useful, defenders having the added threat of his flailing pigtail. Rovers were posing their own threat through the in-form Frear who crossed for Guthrie who mistimed his header.

Carter went closer for Rovers on 24 minutes when Parkin chipped the ball in to Guthrie and Carter, following up, curled his controlled shot inches wide of the right-hand post, with keeper Rafferty beaten. Carter combined well with Frear down the left but could get no power on his header which Rafferty saved easily.

On 30 minutes a Parkin header gathered by Rafferty was quickly sent down field, where Miller saw his well-struck low shot beat Arnold but went narrowly wide. The deadlock was broken on 38 minutes when Modeste was fouled on the edge of the D. Deverdics hit a touched pass around the wall'and past the despairing dive of Arnold. The 150 Dover soles behind the goal celebrated with the players. This signalled sustained pressure from Dover as the goal appeared to have unsettled Rovers. A high ball into the box from a Deverdics free kick slipped through Arnold's hands for a corner. Modeste nearly caught Arnold out at his near post with the inswinging kick. The winger regained possession from the clearance and saw his goal-bound shot blocked away by Wedgbury. It was a relief to hear the half-time whistle.

The surf was up on unprotected beverages whipped by the unrelenting wind. The elements had long extinguished any semblance of daylight and set up TNL as a theatre with dramatic atmosphere under the lights to play out this unfolding encounter. Forest Green took very little time to employ the conditions to their advantage. On 53 minutes a corner on the right saw Frear drop the ball around the penalty spot, and as the Dover defence hit the off switch, Jennings nipped in to flick the ball into the net with the outside of his left foot. Rovers were up and running. Five minutes later they were in front. Carter took a pass midway in the Dover half and pressed forward with Parkin and Guthrie lining up for the cross that never came. Instead he struck a fierc,e low drive inch perfect across Rafferty, inside the right-hand post from 20 yards.

NOVEMBER

On 67 minutes the unfortunate Jones was replaced by Clough after suffering a hamstring problem. Dover were stung into action and all but levelled when Modeste set up Payne, who saw his powerful shot from inside the area tipped over the bar by Arnold. It was a brief respite and on 71 minutes Carter won a corner on the right. Frear stepped up and his in-swinger escaped Rafferty's efforts to claw it away and the ball dropped beyond him into the net. The goal put Rovers firmly in control and Pipe entered the fray in place of Sinclair. Fresh legs were needed as the storm increased, the rain sweeping across the sodden turf in cloudlike murmurations. Parkin tried a flick with the outside of his foot that ended up in the car park to give some indication of the conditions.

Around 80 minutes Guthrie nicked the ball off a defender's toe in midfield and careered goalward on the right; turning inside, his shot from 25 yards beat Rafferty only to rebound off the crossbar to Frear who hit his shot wide. The visitors were still fighting and when a Modeste free kick caused an almighty scramble in the Rovers goalmouth only the woodwork denied Parkinson adding to the scoreline.

O'Connor made a welcome return in the closing stages in place of Parkin. Both teams rode out the final minutes as standing water began to appear, bringing down the curtain on a dramatic afternoon.

Forest Green Rovers are right on track heading for a fixture at Whaddon Road which will be played under circumstances one could never have believed possible just a few seasons ago.

Saturday 21.11.15
Cheltenham Town 1 FGR 1 (El Glosico 2)
CARTER STRIKES TO SEAL EL GLOSICO DERBY DRAW
Richard Joyce

Darren Carter's second-half close-range finish against his former club earned Forest Green Rovers a draw in the Gloucestershire derby at the World of Smile Stadium. The midfield man pounced to net his fourth goal since moving to The New Lawn to ensure the spoils were shared between the National League's two leading outfits for a second time this season. Harry Pell's drilled free kick had given the hosts the lead in front of a crowd of 5,449 early in the second half, but despite having Jon Parkin miss a penalty, Carter's finish helped Rovers to a point.

In what was Forest Green's first visit for a league meeting on Cheltenham's home turf since April 1999, a following of 804 fans cheered on Ady Pennock's side, whose team started the game in impressive fashion. The pressure was all on the hosts early on; however, clear-cut chances failed to materialize for FGR, and just a Carter effort on the turn on 16 minutes represented any attempts on the Robins goal. After ex-Rovers front man Danny Wright had headed the dangerous Billy Waters cross wide, a series of Cheltenham opportunities failed to threaten as Kyle Storer and Wright again struggled in their efforts to test Steve Arnold. Charlie Clough headed well wide from an Elliott Frear free kick on the half-hour mark, and the impressive Carter's overhead kick was gathered by Dillon Phillips, as the interval came with the match again left finely balanced.

Cheltenham, though, set things going early in the second half when Pell broke the deadlock with a free kick, similar to the one he had scored at Southport seven days easrlier. The former AFC Wimbledon midfielder's well-struck effort was out of view for Arnold, who could only feel the ball fly past him and into the back of the net. Rovers didn't stutter, and if anything from this point onward wrestled hold of the tie. Parkin was denied from a narrow angle by Phillips inside the box, while the highly regarded striker blew a huge opportunity to level the scores on the hour mark. After Kurtis Guthrie had been bundled over in the box, he stepped up to take a penalty, which was poorly executed, letting Cheltenham off the hook.

Nevertheless, Pennock's side were not fazed, and parity was restored when Carter swooped to knock the ball in right in front of the goal. Parkin's strike from the left was neither a shot nor cross, but it fell perfectly for Carter, who sent the FGR followers behind the goal into jubilation with the game's leveller. A thunderous strike from Pell almost ruined Forest Green's ambitions to push for the win. His excellent hit slammed against the crossbar and bounced clear to the relief of those in green and black. There was still time in the remainder of the clash for Carter to curl a shot wide, while Guthrie's cheeky handball at the death, which diverted the ball into the net, was witnessed by everyone in the stadium and correctly ruled out.

DESTINATION CHELTENHAM
Rambling Man
El Glosico 2. Rovers' first away league fixture against Cheltenham Town since April 1999, when the Robins were Champions Elect. We nicked a 1-1 draw in front of 3,000 or so, among them my 11-year-old son and me, watching from the Paddock. Back then, Steve Cotterill's side were on the up and up, and we, just Frank Gregan's upstart Villagers, still disbelieving that we'd reached the pinnacle of non-league. The game may be the same but everything else has changed.

**N
O
V
E
M
B
E
R**

Seventeen seasons later, it is Ady Pennock's Rovers who have been frontrunners for promotion, only lately hauled back by The Robins, still smarting over their exit from the Football League. Gary Johnson has an unparalleled record at National League and lower Football League level. He has started to sprinkle his magic dust around the absurdly named World of Smile Stadium – Whaddon Road to you and me.

On a Tuesday night back in September, 3,200 had gathered at The New Lawn to see an exciting 2-2 draw. A largely dominant Rovers were made to regret their poor finishing. But they stayed top with Cheltenham second. El Glosico 2 heralded a reversal of roles – a win would retake top spot for Rovers, a draw or win would cement Town's primacy for the time being. Make no mistake, The County was up for the derby. Egg chasers had been banished from the sports pages of the *Echo*, *Citizen* and *Stroud News & Journal*. Fans Forums, Twitter and Local Radio Stations were abuzz. Nearly 5,500 packed into WR, including some 1000 of South Gloucestershire's finest. A bitingly cold north wind was soon forgotten, the stadium rocking. And both teams delivered.

Rovers had the best of the match for all but 15 minutes before and after the break, the engine room set to warp speed and Frear and Bennett irresistible down the flanks. But as at The New Lawn, they were let down by erratic finishing and a momentary defensive lapse – Pell's free kick parting a timid wall.

Rovers roared back. The Beast of all people spurned a penalty and soon after scuffed a shot, but fortunately into Carter's path for 1-1. Cheltenham's counters were rare, but from one Pell rattled the crossbar. At the other end, Frear tore the defence to shreds again, only to be bundled over. But the referee had given one penalty against the home crowd and was not up for another. The 'hand of Kurtis' was rightly struck off. Parity and frustration remained.

BBC had Rovers controlling 63% of the game and a draw was scant reward. But as at TNL, the match justified the hype and around 8,700 had attended the two games. With any luck, both teams will be locking horns in the Football League next term.

ROVERS IMPRESS DESPITE PARKIN VIOLATION
Jokerman

Just another game? Try telling that to the supporters of Cheltenham Town and Forest Green Rovers. All roads lead to the Spa town for this top-of-the-table encounter where the waters will need to be boosted to around 4% vol to prime the vocals to fever pitch. Both teams scored convincing victories last weekend but Cheltenham start warm favourites this afternoon. After all, inferior and complex spring to mind should they fail against a local village side.

At least 800 FGR fans are in attendance and, let off the leash, they lay siege to the burger bar which is offering a free heart monitor with every bargain bucket. Pennock has indicated that Arnold is the preferred keeper and Parkin, skipper for the day, leads the line with Guthrie. O'Connor remains on the bench though fit again. Nearly 5,500 fans pack the stadium as this much-anticipated match kicks off.

Forest Green Rovers lean on Cheltenham Town. The first 20 minutes are played in the Robins' half apart from a lone corner to the home side. Unfortunately for Rovers they could not take advantage. Carter linked well with Bennett on the right to swivel and shoot narrowly wide across keeper Phillips and from a Bennett cross Parkin glanced a header onto the top netting.

The home side eventually made inroads against the Rovers defence. Waters and Pell were combining well and created a chance for ex-FGR striker Wright who put his header wide. Munns was getting in behind Rovers back line but they were equal to the threat, Clough in particular catching the eye in blocking a tremendous drive from Dickie. Arnold did well to claim the ball off Wright's head following a chipped pass over the top from Waters on 25 minutes. In reply a Frear free kick saw Clough head wide and an overhead effort from Carter was easily gathered by Phillips. Clough again blocked a Waters shot away for a corner which Wright, under pressure, headed wide. At the half-time whistle Rovers fans were well pleased with their team's performance.

On a dry but cold afternoon the visiting fans exhausted Bovril supplies which indicated DV's conversion numbers are very low just now. Manager Johnson had words with his players at the break and they came out all guns blazing. Pressing Forest Green onto the back foot, they were soon in trouble. Carter was booked on 52 minutes for a foul on Pell on the edge of the D. Almost an action replay of last week's free kick for Dover. Pell stepped up and hit a firm low shot at the wall, which very conveniently lifted off its foundations and allowed the ball to zip past Arnold, a helpless spectator. The Robins' supporters behind the goal celebrated big time.

Rovers were not deflected from their task and hit back with intent. Jennings sent Frear down the left who cut into the box; his cross was blocked but Parkin nearly forced the ball inside the near post. Carter raiding down the right forced a corner which Sinclair sent over.

It all resulted in a tangle of bodies all going for a high ball and Dickie

N
O
V
E
M
B
E
R

flattened Guthrie in the melee. The referee pointed to the spot and the usual protests broke out delaying the kick. As things settled down one witnessed the defenestration of experience. Parkin allowed the young keeper Phillips to pick the ball up and push it into his hands making a remark as he did so. Whatever was said Parkin lost his composure and struck the ball wildly over the crossbar. Forest Green fans reached for the sick bags and filled up the swear boxes as the Robins' fans rejoiced.

Rovers were impressively unperturbed and kept pressing for the equalizer and it duly arrived on 70 minutes. Bennett made a great run down the right and put a high cross to the back post. It fell to Parkin who attempted a volley; mistimed, the ball went through a gap and Carter pounced to crack it home from a yard out. The Rovers fans were suitably delirious. It was nearly short-lived as Cheltenham went straight down the other end, and a fierce cross from the right was headed forcibly clear by Clough but it dropped to Pell, who struck a tremendous drive past Arnold only to see it rebound off the underside of the bar.

Rovers, however, looked the more likely winners and the home defence did well to survive immense pressure during a five-minute spell which saw Rovers win four corners, causing some almighty scrambles in the penalty area. In the final ten minutes Carter curled a shot just over from distance. Jennings then sent the ever-dangerous Frear down the left. The winger cut inside; riding one tackle, there was contact with a second. He was looking for it, went down but may have done better keeping his balance as penalty claims were waved away by the referee. No argument when he again got through and smashed a shot cum-cross that Guthrie dived at, putting the ball in the net (with his hand) and got booked. It would certainly have given the Robins fans a laundry problem from their viewpoint at the other end.

The referee blew time on a memorable afternoon. To their eternal credit this Forest Green side overcame a gut-wrenching set-back to earn a worthy point against the league leaders. The defence was outstanding apart from a dodgy bricklayer and with sharper striking should fear no opponents in their quest for the title.

Saturday 28.11.15
FGR 2 Altrincham 0
PARKIN AT THE DOUBLE AS ROVERS CLINCH WIN
Richard Joyce
A Jon Parkin double helped Forest Green Rovers make it seven unbeaten in an eventful encounter with Altrincham that saw three men sent off.

Scoring after only 44 seconds, it was always going to be Parkin's day, as he bagged a brace for the first time this season. His strikes in the first and 18th minute contributed to another successful outing in treacherous conditions at The New Lawn, despite the fact that Dale Bennett was shown a straight red card just before half time. Alty themselves were on the wrong side of the officials. Josh O'Keefe was given his marching orders, while Gianluca Havern's two yellow card offences saw him handed an early shower too.

The visitors had barely had time to breathe by the time Parkin had notched his first in the opening minute. His strong run into the box saw him slip the ball past Tim Deasy from the tightest of angles.

He almost added a second immediately after only for a good save by the legs of Deasy, while as Alty finally moved forward, they came close to levelling on 14 minutes through James Lawrie. The Northern Ireland international attacker saw his low hit deflect off an FGR defender and slam against the post. Keanu Marsh-Brown, back in the starting XI after a good performance in Monday's Gloucestershire Senior Cup win over Bristol City, then forced Deasy into a good stop after a tremendous run down the right flank. From the subsequent corner Parkin added his second. He met Marsh-Brown's corner with a delicate header, which doubled his side's advantage.

It could have been 3-2 minutes later. Charlie Clough headed onto the crossbar from an Elliott Frear free kick. Unbelievably the centre back hit the bar again just before the break. A clever effort saw him lift a chipped attempt from inside the box towards goal, and it clipped the woodwork to the relief of the visitors. Bennett became the first player to see red just before the half-time whistle. He reacted to a late tackle, which had actually seen him rewarded with the free kick, in what was his first sending-off of the campaign.

Kurtis Guthrie came very close to extending Rovers lead early in the second half, only to be denied by a heroic clearance from off the line, and a stunning stop from Steve Arnold prevented Damian Reeves from getting a goal back for Altrincham. There was stand-out defensive work at the other end to note too. Substitute David Pipe made a terrific block at the last moment to stop George Bowerman from slamming home, and Parkin completed his defensive duties with a much-needed header off the line from Nicky Clee's goal-bound strike.

The first of Alty's two red cards in five minutes came when O'Keefe was adjudged to have gone in dangerously on Guthrie, and was given his marching orders. Meanwhile the visitors' skipper, Havern, was shown

N
O
V
E
M
B
E
R

a second yellow card for a needless foul on Frear just outside the area, which saw them reduced to nine men. Any ambitions of a dramatic comeback appeared very unlikely, and after Marcus Kelly had steered a long-distance drive wide in stoppage time, the whistle was blown and the points belonged to Rovers.

ROVERS REIN IN THREE POINTS

Jokerman

Forest Green Rovers have shown good form on soft going recently and as fans head to The New Lawn, heads bent into the driving rain, it is hoped the conditions will prove no hindrance to their continued challenge for the league title. Several clubs have signed loan players to help over the busy Xmas period. Manager Ady Pennock has brought in striker Brett Williams from Stevenage. He is on the bench today while Kelly starts in place of the suspended Jennings. Marsh-Brown starts in a very attack minded line-up. The weather is reminiscent of the Dover game, the rain driven into the away end and its 40-plus Altrincham fans. Rovers choose to play against the wind in the first half.

As at Cheltenham last week Rovers are quick off the mark and Kelly threads a terrific pass through the defence to Parkin who still has work to do. He turns goal-wards and with the finesse of a rampaging rhino, crushes Altrincham skipper Havern before blasting the ball straight through keeper Deasy, low into the net. One minute one nil. Only a minute later he finds himself in the same position but this time Deasy blocks the shot away as Rovers threaten to overwhelm the visitors.

Around 15 minutes, however, Altrincham construct a skilful passing move that ends with Lawrie seeing his low shot from the edge of the area strike the outside of the left-hand post. But it is Rovers in the ascendancy with Frear attacking with impunity on the left flank. Marsh-Brown on the right raced into the area and forced Deasy to concede a corner on 19 minutes. Taking the kick himself he flighted the ball onto the head of Parkin at the near post who glances his header perfectly across goal and firmly inside the left-hand post. The scoreline reflected Rovers' superiority and Alty were reduced to breakaways.

Guthrie was wrestled to the ground challenging for a throw-in and the referee awarded him a free kick. Not satisfied, the player appeared to protest verbally and was booked for his petulance which marked him down with an IQ of about room temperature. On 40 minutes Parkin and Frear combined to win a corner on the left from which the ball fell to Clough on the edge of the box with time to chip a shot over the defence, but unfortunately the ball struck the top of the crossbar. Forest Green suffered a set-back in added time in the first half when Bennett was hard tackled by Richman. Leaping to his feet, the Rovers player appeared to stamp out and the referee sent him off. Pennock had to re-write his half-time team briefing.

The rain continues to sweep in and it is a credit to the club that the playing surface is holding up so well even when waterlogged. Pipe replaces Marsh-Brown for the second half and Rankine replaces Crowther for Altrincham. Ten men makes little difference to Forest Green and they attack from the whistle. Two minutes in and Parkin and Guthrie link up. Guthrie takes the ball round Deasy and shoots but Sinnott appears from nowhere and clears the ball off the goal line. Frear continues to put pressure on, raiding down the left. As the ground takes its toll on stamina, Altrincham have their best chances around the hour mark. Rankine finds room in the box but his goal-bound shot is brilliantly blocked by Clough and the follow-up is blocked well by Kelly. Reeves then cuts free and brings a fingertip save from Arnold.

In reply Frear runs 40 yards down the wing and smashes a shot into the side netting. The rain gets heavier and so do Guthrie's legs. Through on Deasy, he puts a weak shot well wide. More pressure from Altrincham as Sinnott swings a dangerous free kick into the area where it breaks for substitute Bowerman, whose close-range shot is superbly blocked by Pipe. From the corner Parkin heads clear twice as Alty try to batter their way back into the game. On 75 minutes Rovers' goalscorer leaves the field to a standing ovation to be replaced by new signing Williams. Frear sets up Wedgbury on the edge of the box but he hits his shot wastefully wide.

The referee evens up the numbers on 78 minutes when he sends O'Keefe off for a late lunge on Guthrie, who is subbed soon after by O'Connor. To compound Altrincham's misery Havern is also dismissed after bringing down Frear on the edge of the area, and receiving a second yellow card. Carter puts the resulting free kick into the crowd.

The rain finally relents for the closing minutes and Rovers fans have plenty to discuss after an eventful afternoon.

The Bennett incident apart, it was a very good performance by Forest Green. Clough was outstanding again but the whole defence gave Arnold solid protection. Parkin made up for his penalty miss last week and won the MoM award.

The FA Cup game at Oxford on Sunday will be a welcome respite from league action.

D E C E M B E R

A TOPSY TURVY MONTH WITH FEW LEAGUE GAMES. Rovers bowed out of the FA Cup in the second round, edged 1-0 by high-flying Oxford United at the Kassam Stadium. Then a weakened team was humbled at Havant & Waterlooville. Completion of the double over Boreham Wood improved spirits before a crushing 4-1 Boxing Day defeat on the Torbay Riviera. Cheltenham's formidable unbeaten run continued as they stayed out in front while Grimsby looked menacing in third.

Christmas Day
Pitchfork

I
wrote
a poem
in the shape
of a Christmas tree
Borehamwood threatened
but Kurtis chopped them down
3 more valuable points to our
FGR
team
Enjoy your presents
HAPPY XMAS

Sunday 06.12.15
Oxford United 1 FGR 0 (FA Cup 2nd round)
CUP DREAMS ENDED ON THE ROAD AT OXFORD
Richard Joyce
Kemar Roofe's second-half strike was enough to send Forest Green out of the FA Cup at the Kassam Stadium against League Two leaders Oxford United. The attacking midfielder, who is being tracked by a number of higher-level clubs, showed his class with a fine finish that was enough to clinch the home side a place in the third round. An excellent performance from goalkeeper Steve Arnold had kept Oxford at bay, although Rovers will be pleased with their efforts having impressed, particularly in the first half. With Rob Sinclair and James Jennings back in the side, a following of 619 travelled from Gloucestershire, hoping to see the club make it through to the third round for only the third time in the club's history.

From the start Rovers were ambitious and positive. The hosts' Liechtenstein international goalkeeper Benji Buchel was forced into a good one-handed save after only 45 seconds from Darren Carter's sweetly struck volley. And after Aarran Racine's early header was again stopped by Buchel, Oxford forced their first opening after three minutes when Danny Rose's hit dropped wide.

Carter was denied by Buchel again on 20 minutes after a good passing move. This time Jon Parkin set up attacking midfielder Carter whose guided effort was gathered. A disappointing note at the end of the first half saw Dale Bennett stretchered off with what looked like a bad injury near the halfway line. With David Pipe on as Bennett's replacement FGR regrouped, and the first of several superb Arnold saves came on 45 minutes when he denied former Exeter City man Liam Sercombe.

Ady Pennock's side had more than made their mark against a team gunning for promotion to League One in the first half, although the home team did produce a strong second-half display.

They were repeatedly denied by Arnold though, and he made another fine stop on the hour mark from Danny Hylton's header that looked all but sure to hit the back of the net. Arnold foiled another Hylton header minutes later, while Carter was once again unable to beat Buchel with an effort inside the box after Elliott Frear had teed up the former top-flight midfielder. Oxford finally found a way past Arnold when Roofe produced a ruthless strike that flashed into the net. They almost doubled their newfound lead five minutes later. A corner from the right was missed by everyone in the box and slammed against the far post, before eventually being cleared. Jennings came perilously close to netting a late equalizer, but his header from a Frear corner fell just a few yards wide with Buchel and his defenders left stranded. Sercombe wasted another big opportunity for the hosts to extend their lead as he was again stopped by Arnold who nicked the ball off the midfielder's feet with the goal gaping. A Parkin strike with the full-time whistle only minutes away, straight into the gloves of Buchel, was all Rovers could muster in their attempts to force a replay, as Oxford held on to secure their place in the draw for the third round, and to end Forest Green's honourable run in the competition.

DESTINATION OXFORD
Rambling Man

A trip to the Kazzam was FGR's first proper FA Cup 'local' day trip for many a year. And a full team was selected including Foggy, Clegg and Compo (recently returned from the Sub Continent), with me in the role of pilot. We met at the Glider Café and set a course that avoided

D
E
C
E
M
B
E
R

the nightmare of the A40. That meant a fast sightseeing jaunt through Cirencester, Fairford, Lechlade and Farringdon before joining the grind at the charmingly named Botley Interchange. Parked up with 90 minutes to kick-off, a search for wholesome grub was called for. Fair play, Oxford delivered. Haddock & chips plus drink at the chippie discovered in the bowels of the Cinema complex. Delicious, just what was required. So, into the Kazzam to join the 600 or so from the Five Valleys.

It was my fourth trip to the Kassam. Thus far, the highlight was a 2-0 win courtesy of a Danny Carey-Bertram brace, the others a 0-0 and 1-0 reverse. Nothing much had changed around the stadium, still three impressive sides making a square U. The fourth comprises a disappointing domestic close-boarded fence hung with a few advertising banners that look like washing.

At the back of the popular stand, U's fans displayed a bland range of flags and stuff proclaiming the usual street allegiances and optimistic boasts. No offence guys, but I'd expected better from a city of learning and dreaming spires. I have a few suggestions. How about, 'Magdalen College Ultras', 'Class of Bamber Gascoigne' and 'Bullingdon Boys Rule' (they do, don't they?). Personally, I like a bit of Latin and would go with one Oxford University motto I came across, *Domimina Nustio Illlumea*, which, of course means 'My wife is sha**ing the postman'.

In due course, my reveries were interrupted when a game of football broke out. A good one too.

Rovers came out of the traps and came close twice in the opening minutes (Carter and Racine). In the middle, Wedge and Sincs were winning everything and Racine and Clough were bullying the Us's burly front men. The turning point came when Dale Bennett fell awkwardly in an innocuous challenge and was stretchered off. The second period saw some superb stops by Arnold as Rovers soaked up the pressure, the tie being decided by one moment of high-quality finishing by top scorer Roofe. So, a narrow defeat against Division 2's top club on their patch. No shame there and plenty of cause for pride. Somehow, Havant & Waterlooville away seems a rather anticlimactic follow up?

FA CUP MAGIC – "GONE – JUST LIKE THAT"
Jokerman

Just an appraisal – TG, you're thinking – of the game at The Kassam yesterday of which the highlights were well covered by the BBC. This cup tie was a good example to illustrate the marginal differences between the divisions. Oxford United were the better side in possession of the ball.

Forest Green Rovers' defence proved they are up to league two level. Arnold's display will possibly attract interest from elsewhere. Rovers' attack was sporadic and disjointed. So unfortunate to lose Bennett to injury, his input on the flanks was missed. Parkin was given no time to hold the ball up front and Guthrie never threatened. Carter went nearest to scoring but found Buchel in goal equal to the task. It was the difference between the sides: Oxford, with more composure through midfield, enabled the team to attack in numbers. Rovers' attackers for the most part were isolated.

Having said that, FGR gave it a good shot and on another day may have grabbed a replay. The club is clearly in transition and edging closer to DV's goal of league status.

Next week it is the FA Trophy which has lost its attraction for teams vying for promotion to the Football League. Given Saturday priority, the competition causes a log jam every year at the business end of the season. Surely time for a re-think, especially the two-leg semi-final. Cambridge United did win both the play-offs and the Trophy which was a Herculean achievement. Barnet chose a different route to illustrate the dilemma. Onward onward the Six Hundred to Havant & Waterlooville and Victory ... ummmmmaybe not.

Saturday 12.12.15
Havant & Waterlooville 2 FGR 0 (FA Trophy 1st round)
ROVERS LIMP OUT IN EARLY FA TROPHY EXIT
Richard Joyce

A much-changed Forest Green Rovers side were knocked out of the FA Trophy at the first hurdle against National League South side Havant & Waterlooville. For a second consecutive season Ady Pennock's side exited the competition against opposition from a tier below the National League, with goals from Scott Donnelly and James Hayter enough for the Hawks to clinch a second-round place.

Delano Sam-Yorke saw red in the second half after conceding a penalty, which set the hosts on their way to victory. A raft of changes saw nine new faces in the starting XI from the team that started last weekend's FA Cup second round trip to Oxford. Academy graduate Aden Baldwin was handed his first-team debut in the back four, while fellow first-year professional Louis McGrory produced a commanding performance in midfield in his first start for the club.

An uneventful first half provided little entertainment for the small Westleigh Park crowd as both sides struggled to create openings. A

**D
E
C
E
M
B
E
R**

tricky wind made life difficult as front line duo Brett Williams and Aaron O'Connor struggled to latch onto steady build-up play from Sam-Yorke and Keanu Marsh-Brown.

The clash came into life in the second half though. Marsh-Brown slammed over the bar early on from a well-weighted ball forward from Baldwin, while a brilliant save from Jonny Maxted denied former FGR loanee Matt Paterson who had broken through in the box. There was another tremendous stop, this time from Havant's Ryan Young, to deny Rovers what looked to be a sure goal after a good move just past the hour mark. David Pipe's excellent run down the right saw him clip a ball into the area that was prodded towards goal by Williams, although Young got across to make a superb stop.

The game turned, though, midway through the half when Sam-Yorke was given his marching orders by referee Nigel Lugg for a foul in the box. Donnelly produced the punishment, slotting from 12 yards, to put the home side in the lead. Forest Green struggled to find a way back into the tie as Havant confidently dealt with the little forward advances that were thrown at them. And they confirmed their place in the next round with a second right near the end when the experienced Hayter got in on the goal-scoring act. The former AFC Bournemouth forward picked his spot after receiving the ball on the edge of the box.

DESTINATION HAVANT
Rambling Man
In the course of six days, Rovers changed their casting from hopeful giant-killers at Oxford to vulnerable Goliaths (relatively speaking) at Havant. The hunters became the hunted. Foggy, Clegg and I met at the Glider Café, the former drawing the short straw to become chauffeur du jour. Two hours of virtually traffic-free cruising saw us arriving at downtown Havant, otherwise known as Westleigh Park, the stamping ground of Havant & Waterlooville FC.

A tie like Havant serves to underline how far Rovers and their supporters have to travel to reach footie heartland. I think of the South Coast as being relatively local and home of course to the feuding football cities of Portsmouth and Southampton. Yet the mileometer clicks to 115. That many miles north will get you to Crewe, eastwards as far as Wimbledon or westwards to Dartmoor. Nope, with the exception of Cheltenham, when you play at our level do not expect many local derbies.

Westleigh Park is a compact, fully enclosed stadium bedecked in blue. The hosts play in National League 2 where they are perilously close to the trapdoor. There are plenty less impressive venues in NL Premier albeit Westleigh Park has a pronounced downward slope from north to south. On arrival, a quick perambulation showed many areas of the pitch to be soft and oozing water, oddly worst at the top of the slope. Keeping your footing and getting the ball to travel across the surface would present a challenge. This would not be an easy game regardless of the relative position of the adversaries.

Ady picked an XI from the first team squad, of which only Racine and Clough had started recent first-team games. Academy graduates Louis McGrory and Aden Baldwin claimed midfield and right-back berths. The first half had Rovers in the ascendancy. McGrory saw a lot of the ball and released Sam-Yorke and Marsh-Brown on frequent raids. All too often though, their dangerous crosses found a penalty area devoid of their colleagues. 0-0 at the break.

The Hawks really gave it a go in the second half against an away side that had lost its appetite. Sam-Yorke's mistimed challenge brought a penalty and an unfortunate red card for Rovers' hardest worker, but the 1-0 lead was deserved. As was the breakaway second which assured victory for the jubilant home supporters. So, a dispiriting showing by Rovers that did little to advance the case of those currently unfavoured in the League starting XI. No doubt Ady will be doubly keen to rediscover winning ways against Boreham Wood, the last fixture before Christmas.

ROVERS HAVANT A CLUE
Jokerman

The FA Trophy, once the Holy Grail for Forest Green Rovers has apparently lost its appeal as league ambitions take priority. Manager Ady Pennock made clear his intentions to field a much-changed side for the trip to Havant & Waterlooville. This is not lost on the supporters and many have no doubt chosen the crush on the High Street instead as the commercial maelstrom of Xmas begins to bite. And so it came to pass that the supporters' ship sailed south with a skeletal crew, hoping to plunder a victory in the shadow of the same. The Westleigh, adjacent to the ground, had the excellent Doom Bar ale on tap, so a good start at least.

The playing surface was soft and cutting up as the players worked out. Mercifully the rain held off despite a blanket of heavy cloud over the stadium. The youngsters Baldwin and McGrory were given a start and Williams and O'Connor led the attack supported by Sam-Yorke and Marsh-Brown. Unsurprisingly Arnold was rested having had his nuts

**D
E
C
E
M
B
E
R**

cracked early for Christmas in the match at Oxford. Maxted played in goal.

Portsmouth were at home which may have had an impact on the attendance, as less than 300 were present as the game kicked off. The first 45 minutes were utterly forgettable as both sides failed to string together any passing movements of note. Both goalkeepers were redundant with no direct shots at goal. The only player for Rovers to catch the eye was McGrory who worked hard to make an impression.

At half time the discussion was concentrated around the word 'dire'. The second half started far more brightly. Baldwin made a run down the right and lofted a pass to Marsh-Brown who was into the area but blazed over when he should have done better. H&W replied when Medway raided on the left and crossed to the back post for Patterson to head across goal to Donnelly whose shot was blocked over the bar. This was followed by another good move by the home side that saw Patterson clean through only to have the ball picked off his toe by Maxted. Around the hour mark Forest Green should have taken the lead. A quick break from defence released Pipe who took the ball across the corner of the box on the right before cutting it back into the path of Williams who looked certain to score, only for Young in the H&W goal to save brilliantly and the ball was scrambled clear.

On 68 minutes H&W, who were certainly looking the more likely side, went in front from the spot. Sam-Yorke brought down Donnelly and was shown a red card. Donnelly picked himself up and fired the ball low past Maxted into the right-hand corner. With the extra man the home side never looked in danger.

Pennock replaced Baldwin with Wedgbury but their heads looked disinterested. 88 minutes and Havant & Waterlooville clinched the victory. A Rovers attack was cleared downfield and an overhead kick on halfway sent Donnelly and substitute Hayter free. They exchanged passes and Hayter from the edge of the area guided the ball low past Maxted into the right-hand corner. The same player could have had a second at the death when clean through but Maxted saved with his legs outside the box.

It was the last action and as Rovers trudged off they could have no complaints. It was an underwhelming display but no blame could be attached to the youngsters Baldwin and McGrory who did well in the light of their experience. To bury this result Forest Green Rovers need a positive winning run when they return to league business. For those who braved the journey today it just remains to get wrecked on Doom Bar.

Saturday 19.12.15
FGR 1 Boreham Wood 0
GUTHRIE SWOOPS TO SEAL ANOTHER KEY WIN
Richard Joyce

Kurtis Guthrie's introduction from off the bench as a second-half substitute helped Forest Green Rovers to a key home win over Boreham Wood. The young attacker, who scored the only goal in a similar win over last season's Conference South play-off winners earlier in the season, nodded home to make it six league games unbeaten for Ady Pennock's side. Another three points helps FGR into the festive period in a fulfilled mood, with a frantic schedule now set to see the side in action three times in seven days.

A simple header right in front of goal from Guthrie was enough to separate Rovers from a Boreham Wood side making their first ever visit to The New Lawn. Earlier, Keanu Marsh-Brown had guided Elliott Frear's looping cross wide, while the dangerous Conor Clifford saw his curving free kick for the visitors only just whip past Steve Arnold's left-hand post. There was little between the two teams, although towards the latter stages of the opening period, FGR began to wrestle control. Aarran Racine forced Wood keeper James Russell into a good save with a header from a Rob Sinclair free kick, and Frear's jinking run saw him power an effort over the bar. A moment of brilliance from Jon Parkin almost then saw the experienced front man hand his side the lead. He hit a first-time shot from Russell's poor clearance that looked set to send the watching crowd to their feet, however the goalkeeper made up for his error with a fabulous one-handed stop. The away side then made Arnold produce a marvellous save at his near post. Luke Howell's guided attempt from an Anthony Jeffrey cross was stopped well by the feet of Arnold. Both teams were edging closer to a goal, and Parkin was literally inches away from opening Forest Green's account on the stroke of half time, only to see his hit bounce back off the post.

Despite the increase in chances towards the end of the first half, there was little to suggest a goal would be scored by either side given proceedings early in the second half. However, the introduction of Guthrie changed that. The Jersey international was first denied a goal by an awesome Russell stop after he had got on the end of a good Frear cross, but from the next phase of play he made sure he would find the net with a simple header from a David Pipe cross into the six-yard box. It was a goal that delivered Forest Green the urgency to go on and seal the three points, and they nearly doubled their advantage when Racine met a Frear corner, but could only head narrowly over the bar. Racine tried his luck again

D
E
C
E
M
B
E
R

in the tie's final major chance, but Russell, who had produced several good saves over the course of the afternoon, pulled off another one as he denied the former Southampton defender who had steered another header on goal.

ROVERS FIND SOLUTION TO BOREHAM'S PUZZLE WOOD
Jokerman

Oxford excusable. Havant & Waterlooville? Let's not dress this up, it would have had Banksy rethinking his Trip to Dismaland project. Today is redemption day, payback time for the fans who endured. The wind is whipping the corner flags and with luck Pennock is whipping his players into line inside the dressing room. A room full of egos and tantrums, therein lies the key to success or failure. Four points off the leaders, no time for slip-ups. Tom Long is the beer of choice in the bar, talk is that nothing but a victory will suffice and FGR long odds on with the layers. The line-up reverts to type Parkin and Marsh-Brown in attack with Guthrie on the bench with O'Connor who is right out of favour.

Rovers start with the wind at their backs and a crowd of 1,300 urging them on. Frear is making inroads down the left flank and on eight minutes loops a cross to the back post to Marsh-Brown who from six yards hits a low shot across keeper Russell but wide. Clifford replies for Boreham Wood, curling a free kick from 25 yards but just wide, though Arnold was covering. Jeffery the Boreham left winger soon discovered he had the beating of Pipe, passing him to the by-line and pulling the ball back to Clifford who hit his shot wildly over the bar. Racine went closer at the other end, Russell tipping his header over the bar from a Sinclair free kick. Jennings on the overlap crossed for Parkin whose header was cleared out to Frear but his fierce shot was blocked.

The visitors hit back through another free kick from Clifford that Arnold gathered. Shakes then muscled his way past Jennings into the area but Arnold positioned himself well and made the save. Around 40 minutes Russell the Boreham keeper miss-hit a clearance straight to Parkin. He immediately hit the ball from 25 yards towards the top corner. Russell redeemed himself with a fingertip save.

Pipe's nightmare continued as Jeffery twice in a couple of minutes passed him to put in dangerous crosses. Jennings beat Shakes to clear the first but only a goal line block by Arnold at his near post prevented Howell opening the scoring. In the added minute to the first half a melee from a Sinclair corner ended with Parkin hitting a shot through a ruck of bodies to see the ball hit the left-hand post. It remained goalless. Most agreed at half time that the difference in league positions between the sides was not in evidence on the field of play.

The second half started brightly and Boreham pressed Rovers back, winning two free kicks in succession on the edge of the Rovers penalty area. Clifford struck the first into the wall and the resulting corner was cleared. The second was left to Tiryaki who was a worthy challenger to Parkin at the weigh-in. He put his substantial mass behind a thunderous drive into the already battered wall. Whoever it struck will probably carry the mark into the New Year. Brave defending indeed.

Carter had been a peripheral figure throughout proceedings and was replaced by Guthrie on 63 minutes in an effort to break the deadlock. Lo and behold, Parkin near halfway placed one of his visionary passes into the path of Frear down the left. The winger cut inside and crossed superbly to Guthrie six yards out; certain to score, he didn't quite connect with sufficient power which enabled Russell time to make a good save. The ball was only cleared away to Wedgbury and Marsh-Brown on the right and they linked with Pipe whose excellent cross eluded Russell and Guthrie made no mistake, this time heading the ball firmly into the back of the net. The relief from the home support was palpable.

The goal lifted the team and knocked the fight out of Boreham Wood who were lucky to finish the game with eleven players. Frear anticipating a back pass was brought down by Russell outside the area. One can only assume the referee reaching into his back pocket while running towards the keeper mistakenly pulled out the wrong card and was too embarrassed to change his mind. Rovers nearly added a second goal when Racine, always a threat at set pieces, brought a good save from the fortunate Russell following a Frear corner.

On reflection FGR just about deserved the three points but they looked far from comfortable. They gave the ball away too easily and never looked in control. Wedgbury is a workaholic and demonstrated that today and the defence in general is dependable. Parkin was explicit in his advice to Marsh-Brown and it is clear that improvement must be made in attack. The three Christmas fixtures are against the bottom two clubs in the league. If today was a measure of that level Forest Green Rovers need to steer clear of a Turkey just now.

FGR V BOREHAM WOOD

FGR Student Ambassador Evie Urquhart Gordon

My name is Evie. I'm the ambassador for King's Stanley Primary School. Our school is one of the luckiest schools to have received the green flag

DECEMBER

award which Dale Vince celebrated with us. As part of my ambassador's role I recently held a sports themed raffle for Children in Need where I sourced all the prizes myself and we raised £76.50. The main prize was a family ticket to FGR that was won by my French teacher. I live down the road from The New Lawn where the Old Lawn used to be, around about the halfway line. I have been going to matches since I was five and now I'm nearly eleven.

Match report: A great start for FGR; in the first ten minutes we had already been given two corners. The first was taken by Rob Sinclair whom I paraded with and the second by Elliott Frear. The first hit the crossbar and Keanu Marsh-Brown went wide. Twenty minutes in we had our first free kick which also went sadly wide. After half time we had our first substitution, Kurtis Guthrie (17) came on and Darren Carter (24) went off. Straight after Guthrie had come on he went for a goal but unfortunately it just missed, but thankfully he soon followed up with a great first goal. Disappointingly Kurtis had a clash of heads but after five minutes he was back up on his feet sprinting forward. With ten minutes to go FGR worked well to get the ball to the other end of the pitch, this was shortly followed by Elliott racing down the wing and he made the goalie save a great shot. Instead Boreham Wood nearly scored a second goal for us, whoops! With seven minutes to go there was a clear hand ball but nothing was done by the referee. With only two minutes to go we got another corner by Elliott Frear, our Man of the Match. The corner should have gone in but it was deflected by a Boreham Wood player unfortunately! Then the fourth official announced that there was going to be four minutes of time added on. These last few minutes were tough, but FGR did it – they won!

We are still creeping up on Cheltenham only four points difference. The final score was FGR 1 Boreham Wood 0; it was an excellent game with lots of action. Attendance: 1,356 Away: 40.

Saturday 26.12.15
Torquay United 4 FGR 1
POOR ROVERS SUFFER AGAINST THE GULLS
Richard Joyce

There was to be little Christmas cheer at Plainmoor as Forest Green Rovers' unbeaten league run was brought to a halt by relegation-threatened Torquay United. Backed by a buoyant home support, the former Football League side fought back from being a goal down to deliver a bad blow to Ady Pennock's side's progress. Keanu Marsh-Brown's stunning opener had looked to set Rovers on their way to extending their impressive run of form in the division. However, Torquay hit back instantly, and they never looked back, as they basked in the glory of what was their first win on home soil since the opening day of the season.

A promising start saw FGR dominate the early exchanges, and Darren Carter's long-distance drive only just whistled past the post after eight minutes. Only a couple of minutes later Jon Parkin headed off target after a wonderful flowing move had seen Elliott Frear and Marcus Kelly combine to set up the target man. A powerful south coast wind almost gifted Forest Green the opener as they continued to pile on the pressure. Frear's corner looked set to drift into the net, although Durrell Berry made a crucial clearance off the line.

The goal Rovers deserved for their early efforts came just before the midpoint of the half. Another Frear corner dropped to Marsh-Brown 25 yards from goal, and the former Fulham man executed a spectacular volley which found the top corner and put Rovers in front. Torquay's response was swift and effective – as they struck a leveller less than 30 seconds after the restart. West Bromwich Albion loanee Andre Wright's powerful burst down the right saw him cross for Tyrone Marsh, who was on hand to tuck in despite Steve Arnold's best efforts from close range.

The goal had given the Gulls some belief, and further inspired the Boxing Day crowd, and they took the lead when Marsh grabbed his second, eight minutes before the interval. A fine cross found the unmarked ex-Oxford United man, and he had the simple job of nodding home.

Forest Green's second half showing lacked inventiveness and design, although were it not for a stunning stop from Torquay's young goalkeeper Dan Lavercombe early on from a Kurtis Guthrie smash on goal, the story of the game could have been very different. Substitute Aaron O'Connor offered a rare shot on the Torquay goal in a frustrating period where FGR struggled to carve up any openings. And they were punished when the hosts scored twice in the last ten minutes to seal a deserved victory. Arnold had made two fine blocks to deny Louis Briscoe from netting; however, he couldn't keep Berry's follow-up out as the defender made it 3-1. Wright wrapped up a fine display with Torquay's fourth, at the end, when he drilled home with a right-footed finish into the bottom corner.

DESTINATION TORQUAY
Rambling Man
First time I've missed a Rovers Boxing Day fixture for ... well, since the last millennium. But, greater powers than I decreed that a family

D
E
C
E
M
B
E
R

gathering would take place in Italy with the 1,000-mile outward drive commencing inconveniently on 26 December. Of the regular foursome that usually make up our car-load, that left just Foggy to head for the English Riviera. He also accepted scripting duties for my rambling views for this FGR away fixture. So, as I loaded the car with skis and countless bags (oh, and Mrs R-M) and set course for Dover, Foggy travelled in hope to lovely Torbay. Now, the Torbay area is a jewel of the English coastline; no arguing with that. But who in the name of all that is sane decreed that it should be Rovers' Christmas/New Year double header? Torquay is 130 miles from Nailsworth, similar in fact to our journeys to Chester, Altrincham and Macclesfield. Salisbury is nearly 20 miles closer to Torquay, while fellow Gloucestershire club Cheltenham, or Harriers or even Aldershot would have knocked an hour and scores of miles off the fans' travelling. Remind me to send the National League a roadmap of Britain. Geography aside, all followers from TNL would have travelled in good heart. Last year's 3-3 draw had been a terrific game - a warm welcome by the loyal Devonian fans, brilliant entertainment and a maiden double strike by Kurtis Guthrie. Sadly for the Gulls, their club's financial fortunes have nose-dived this term, and National League South yawns like a big, yawny thing. Yet stalwart supporters of both teams will wish ex-FGR skipper and now Gulls' player-manager, Kevin Nicholson, can revive their fortunes and maybe avert the 2016 trapdoor.

No one expected the 4-1 thrashing dealt by the hosts as the Gulls meted out similar treatment as at Macclesfield in the season's 11th game. In the League, Rovers had been in a lengthy unbeaten run while Torquay were in dire form, their small squad beset by injuries. As in Cheshire, Keanu Marsh-Brown made early inroads and gave Rovers the lead. But for the away fans, that is where both games should have finished. Instead, a sorry collapse took place that put the home supporters into delirium while their rivals choked up their Christmas dinners. None of which did much for good Foggy's disposition. I have searched his notes for something relatively savoury to use in this 'ghosted' account. However, about the only phrase I found that will not invoke censorship is "all in all it was abject". From what I read on the Forum, few eyewitnesses from the Five Valleys would disagree.

So, it falls to me to find the shaft of sunshine to light up Foggy's gloomy place. And, this is it. In 2014, a poor autumn saw Rovers fall at home to Kidderminster Harriers. Yet that was the zenith of their fortunes and the lowest ebb of Rovers'. Thereafter, Rovers claimed a revenge win at

Aggborough before embarking on a great run that saw them to the play-offs for the first time. If we can bounce back in a similar way in 2016, an automatic promotion place would be the result.

How's that for mindless optimism?

GULLS GORGE ON ROVERS RUBBISH

Jokerman

Boxing Day, what happened? Well, something like this is a point of view. On a day when thousands are repacking unwanted presents to claim a refund, over a 150 Forest Green supporters head south to Plainmoor and the Riviera that is Torquay. Nearly 40 are aboard the Kendo Express that arrives in good time for some refreshment. The club bar welcomes visiting fans and has a friendly atmosphere but scores zero on real ale, though Irish Tar is on tap.

Rovers are odds-on favourites for their next three fixtures against the bottom two clubs in the National League. Not surprisingly given their lofty status. Gamblers know, however, that nothing is certain and only a third of odds-on shots win. Studying the form, the Boreham Wood win looked a little shaky. Confidence can be so brittle. Team changes mean Kelly replaces Jennings who is ill, Sinclair drops to the bench and Guthrie plays up front with Parkin and Marsh-Brown. Carter struggled last week but keeps his place.

A crowd of 2,000 see the kick-off on a pitch that survived a precautionary inspection but is not cutting up. The opening 15 minutes see a Carter shot clear the bar and a Parkin header from a Frear cross do likewise. Two quick corners for Rovers are dealt with confidently by Lavercombe, the Torquay keeper. Torquay's only reply is a dangerous cross from ex-FGR star Nicholson that is well gathered by Arnold.

On 20 minutes the game sparks into life when a corner for Rovers on the right is crossed by Frear to be cleared only as far as Marsh-Brown 25 yards out who promptly hits a terrific shot past Lavercombe into the left-hand side of the goal. His ideas of grandeur last for as long as it takes to restart the game. Torquay, in the shape of Wright, true to his name, goes marauding down the right flank and hits a fierce low cross to the back post, where Marsh is on the spot to force the ball over the line despite Arnold's heroic efforts to prevent the equalizer. What a day to land a sucker punch: FGR were undone as the home side, without a home win since August, were visibly lifted. Wright was inspired and cutting inside two defenders, forced Arnold to make a good save at his near post. Rovers replied when Racine headed another Frear corner over the bar.

**D
E
C
E
M
B
E
R**

There was no denying Torquay and on 37 minutes they were in front. A well-rehearsed corner routine between Butler and Richards saw the ball crossed to the back post where Marsh was unguarded and deftly headed the ball past Arnold. Torquay had the initiative and Heslop was only narrowly wide with a shot from the edge of the box as half time approached. Rovers looked ragged and were glad of the half-time whistle.

For FGR fans being beside the seaside was losing its appeal. Frear was Rovers' only consistent threat and at the start of the second half he again beat his man and crossed to the near post for Guthrie, who was only denied by a brave block from Lavercombe. The keeper was also on hand to save a downward header on the line from Racine following another Frear corner as Rovers chased the game. For all their pressing, the passes were wayward, especially the long ball which was resorted to at times. Guthrie looked lightweight and Parkin deadweight while Carter and Marsh-Brown faded. Around the hour Pennock had seen enough and replaced Marsh-Brown with O'Connor. Whatever words were exchanged between M-B and the bench, protocol was shelved and the striker walked away from the bench to the dressing room. To FGR supporters it looked like a pram disappearing over a cliff.

Not much altered for Rovers who continued to win corners to no avail. Frear, perhaps a little late, took it on himself and cut inside to whistle a shot only inches wide across goal. Soon after, playing on the break, Torquay sealed a deserved win on 83 minutes.

Brisco on as a sub was put through, held off his marker but was thwarted by a double save from Arnold, the second a brilliant one-handed block that didn't deserve to run to Berry, who blasted the ball into the unguarded net.

The knife was given a final twist when the hapless O'Connor gave away possession on half way, and could only watch as Wright bore down on goal and ruthlessly blasted the ball past the exposed Arnold on 89 minutes. It was all over. The four added minutes were played out to a dozen masochists and a bunch of tumbleweed as the wind blew along the away terrace.

Another odds-on shot bites the dust and Mr Hockaday is back in town on Monday. The club do not want supporters to view this game from behind their new DFS sofas but it is understandable. In context there are still 63 points to play, for anything is possible … mmmmh. As Timb would say, "Keep calm. But for goodness sake, let's not carry on like this."

Monday 28.12.15
FGR 3 KIDDERMINSTER HARRIERS 0
Rovers make it five wins in a row at home
Richard Joyce

A disappointing Boxing Day defeat at Torquay United was well and truly flushed out of the system at The New Lawn with a comfortable victory over bottom-of-the-table Kidderminster Harriers. Goals from Jon Parkin and Kurtis Guthrie, as well as a first goal for Brett Williams, saw Forest Green make it five straight home victories, and move past the 50 point mark. It was the ideal way to close 2015 at FGR, as Ady Pennock's side go into the New Year firmly in the race for promotion to the Football League.

Rovers were ahead from as early as the quarter-of-an-hour mark courtesy of Parkin's accuracy from the penalty spot. The menacing Elliott Frear was dragged down on a run into the box, and referee Constantine Hatzidakis pointed to the spot, allowing Parkin the chance to open the scoring. Kidderminster's uphill challenge got even harder when on 19 minutes they were reduced to ten men. Matt Young picked up his second yellow card and the right back's afternoon was quickly over. The visitors, managed by former FGR boss David Hockaday, struggled to create openings – although Elton Ngwatala did fire a shot off on goal on the half-hour mark, which was watched wide by Steve Arnold. Dale Bennett's return to the side saw his attacking presence on the right add danger, and his fine cross shortly before the interval was only just turned wide by Williams.

Throughout the second half Forest Green continued in their attempts to further the lead, and Charlie Clough almost nodded home with a powerful header five minutes into the half after he'd met Frear's set piece. The second finally came when Williams notched the first goal of his loan spell at The New Lawn, as his unstoppable header from a Rob Sinclair corner flashed into the top corner. And he almost doubled his tally minutes later, when having been set clear down the left, he couldn't hit the target despite the fact that Harriers stopper Dean Snedker has been left stranded. Kurtis Guthrie was introduced as a substitute in the final ten minutes, and the young attacker provided an effective late influence. He firstly forced Snedker into a good stop with a snap shot on the turn, while he completed the win when he scored a third early on into second-half stoppage time. Keanu Marsh-Brown's pinpoint free kick received the perfect touch from Guthrie, who has now moved onto nine goals for the season.

**D
E
C
E
M
B
E
R**

HARRIERS AN ENDANGERED SPECIES
Jokerman

Forty-six hours after the Torquay trouncing, Forest Green fans are expecting a positive response from their team against bottom club Kidderminster Harriers at TNL today. Nothing but a victory will suffice. Having surveyed the wreckage of his team, manager Ady Pennock has made changes. A much-needed boost is provided by the return of Dale Bennett. Marsh-Brown and Guthrie return to the bench and Williams is given a start up front alongside Parkin.

A crowd of over 2,000 are present as the game kicks off on a cloudy but dry afternoon. The opening 15 minutes produce nothing of note. Frear, the jewel in Rovers' attack, races into the area and is pulled back by Young. The referee has no hesitation in pointing to the spot and books the errant defender. Parkin steps up and confidently strikes the ball past keeper Snedker into the right-hand side of the goal on 16 minutes. Five minutes later Young is booked again for another foul on Frear and goes in search of the shampoo. The game is effectively over as a contest.

A rare Kidderminster attack down the centre ends with an Ngwatala shot clearing the bar. Frear and Carter then create an opening for Wedgbury who screws his shot wide from a good position. Bennett is making his presence felt both in defence and attack. Linking with Carter and Wedgbury, he crosses from the right to Williams but his effort is wide. Carter has a fierce shot blocked away as the first half ends. Fans bemoan the fact that Rovers have not pressed home their advantage against a struggling Kidderminster side following an uninspiring half.

Hockaday brings on sub Maxwell for the restart and they look lively for the opening few minutes with Whitfield their best forward firing in a defiant shot from distance that Arnold gathers. The effort is short-lived and Rovers again dominate possession for long spells. Their finishing, however, leaves a lot to be desired and Parkin would probably admit that his eye and head coordination are well out of kilter today, missing several opportunities. Bennett takes a knock raiding down the right and winning a corner, remaining on the sidelines as Sinclair takes the kick. He flights it perfectly on to the head of Williams who guides it powerfully past Snedker on 58 minutes.

Bennett returns and runs off the pain. On 66 minutes Marsh-Brown replaces Frear who leaves the pitch to a standing ovation. Rovers continue to dominate and Racine flashes a header wide from a corner and Kelly puts a great ball over the defence to Williams. Snedker comes out of the area and is beaten by Williams, whose 'brain' shuts down immediately, and he hits the ball from the edge of the area out for a throw-in on the far side of the field, which is worrying. Pipe comes on for Bennett who has taken another knock. It is to be hoped this Iron Man, so essential to Rovers, is only bruised. Guthrie replaces Carter and is soon in action during the final ten minutes, hitting a powerful low shot from the edge of the penalty area that Snedker does well to save. In time-added-on Rovers win a free kick midway in the Kidderminster half. Marsh-Brown hits a splendid cross towards the top right-hand corner where Clough and Guthrie are attacking on the run. The ball drops for Guthrie and he joyfully thumps a header into the net.

FGR V KIDDERMINSTER HARRIERS
FGR Student Ambassador Oliver Beere
My name is Oliver Beere. I am ten years old and currently attend Kingswood Primary School and have been in the ambassador role since mid-August. I have been supporting Forest Green for three years now and I play football for Wotton Rovers U10s. I am looking forward to walking out with the team in February against Eastleigh. My favourite player is goalkeeper Jonny Maxted and I hope that he gets to play again soon. My most memorable game – but not my favourite – was seeing Forest Green play in the semi-final promotion leg away against Bristol Rovers last season which unfortunately we lost 2-0.

Match report: Forest Green started the game 7 points behind the leaders, Cheltenham Town, but with a game in hand. It took 13 minutes for the first real action to come when Frear was cut down inside the area and a penalty was awarded. Jon Parkin stepped up to take the penalty, placing the ball to the bottom right corner taking the score to 1-0.

In the 18th minute Frear again was brought down by Kidderminster's number 24 and the referee didn't hesitate to show him a red card. Twelve minutes into the second half a Rob Sinclair corner was met by an unstoppable header from Brett Williams that was placed into the top corner of the net. On 75 minutes Williams rounded the keeper just inside the area but was unable to convert his left-footed half volley shot in. At 84 minutes Williams again was one-on-one with the keeper in the six-yard area but got his feet tangled up and eventually put the ball wide. One minute into injury time the substituted Guthrie tapped home a Marsh-Brown free kick. Man of the Match went to Sam Wedgbury, and Frear and Bennett also had a good game. I am very proud to be the ambassador for Kingswood Primary School and wear my FGR shirt with pride. Full time: FGR 3 – 0 Kidderminster / Match attendance: 2,110

Some crusty antiques near Halifax? Travelling companions Compo, Foggy and Rambling Man, as captured by Deep-Throat.

Some big old piles plus Foggy and Rambling Man at Hever Castle, also by Deep-Throat.

3 FGR 1st squad and management. Back row, from left: Dale Bennett, Darren Jones, Aarran Racine, Danny Coles, Kurtis Guthrie, Jon Parkin, Delano Sam-Yorke, Aden Baldwin, Sam Wedgbury. Middle row, from left: Neil Withington (strength & conditioning coach), Charlie Clough, Tom Bender, Paul White, Steve Arnold, Jonny Maxted, Keanu Marsh-Brown, Clovis Kamdjo, Ian Weston (head physio), Glyn Jones (goalkeeper coach). Front row, from left: Matt Rainey (groundsman), Louis McGrory, Elliott Frear, James Jennings, David Pipe, Ady Pennock (manager), Dale Vince (chairman), Jamie Day (assistant manager), Corby Moore, Marcus Kelly, Rob Sinclair, Aaron O'Connor, Chris Novoth (video analyst)

Dale Eve.

Darren Carter.

Brett Williams.

Kieffer Moore.

Ben Jefford.

Lenny Pidgeley.

Anthony Jeffrey.

Defeated – Margate mascot seems to say it all.

Joe Stokes.

The Kassam: 600-plus FGR fans at FA Cup round 2.

The Racecourse, a fine gesture by Wrexham who invited families of opposing brothers James and Connor Jennings to mark the occasion prior to the match.

The Shay – vast, 90% empty and very angry.

Segregation Braintree style.

Silverlake's playing surface was a nightmare much of the season. But Jonny Maxted did not have to put up with this goalmouth wasteland behind the stand.

Welling's main stand – a forest of stanchions.

The Silverlake – disproportionately large end stand with vision-obscuring columns, not my favourite ground.

Havant & Waterlooville – 'keepers Arnold and Maxted warming up.

Braintree's Avanti – the teams line up.

Dover, another friendly little club on a hill, cut into the local chalk.

Little Moreton Hall near Congleton.
(*With kind permission of the National Trust*)

Brockhampton Estate near Bromyard.
(*With kind permission of the National Trust*)

Lyme Park House, Disley.
(*With kind permission of the National Trust*)

Tattershall Castle near Sleaford.
(*With kind permission of the National Trust*)

Furness Abbey, Barrow.
(*With kind permission of the National Trust*)

Illustration of the blindingly obvious – en route Guiseley, the National Coal Mining Museum at Caphouse Colliery, 450 feet down with the lights out.

Hever Castle, Kent.
(*With kind permission of Hever Castle*)

Paycocke's House, Coggeshall near Braintree.
(*With kind permission of the National Trust*)

Dover Castle.
(*With kind permission of English Heritage*)

At Anne Boleyn's Hever Castle, Foggy and Rambling Man interview local serving wench for the post of Mistress to the Honourable Order of Ye Olde Forest Green Rovers Supporters.

Student ambassador Wilf Doble with Elliott Frear.

Student ambassador Oliver Beere with Joe Stokes.

Student ambassador Evie Urquhart-Gordon with the Green Devil itself.

Notable FGR-inspired donations at Gloucestershire Deaf Association's Promises Auction at Stroud Auction House, 6 November 2015. Centre: Skipper David Pipe presents Rambling Man with FGR shirt signed by the squad. Above: Bristol City and FGR supporter Ian Ridler made this unique FGR Subbuteo set – he has an all-important licence to do so – which was purchased by Dale Vince.

Play-off semi-final v Dover.

The fantastic crowd scenes before the game.

Cruel despair for Rovers as Grimsby celebrates.

SIX STRAIGHT WINS BROUGHT ADY HIS SECOND Manager of the Month award and took everyone by surprise (after the Boxing Day Torquay debacle). With Cheltenham dropping points, Rovers regained top spot for a few games. None of the other teams could live with the pace being set by the Gloucestershire duo, with a 15-point gap separating them from the rest.

However, the means of Rovers' success had undergone change. The defence remained mean but attacking play was attritional with the team indebted to a run of late goals. That was in contrast to the thumping wins achieved by Cheltenham whose goal difference was becoming vastly superior. Supporters are always hard to please and the Forum was beginning to get jumpy about the style of play and squeaky wins.

Top of the league, top of the league top of the league, nearly
Forest in the Vale of the Green
They thundered and they plundered
Forward my brave bonny boys
Strike at their defence, our general said
Forest in the Vale of the Green
They plundered and they thundered

(Excerpt from 'The Charge of the Green Brigade' by the Lord Farmcotian, after Tennyson)

Friday   01.01.16
FGR 3 Torquay United 1
FGR FIGHT BACK TO CONTINUE FINE HOME FORM
Richard Joyce

A late comeback saw Forest Green Rovers get 2016 underway with an excellent win over Torquay United in front of the BT Sport cameras. Ady Pennock's side gained revenge for their Boxing Day mauling by the Gulls by claiming all three points, despite having fallen behind early in the second half to Aman Verma's back-post finish.

A Ben Gerring own goal, then Darren Carter penalty saw Rovers seize hold of the tie, and Keanu Marsh-Brown's stunning finish at the end was the icing on top of the cake. It was a sixth straight home win in the league for FGR, whose home form since a mid-October defeat to Tranmere Rovers has been exceptional.

The TV cameras would have struggled to capture any exciting footage from an uneventful first half that saw Torquay's Tyrone Marsh test Steve

Arnold with an early shot he comfortably dealt with. A fiercer Marsh shot from a narrow angle minutes later forced Arnold into another stop – and the former Stevenage keeper managed to claw the ball away at his near post. Young Gulls keeper Dan Lavercombe was very much a spectator in the opening 45 minutes as FGR struggled to find a way through.

The relegation-threatened visitors claimed a hugely important goal soon after the break. Verma, who scored at The New Lawn last season for Kidderminster Harriers, was on hand to finish off a Torquay cross into the box through a sea of bodies, as he turned in past Arnold.

Rovers again struggled to respond, although the introduction of Guthrie and Marsh-Brown as a double substitution from off the bench raised hopes. The decision worked, as on 66 minutes Marsh-Brown's brilliant free kick found Guthrie in the area, whose touch towards goal slammed into Torquay defender Gerring who couldn't keep the ball out of his own net. Frear looked to build on the ascendancy that was now with his team, and the left winger came close to finding the net with a powerfully hit strike on his right foot after he had cut inside.

But the big break Forest Green needed finally came: Durrell Berry's blatant handball from a Frear shot left referee Steve Rushton with no choice but to point to the spot, and Carter stepped up to send Lavercombe the wrong way.

Quality tells at whatever level, and having taken the lead in the final ten minutes, Rovers extended it with a superb effort in stoppage time. Marsh-Brown picked up the ball 25 yards from goal and drove a stunning effort that curved away from Lavercombe and sealed a magnificent way to start the New Year.

MARSH-BROWN SWAMPS TORQUAY

Jokerman

New Year's Day at TNL and the reverse fixture with 'near' neighbours Torquay United is being broadcast 'live' on the BT sports channel. The car-park-full signs are up over 90 minutes before kick-off despite the cold wet and windy weather conditions. The Green Man bar has been taken over by a contingent of raucous visiting supporters who will be hoping for a repeat of their Boxing Day triumph against Rovers. The odds suggest otherwise but FGR fans still need convincing their team has what it takes to tackle a daunting run of fixtures in the coming weeks. Jennings returns to the starting line-up and Pennock persists with Williams and Parkin up front. The weather is taking its toll on the playing surface and will prove a stern challenge for the groundsman if the rain prevails.

Rovers attack the away end containing over 250 Gull fans. It is an inauspicious start as Torquay look the better side with Marsh, who scored twice on Boxing Day, again looking dangerous in attack. He is the first to hit a shot on goal that Arnold gathers comfortably. A Sinclair corner is punched clear confidently by Lavercombe whereas, soon after, Arnold at the other end is anything but when he is caught flailing at a looped cross that fortunately goes unpunished. On 20 minutes the Rovers keeper is almost caught out by a Marsh shot from distance at his near post. Bennett replies for Rovers with a raid down the right and a cross-cum-shot that Lavercombe tips over the bar. Frear is playing well and supplying crosses but with Williams out wide and Parkin heavily – well, he would be – marked there was no end result. The half-time whistle signalled a rethink.

From the restart Torquay took the lead while many were still finishing their drinks in the bar. An attack down the left saw Butler cross the ball low that somehow eluded Clough, and was slid home at the back post by Verma. Players and supporters celebrated with a 'love in'. Forty-eight minutes gone. On 59 Pennock changed it after no little encouragement from the home fans. Williams and Parkin were replaced by Guthrie and Marsh-Brown

The whole complexion of the game changed and the Forest Green attack was galvanized. On 66 minutes a free kick to Rovers, identical to the one against Kiddy, was again launched with precision by Marsh-Brown, this time dropping the ball low in front of inrushing bodies. Torquay defender Gerring beat Guthrie to the touch but could only direct the ball into the net and Rovers were level. It gave FGR the lift they were seeking and Marsh-Brown went on his very own advertising campaign.

He was unplayable and had the Gulls in a real flap. Ably assisted by Guthrie and Frear, Carter also became involved in proceedings. Eighty minutes saw Marsh-Brown launch a 40-yard pass to release Frear on the left, who cut inside and ignored his supplier's run for the return to rip a shot over Lavercombe's bar. Unperturbed, he turned the Torquay defence down the right and cut the ball back across the area to the unmarked Frear, who swept the ball goalward only to be denied by Berry who deflected the ball wide with his hand. The referee pointed to the spot with Torquay players protesting; they had some gall: their man wasn't booked when he could have seen red. On 84 minutes Carter stepped up and hit the ball low into the right side of the goal and Rovers had turned it round when it looked unlikely. Torquay were not done with and might well have levelled with more composure from Berry, who failed to make amends by blasting the ball into the car park from an excellent position to score. Marsh-Brown was far from done as the game neared the end. He again caused havoc on the right and crossed to the unmarked Frear in acres of space. Instead of taking a touch the winger bowed to temptation and attempted the volley. Less said.

Marsh-Brown was then announced as Man of the Match as the game moved into added time. He saved the best till last and made BT's night. Gaining possession 25 yards from goal on the right, he struck a shot with such velocity that Lavercombe did well to avoid, if indeed he saw it, as the ball fairly burst the net. It was over and Forest Green Rovers had answered a few questions but raised many more regarding the way forward into the second half of the season.

Saturday 16.01.16
Lincoln City 0 FGR 1
GRITTY ROVERS SECURE MAGNIFICENT IMPS WIN
Richard Joyce

A moment of real class from Keanu Marsh-Brown helped Forest Green Rovers to a superb three points in a fine away win at Sincil Bank. The 23-year-old's sensational 78th minute volley proved to be the difference on a difficult and tense afternoon against a direct Lincoln City side. Aarran Racine's red card in the second half looked like it could peg Rovers' ambitions of clinching three points back; however, a fabulous finish from Marsh-Brown and an excellent defensive and goalkeeping showing proved to be the perfect formula for victory.

Now two points off the top of the table, Forest Green started brightly, but it was the home side who produced the game's first notable chance as Craig Stanley's curling effort brought a fine stop from the flawless Steve Arnold. Jack Muldoon's burst into the box on 18 minutes saw the Imps attacker find a way through on goal, but they were again denied the opening goal by Arnold's crucial intervention. A slow half developed some momentum in its closing stages, and it was sparked by Elliott Frear, whose well-hit shot struck Lincoln keeper Paul Farman's post after Marsh-Brown had fed the left winger. Farman was then called upon to make a crucial stop after Marsh-Brown had burst through. He looked all but set to score but at the final moment Farman smothered the ball fantastically. A suddenly open contest saw the chances keep coming. Frear's attempt was deflected just wide from Darren Carter's set-up, while Lincoln's Terry Hawkridge then whipped a shot narrowly wide in the same minute.

The second half appeared to be a repeat affair of the opening 45 minutes, as James Jennings's key clearance off the line denied Lincoln's Luke Waterfall from heading in early after the break. Marsh-Brown's influence gradually began to tell, and he tested Farman with a fine effort from 25 yards just before the half-hour mark, with the ex-Gateshead stopper equal to his strike.

The game was calling for a moment to help it burst into life, and that moment very possibly came when FGR were reduced to ten men, with quarter of an hour still to go. Racine's attempted tackle away from goal on Patrick Brough was deemed worthy of a straight red, and Ady Pennock was forced to regroup his side for what looked set to be a testing end to the tie. The numerical difference should have given the hosts the edge, but instead it inspired Forest Green and particularly Marsh-Brown, who demonstrated his exciting ability by firing a stunning volley into the back of the net having broken clear of the Lincoln back line. It was a wonderful moment for the supporters who had made the trip, as a struggling Lincoln side tried their best to steal something from the game with a late comeback. They couldn't find a way through, as Arnold stood tall to block all that they could throw at the FGR goal, to help seal a marvellous first away win of 2016.

DESTINATION LINCOLN
Rambling Man

It is a month since I last saw Rovers in action, including a fruitless 388-mile round trip to Guiseley. Thankfully, the weather saw sense and permitted our away fixture at the lovely City of Lincoln. Compo's back was playing ball too, and he took the helm in the silver Beamer. We were joined by Foggy and a first-time companion in our stalwart local reporter. He shall be called Deep-Throat.

We met at a frosty Stonehouse Court Hotel and set a course across country via your favourite Ms – featuring 5, 42, 6 and 69. Done with the Ms, we tried an A, 46 to be precise, aka Fosseway, built by the Romans, and maintained by the Highways Agency.

Boredom kicked in, not helped by the featureless landscape. Time for a watering hole. Compo spotted one of those brown tourist signs sporting a knife and fork. That led us miles into the uncharted depths of Leicestershire to the Viking-founded village of Thrussington. Specifically, to the Star Inn built in 1744 at the village centre, on the green. Serfs eyed us with uncertain gaze and the street urchins stopped playing to take in our new-fangled horseless carriage. Unfazed, we entered the inn, surprising the friendly landlord who was unused to four customers at a time, especially before noon. We admired the exposed oak beams and panelling around us and enjoyed tea, coffee and hot chocolate. I suspect that was the first and last time any of us would visit Thrussington, nice though it was.

So to Lincoln. The view of the cathedral, set on an ancient citadel above the town, is iconic. Sadly, the massive waste-recycling centre that looms as you approach the city is monstrous. God help Haresfield. Fortunately, Sincil Bank enjoys of view of the former.

In recent years, Lincoln City has acquired a reputation for robust play on an often uneven home pitch. Current arch-villain is prolific top scorer Matt Rhead, a large gentleman who clearly has a good appetite. He would have intimidated Rovers teams of old, not known for their size or strength.

Not now though. Where the situation calls for it, we have bruisers that can bully better than Flashman, namely Charlie Clough and Arran Racine – the Kray twins. Their battle with Rhead was pivotal in the match (as it was at The New Lawn). Like implacable doormen, they refused the striker entry to the penalty area, though helping him to his feet each time he bounced off them. Great fun.

One enthusiastic lunge too far saw Racine ordered from the pitch with three-quarters of the game gone. But quicker than you can say "the bleeping defender's elbowed Kurtis in the neck again", the mercurial Keanu had smashed in yet another spectacular goal to win the game. An important win and one that will make our friends at Cheltenhamshire just a tad uneasy.

ROVERS' ACES WIN GAME OF CARDS
Jokerman
Saturday, 16 January 2016. 0915. The Cathedral Express is pulling out, diesel-hauled. Kendo gives her the heel and toe heading north and east, destination Lincoln. A county joyfully celebrated in verse by 'Amazing Blondel' in the twentieth century. Such cities always echo days of yore but none of the pilgrims aboard will climb Steep Hill to seek celestial enlightenment. Our game is a different religion where salvation is dictated by ££££s. The rich man really can buy his way to the Premier Land, and the multitude, they stand in line and donate alms to the almighty Sky Master. Armageddon? When the sky comes falling in, of course. Meanwhile we sinners enjoy the ride as Kendo eases into the sidings at Sincil Bank.

J
A
N
U
A
R
Y

Freed from the vegan constraints, most of the Forest Green faithful go in search of the hearty liver diet, burgers and beer. Over a beer or three the team news declares Marsh-Brown replaces Williams as the only change from the Torquay line-up. The Stevenage swap, Williams for O'Connor caused much spleen-venting on the forum … fascinating. Both Parkin and Rhead start for their respective teams which triggers a seismographer alert (can't help it).

With sunshine striking the twin towers on high and the temperature threatening the brass monkey, the game kicks off in front of nearly 2,000 fans. It is a lively start by Rovers who win an early corner and then M-Brown and Bennett combine to cross for Parkin to head the ball narrowly over the bar.

M-Brown sets up Parkin who shoots wide while Rhead at the other end does similar with a volley from an equally good position. Lincoln exert some pressure 15 minutes in and a fierce shot from Stanley is spectacularly palmed away for a corner by Arnold.

Muldoon then picks up a defence-splitting pass which has Arnold and his defender scrambling to clear. He is more comfortable when Howe puts a free header from a long throw straight at him.

Twenty-seven minutes and Rovers come closest to scoring when M-Brown threads a sublime pass across a crowded penalty area to Frear closing in on the left. His shot beats Farman, the Lincoln keeper, but rebounds off the left-hand post. Arnold, trying to claim a cross under pressure from Rhead, ended up on the floor and was fortunate the referee stopped play thinking he was injured; it was no foul and the Lincoln fans were not happy.

At the other end Carter slipped a pass to M-Brown who was through on Farman but the keeper dived at his feet to deny him. He quickly moved the ball upfield and Hawkridge was only inches wide with a curling shot from the edge of the area with Arnold beaten. A low cross from the right saw Rhead step over the ball that ran to Power with a clear sight of goal. He blazed the ball wildly over the bar when his side could easily have gone in at half time a goal to the good.

Hot Bovril was the order at the break with the game finely balanced. Lincoln were soon on the offensive at the start of the second half and Racine was booked when Rhead crashed to earth for no apparent reason other than to spill all the coffee in the press box. From the free kick Waterfall at the back post beat Arnold with his header only for Jennings to head clear from under the bar. Power following up hit his shot wide from 20 yards.

Rovers replied when Parkin on the left combined with M-Brown whose shot was tipped round the post for a corner. Sinclair stepped up and failed in three straight attempts to beat the first defender. On the hour Rhead fouls the excellent Clough but ends up flat on his face. Clough is then booked while Rhead is attended to by the vet (don't); it must have been something he said. The game was becoming a little feisty. Sixty-seven minutes and Muldoon fouls Arnold and was booked very quickly as several players were keen to join the discussion. On 70 minutes Pennock replaced Carter with Guthrie. Five minutes later Racine overstretched into a challenge on Brough and the referee bypassed the second yellow and showed a straight red card.

While Lincoln were digesting the implications and tactical changes that would now have to be applied to their game, Forest Green went up the other end and scored a goal on 77 minutes. Parkin facing a retreating defence lofted a pass to M-Brown running in the inside right position, who expertly hit the ball on the volley over Farman and into the net. Rovers fans were very pleased indeed. For Lincoln it was a dagger to the heart. Understandably Lincoln went all out for an equalizer and Arnold saved a powerful downward header from Howe on his goal line. Pipe had replaced Frear to help the defence in which Clough was outstanding.

Frustration set in for the home side as the clock ran down and there was a mighty handbags job in the Lincoln half of the field involving Guthrie and 20 others. The referee was spraying cards like confetti and his report will be longer than these ramblings. After filling several swear boxes, the game resumed. Wedgbury gave away a free kick on the edge of the area which had Rovers fans clenching. The kick to the back post came back across the box to Waterfall who hit a full-blooded shot from close range that Arnold was equal to at his near post. A fine save.

Five added minutes but Forest Green were resolute and took the points and extended Lincoln's run to nine games without a win. For all the criticism this team did the business today and Pennock and his staff will take satisfaction from that. Many twists and turns lie ahead but Forest Green are still within touching distance of Cheltenham so bin the sackcloth and ashes and keep the faith.

Saturday 23.01.16
FGR 1 Braintree Town 0
HIGH-FLYING ROVERS CLINCH ANOTHER HOME WIN
Richard Joyce
Jon Parkin's second-half header made it a fantastic seven straight home wins for Forest Green Rovers against Braintree Town at The New Lawn.

The unstoppable forward pounced at the perfect time to convert from close range to return his team to the top of the table for the first time since November.

A couple of fine saves from the Irons on-loan goalkeeper Michael Crowe denied FGR what would have been a more emphatic-looking victory, but boss Ady Pennock will care little for the size of the win, as he watched his charges produce another confident and overpowering performance.

Kieffer Moore was handed his debut after signing on Monday, as he lined up alongside the unbeatable Charlie Clough in the middle of the back four. And there was also a place on the bench for teenage midfielder Charlie Cooper, son of former Rovers great Mark, who had joined on loan from Birmingham City on the morning of the game.

The contest took time to get going, with Braintree's Dan Sparkes looking to convert from a wide area, and Clough's header from a Sam Wedgbury free kick for FGR failing to set the pulse racing too much in the early exchanges. Following his stunning winner last weekend, Keanu Marsh-Brown was beginning to threaten, and his magnificent solo run and long-range attempt on 28 minutes slipped just wide.

After the break, Rovers took command, and came close to breaking the deadlock just a couple of minutes into the second half. Elliott Frear's piercing drive inside the box was blocked away at the last moment when it looked like the winger was set to convert Wedgbury's lay-off.

The goal Rovers needed to secure the win did come, though only minutes later, as match-winner Parkin demonstrated how vital he is to this Forest Green set-up with a neat headed finish. Darren Carter's sweetly struck shot was well saved by Crowe; however, the on-loan Ipswich Town keeper couldn't deny Parkin who pushed his side in front. Leading goalscorer Parkin was almost at it again a short while later. James Jennings's excellent cross was hooked towards goal by the front man, although Crowe this time was able to keep the ball out of his net.

And Crowe kept his side in the tie with another marvellous save on 74 minutes. Again it came from a Parkin effort, who had slammed a shot on goal from Rob Sinclair's ball into the area.

Of late, FGR seem to have become experts at seeing out games with tight scorelines and again they confidently clinched the three points in this clash, although they could have doubled the scoreline in stoppage time.

Excellent work from Frear down the left saw him pull the ball back for Marsh-Brown, who couldn't add to his goal tally this season as he drove over the bar.

IRON DEFICIENCY BOOSTS ROVERS
Jokerman

A chance to return to the top of the league looms today with Cheltenham Town playing on Sunday.

Forest Green manager Ady Pennock has been busy signing additions to his squad this week: Kieffer Moore, a versatile player in both defence and attack, and Charlie Cooper is on loan for a month from Birmingham City, son of Mark Cooper who served FGR so well towards the end of his playing career. Today's opponents, Braintree Town, whose fans consider them a pub team, have one of the best defensive records in the league but conversely are weak in attack.

The win at Lincoln last week will have done Rovers confidence no harm and a win today will give them a psychological edge over Cheltenham who face a difficult fixture away at Dover tomorrow. New signing Moore is straight into the starting line-up in place of the suspended Racine, while Parkin again leads the attack.

Fifteen hundred fans witness the kick-off. The forecast is dry which is as well for the playing surface is already soft. A low-key start as both teams probe for openings, Braintree the more cautious. On eight minutes the first threat is from Rovers when Wedgbury passes inside to Parkin who hits a shot over the crossbar. Braintree reply when Sparkes attacking down the left puts in a dangerous cross that has Arnold stretching to palm over his bar. From the corner the ball eventually finds Woodyard who crosses for Cheek but his header is weak and goes wide from a scoring position. A Wedgbury free kick from near halfway picks out Clough coming in on the blind side of Braintree's defence but his header is just wide of the upright.

Any doubts concerning Moore's ability are soon dispelled. He slots in seamlessly alongside Clough looking strong in the air and more than assured in possession. Arnold uses him a lot today in distribution. Frear's skill usually makes him Rovers' main threat in attack and so it proves again. Crossing for Parkin who heads on to Carter whose header, though on target, has no power and is easily gathered by Crowe, the Braintree custodian. Clough spurns a good chance from a Frear corner, putting his header over the bar. Marsh-Brown, not short on confidence, jinks his way through a crowded midfield and hits a good shot narrowly wide of the left-hand post.

Braintree are offering little in attack where Clough and Moore are dominant, enabling Bennett and Jennings to add support to Rovers' own efforts to break down a stubborn defence. Parkin heads a Bennett cross

JANUARY

too high as half time approaches, with Forest Green looking the more likely side to prevail.

Pennock's half-time team talk certainly sparks a positive response from his players who come out on the offensive at the restart. Parkin sets up Frear whose powerful shot inside the area is blocked away for a corner. 52 minutes and Rovers find the key to unlock The Iron defence. Frear beats off two defenders to reach the by-line where he pulls the ball back into the path of Carter, who hits a thunderbolt that Crowe somehow blocks at full stretch, but only to see the ball sit up invitingly for the lurking Parkin who scores with a close-range header over the stricken keeper. It is a deserved lead and Rovers continue to dominate possession, keeping the ball for prolonged spells and denying what is a blunt Braintree attack any clear-cut opportunities. The visitors employ all three subs with 20 minutes left in an effort to alter their situation but Arnold, handling confidently, and his defence are untroubled.

On 70 minutes Frear sends Jennings on the overlap and his cross is hit first time by Parkin from six yards, bringing a superb save from Crowe. Rovers could well have increased their advantage but Carter hit his shot wide following a break down the middle, and another volley from Parkin was again kept out by heroics from Crowe in the Braintree goal. He must be a prime reason for their mean defence. A desperate late flurry by the visitors troubled the Rovers fans more than their defence. Rovers should have finished with a flourish when Williams, on as a sub, sent Frear down the left to cross sublimely for M-Brown. His game-set-and-match shot careered over the bar, leaving the striker to beat himself up in disgust.

As the final whistle sounded Forest Green returned to the top of the league table. Make no mistake, this was a confident performance and Pennock has denied Johnson at Cheltenham the signature of Kieffer Moore. His credentials were obvious against today's opposition at least and Clough will not begrudge him MoM on his debut. The team is surely improving and it is not beyond them to burst the Southport bubble on Tuesday night.

FGR V BRAINTREE TOWN
FGR Student Ambassador Paul Westoby
My name is Paul Westoby and I am eight years old. I have been the FGR ambassador for Lakefield Primary School in Frampton-on-Severn since October. Being an ambassador has not only given me a great opportunity to recruit more young Rovers supporters but has also shown me how FGR can support my school. I put up posters around school and the

community, and keep everyone updated with a newsletter and posts on our PTA FB page. I'm currently planning a stadium tour for my school Eco Council, I have asked for players (including ladies) to visit and inspire us, and have encouraged our head teacher to join the brilliant Fit2Last programme. I'm also organizing an FGR-themed sponsored 'all day football match' for Sport Relief and the school. When I'm not watching Rovers I love playing for Frampton Youth U9s. I play in defence so I'm always watching the FGR defence to pick up tips. It's hard to pick a favourite player though because they all work very well as a team. I am really excited to be walking out with the players on the 20 February against Eastleigh!

Match Report: A bright, sunny afternoon at The New Lawn saw the visit of Braintree Town. The Irons had very good away form with only three losses so far this season. It was a quiet start to the game with the first chance coming after seven minutes which was fired over the bar by Parkin. New signing Kieffer Moore worked very hard throughout the game, managing the defence well and stopping Braintree threatening the goal. Bennett and Frear made some great runs up the lines as we built up the pressure, with Carter and Clough coming close but not managing to finish. Despite several Forest Green chances, it was still nil-nil when the whistle blew for half time.

FGR started the second half strongly with a shot that was saved by the keeper but Parkin was there for the rebound which gave us a well-deserved lead. Braintree's best effort of the game was probably from their goalkeeper whose brilliant kick from the goal tested Steve Arnold's judgement for a clever save. A great defensive performance for the rest of the game prevented Braintree from scoring and made sure of a Rovers well-earned win.

Tuesday 26.01.16
Southport 0 FGR 1
GUTHRIE STRIKES TO SEAL A FINE BATTLING WIN
Forest Green Rovers returned to the top of the National League table thanks to Kurtis Guthrie's dramatic late goal at the Merseyrail Community Stadium against in-form Southport. The 22-year-old striker swept home in the most climactic of finishes to make it five wins in a row in a truly gruelling encounter. Horrendous conditions throughout turned what was a football match between two sides with excellent recent records, into a battle full of grit, fight and desire. Southport have been re-energized since the appointment of Dino Maamria as their new manager. But they saw

JANUARY

their brilliant unbeaten run ended by an Ady Pennock side who recorded their third consecutive clean sheet.

In truth it was the Sandgrounders who performed best in the early stages, as the pitch deteriorated quickly under the constant falling rain. However, they couldn't work any real openings to test Steve Arnold, despite their inventiveness from set-piece situations. Parkin snapped up the opportunity to force Rovers' first real opening on goal on the half-hour mark; however, his free kick never threatened Crocombe.

The conditions continued to offer challenges to both sides, and after the interval Parkin produced an early strike on goal, which Oxford United loanee Crocombe was equal to. Down the other end Arnold then made a fine stop to prevent Louis Almond from opening the scoring after he had been left with too much room in the box. The save of the night though would fall to Crocombe only a couple of minutes later, as he denied what looked to be near enough the opener. Parkin looked to have turned a pass into the box past the New Zealand youth international, only for him to produce a wonderful save diving to his left.

After Arnold had again saved well from Paul Rutherford, and Keanu Marsh-Brown had skied over in an FGR foray forward, suddenly a point on a torrential night on Merseyside would have represented an impressive effort. Guthrie though had other ideas. James Jennings's shot from distance was parried by Crocombe, and Guthrie was on hand to thunder the ball into the back of the net via the crossbar. It was an awesome moment to wrap up another marvellous win for Pennock's charges, who'll be desperate to extend their winning run when Macclesfield Town visit The New Lawn on Saturday.

DESTINATION SOUTHPORT
Rambling Man

Our December cup tie at Oxford United had displaced the Saturday Southport away fixture. That meant a cruel trip for the faithful on a sodden, wind-blown Tuesday night in mid-January. And regretfully, for only the second away fixture of the season, I was not among them. Instead, I had an evening meeting of the charity for whom I am Chair of Trustees. Subject: pros and cons of registering for VAT. Even if Southport had been hit by a tsunami, I know where I'd rather have been. Mind you, in recent years the Southport weather has fallen inches short of catastrophic. Southport is also a club I enjoy visiting. The town has impressive streets and architecture, heritage from its Victorian heyday as a favoured seaside resort. The club is one of those overtaken in scale by FGR, but it is old-fashioned in the nicest sense. I always seem to meet the same friendly buffers in ties and blazers who greet you warmly, appreciative of how far you have travelled. One is a dead ringer for Captain Mainwaring and I hope he is well and enjoying his club's best league run in years.

Those of us with many rings around our trunks will remember the well-travelled striker, Dino Maamria, now the latest manager at Southport. What a job he has done! Mired in the relegation places earlier in the season, his charges are on a lengthy unbeaten run that has taken them to the safety of mid-table. So, if Ady needed any reminder what a tough fixture his team was facing, the statistics said it all.

My absence was compounded by Compo and Clegg, leaving Foggy temporarily isolated. Club Secretary James (he of the WG-type beard) came to the rescue and played chauffeur.

I'm delighted to say that Foggy's notes to me contained a much higher percentage of printable text than had been the case after the Torquay defeat. Not surprising as he was able to purr in contentment over Rovers fifth win on the bounce since the Torbay massacre, four being clean sheets, too. By Foggy's account, Southport played with expected confidence in the first half. As at The New Lawn, the main threat was Phenix. But Rovers were as mean as in recent games and the longer the match went on they looked the likelier to score. Not that Foggy, James and the terrific 32 travelling fans would have wanted settlement left as late as the 92nd minute. Jennings's thumping drive was parried, only for Kurtis Guthrie to prove the saviour as he has done on so many occasions this term.

At that point in the game, I was on the way home from my Gloucester meeting. BBC Glos was giving me an uninteresting commentary on Oxford City trouncing Cheltenham at Whaddon in their delayed FA Trophy replay. Then the trivia was interrupted by the score flash: I think my impromptu swerve might have frightened a few pedestrians, to whom I apologize. No matter, for the second time in a few days, Rovers had regained top spot from The Robins and given Gary Johnson something more to moan about. Sixteen more nerve-jangling games to go.

Saturday 30.01.16
FGR 2 Macclesfield Town 1
ROVERS LEAVE IT LATE TO SEAL ANOTHER WIN
Richard Joyce
Charlie Clough's stoppage-time winner helped Forest Green Rovers make it a stunning six wins from six at the start of 2016. The resilient defender poked home a euphoric late winner to seal a crucial three points in a hard-

fought battle against a disciplined Macclesfield Town side. On Tuesday Kurtis Guthrie's dramatic late strike had earned Rovers a victory in the final seconds at Southport, and it was a repeat story at The New Lawn as Ady Pennock side's reign at the top of the National League continues.

With Guthrie's winning goal on Tuesday having earned him a return to the starting XI, his strike partner Brett Williams had a huge chance as early as the second minute to put FGR in the driving seat early on.

Keanu Marsh-Brown's corner was headed on by Kieffer Moore; however, he couldn't keep his reactive header down and it zipped over the bar.

The well-built Jack Sampson was proving a threat for the away side, and his header on 17 minutes from a Chris Holroyd cross dropped just wide. Danny Whitehead's dangerous shot a short while later was stopped by Steve Arnold, as the Silkmen, who are keen to cement a play-off slot this season, illustrated the threat they carry all over the park.

There would be no first-half goal despite Guthrie's best attempts just before the break – he got up well to meet Marsh-Brown's corner but nodded wide.

Moore produced the first opening chance of the second half only to fire off target, but he was involved in the tie's opener when an unfortunate error allowed Sampson the opportunity to put Macclesfield in front.

His miss-hit pass back to Arnold was seized upon by former Morecambe man Sampson to guide the away side into the lead.

It was a goal that kicked FGR into life, and they produced an effective final 15 minutes that proved essential to winning the game. Elliott Frear's delivery from a free kick was poorly handled by the Silkmen defence, and Jennings, wearing the captain's armband for the first time, was allowed to ghost in unmarked to tap home.

With the clash back on level terms, it was there for both teams to win it, and Macclesfield's best opportunity came from a Danny Whitaker long-range effort that Arnold did well to save.

It looked like Rovers' chance had gone when Clough couldn't convert a Marcus Kelly free kick, having found room at the back of the box. However, the highly thought-of centre back did find the goal all of the home supporters craved in the dramatic closing moments of stoppage time.

Sam Wedgbury's pinpoint cross from deep inside the Macclesfield half against his former club landed in the perfect area for Clough to guide the ball home, and to confirm a superb sixth consecutive win.

ROVERS TURN PIG'S EAR INTO A SILKY THREE POINTS

Jokerman

On the back of a late, late show and a magnificent three points at Southport on Tuesday night, Forest Green Rovers will not lack for confidence today against a Macclesfield side on a losing run. Prior to the game Ecotricity held a presentation in the Carol Embrey Suite to glean support to move the football club to the hard shoulder of the M5 at Junction 13 west of Stonehouse. No worries, it's only a number. Isn't it?

Over an ale today's team selections are announced. Now what all the critics have to understand is that Mr Johnson is working to a proven formula whereas Mr Pennock is having to make it up as he goes along.

A glance at the league table is a measure of how well he is doing. He flips down another googly today: Parkin the Cart on the bench for a rest, playing Williams and Guthrie up front and appointing Jennings captain for the day. Who are we to argue.

The teams paraded in front of 1,600 spectators on a dry but fresh afternoon edged with a bitterly cold breeze. After a bright opening couple of minutes that saw Williams head the ball narrowly over the bar from a corner, Rovers faded and Macclesfield looked the more likely side.

On 15 minutes Holroyd crossed from the right to Sampson who put his header wide. The visitors kept the pressure on with two corner,s ending with Whitehead firing in a shot from the edge of the area that Arnold fumbled.

Fortunately Clough was on hand to blast the ball clear for yet another corner. Rovers only reply was a weak header from Guthrie that Jatal the Macclesfield keeper gathered easily

Askey the Macclesfield manager had clearly done his homework and was allowing Frear and M-Brown no time on the ball. His side certainly shaded the first half and might have been in front had Sampson not put the ball wide from a great position.

Pennock put the hard word on his players as they enjoyed their half-time soya, for they started very positively from the restart. A M-Brown corner saw Clough miss his kick but Moore was on hand to hit a fierce shot across the goal just wide of the right-hand post.

Rovers' best chance of the game fell to M-Brown who received the ball from a precision cross from Frear to the back post. Instead of taking a touch and scoring, he hit the ball with so much top spin it looped over the stand, took a wicked deflection off a wing mirror and disappeared into the stinging nettles.

In reply Whitehead sent in a brutal shot from distance that Arnold

J
A
N
U
A
R
Y

gathered low down at the second attempt. Macclesfield striker Holroyd pulled up lame on 55 minutes which saw the introduction of ex-FGR man Reece Styche. He entered the arena wearing more canvas than the *Cutty Sark*, Arsenal in the '30s kit it looked like. To be fair to him he proved a real thorn in the side of the Rovers defence. He literally sailed past Moore to the by-line to cross dangerously and often tacked inside to cause more consternation among Rovers' ruffled defenders.

On 69 minutes he will no doubt claim an assist for the opening goal of the game. His pass down the channel was intercepted by Moore who suffered a massive miscalculation when he turned to pass the ball back to Arnold. Under hit, Sampson stepped in and poked the ball past the stranded keeper. It was a kick in the guts for the whole team, Moore especially who had done so well since arriving at the club.

It shook any complacency out of the home side but Williams and Guthrie, although showing plenty of endeavour, were not solving the problem of goalscoring.

Pennock changed it on 70 minutes, replacing Williams with Carter and soon after M-Brown with Kelly. It brought a better balance to the play and soon paid off on 77 minutes. A Frear free kick on the right to the back post cleared the main attack but dropped nicely for Jennings who merely ran the ball over the line.

It was all to play for but Macclesfield were not sitting back and it needed a fine save from Arnold diving to his left to deny Whittaker, who struck a good shot from the edge of the box. Forest Green were now playing with more purpose and as the game entered added time of five minutes, Parkin entered the fray and was actually seen running at one point, such was the urgency.

On 93 minutes a booted clearance from Macclesfield reached Wedgbury near halfway via a quick throw-in, and he fired the ball into the danger zone where Moore, desperately trying to make amends, caused enough distraction for the ball to drop for Clough at the back post.

Under pressure he would not be denied and gleefully smashed the ball into the back of the net. It ripped the Silkmen to tatters and the RSPB immediately issued an arrest warrant for inflicting gratuitous mental harm on a local family of robins.

Whatever happens next one should really savour these moments.

Next week Forest Green are off into the wilderness, crossing the dyke to slay some dragons.

ROVERS' REMORSELESS FORM CONTINUED with three further wins and draws at Wrexham and Barrow, now unbeaten in 11 including nine wins. But the two draws were conceded from winning positions and Cheltenham took advantage to retain first place. Grimsby and the nearest rivals had already conceded that the title was a two-horse Gloucestershire race. The competition for automatic promotion would be decided over the season's final quarter

Pipey is a warrior,
A slave he'll never be
A soldier and a conqueror
A hero to thee and me

(Excerpt from 'The Warrior' by Farmcotian)

Saturday 06.02.16
Wrexham 2 FGR 2
WILLIAMS STRIKES TO MAKE IT SEVEN UNBEATEN
Richard Joyce

For a third game in a row Forest Green Rovers scored a valuable stoppage-time goal, as Brett Williams's finish sealed a last-gasp point at the Racecourse Ground. With Rovers' marvellous unbeaten run looking set to come to a crashing end against out-of-form Wrexham, January addition Williams popped up with a dramatic finish to make it seven games without defeat for Ady Pennock's men. Darren Carter's first-half goal had given FGR the lead in an opening 45 minutes that should have ended with a larger Rovers advantage at the break. However, a rejigged Wrexham side managed to find the net from two set pieces through central defender Blaine Hudson to complete what looked like an unlikely turnaround. The never-say-die attitude in the FGR squad prevailed once again when Williams slotted at the death.

From as early as the third minute Rovers were putting pressure on Rhys Taylor's goal, as James Jennings saw his header slam onto the woodwork from an Elliott Frear corner. Jon Parkin, back in the starting XI, skewed an effort wide, while Mark Carrington's strike from distance for the hosts never looked likely to threaten Steve Arnold's goal. Carter then handed his side the lead midway through the half. Keanu Marsh-Brown's corner was headed back into the path of the former top-flight midfielder, who applied a simple header to break the deadlock. Wrexham's best chance yet fell to young forward Kayden Jackson, but he couldn't find a way

**F
E
B
R
U
A
R
Y**

past Arnold who produced a solid stop. One of the biggest remaining opportunities of the half fell to Parkin inside the Wrexham area. The big striker had peeled away to find some room in the oppositions box, but he couldn't hit the target through a sea of bodies.

An overrun Wrexham side reshuffled their pack at the break with a new set-up that proved influential in their second-half performance. It was from a set piece where they levelled, as Hudson scored his first with a strong header at the near post. He grabbed his second to complete the Welsh team's turnaround only a few minutes later. Rovers couldn't clear the ball from a deep free kick, despite the best efforts of a great stop from Arnold, and Hudson forced home over the line.

The previously despondent home fans were now fully behind their troops; however, they couldn't extend their lead as the game entered its final stages when Arnold saved terrifically from Jackson.

With the match heading for stoppage time it looked as though Forest Green's magnificent start to 2016 was coming to an end, especially when Sam Wedgbury was sent off right near the finish after picking up his second yellow card.

But this FGR side do not know when they're beaten. And Bennett's low ball into the area in the depths of stoppage time was turned home triumphantly by Williams to earn a breathless late point.

DESTINATION WREXHAM
Rambling Man

For the second time in Rovers' season, a run of wins had netted Ady the feared Manager of the Month award. Last time – September – more wins followed before an autumn stutter. So we travelled, optimistic that six wins on the bounce would become seven.

'We' comprised most of the usual team: Compo at the helm, Clegg and me. We had left Foggy at Stonehouse Town Hall, where we'd been helping with the latest Junction 13 Exhibition. He would travel later.

The journey to North Wales was memorable for one thing: rain so hard that we expected the silver paint to be scoured from Compo's Beamer. We hoped against hope that the Guiseley farce was not to be repeated. Happily, faultless preparations by Wrexham's directors and ground staff enabled the referee to pass the pitch as playable. But, we were told, it was a close-run thing.

As usual, the Welsh boyos were professional and welcoming (albeit quietly, Compo was asked to prove that a tie lurked below his lambswool jumper).

In the run-up to kick-off, the hosts amassed more credits. Wrexham's skipper is Connor Jennings, younger brother of Rovers' left back James. The neon scoreboard flashed familial greetings to both, and family and friends assembled on the pitch in both teams' colours. Those courtesies spoke volumes about Wrexham FC and its sportsmanship. I for one applaud them.

The pitch proved tricky, but not unduly so. An excellent game played out despite some indifferent officiating that was to neither set of supporters' satisfaction. Rovers bossed the first half playing some expansive football; they lead by Carter's header, midway. But the Beast's Satnav was off, and we worried that the chances he and his mates spurned might come back to haunt the team. Spot on.

Wrexham roared back in the second period. A string of excellent crosses brought parity, the lead and nearly went on to secure a comfortable win. The irrepressible Wedge leapt after one unwinnable challenge too many, leaving Rovers down to ten and game over? Not for the class of 15/16.

Guthrie, Moore and Williams all trooped on and the siege was laid. For the third successive match, Rovers scored deep into time added on, in this case minute 93 of 94. Point saved: 100 joyous travelling Gumps, 3,800 deflated Dragons.

Nonetheless, a fine game. The return journey mirrored the outward one. However, treacherous flooded patches were added to the stair-rod rain as we submarined home. Halifax next Saturday will give no relief

ROVERS MISFIRE IN DRAGONS' DEN
Jokerman

Forest Green Rovers fans head north today and will do so for the next five away fixtures over a six-week period. One doubts Ady Pennock will be sending a thank-you card to the compilers of this ridiculous situation. The conditions are relentless as Kendo drives on through the pouring rain. Talk is of pitch inspections as the border is crossed but lighter precipitation on arrival gives reason to hope the game will go ahead.

Away fans are welcome to share the club bar which is a large, windowless cavern. To its detriment the excellent Welsh real ales are ignored in favour of larger plonk. Compensation comes from the twenty 'screens' showing Leicester City destroying Man City in the early kick-off. Such is the uncertainty of the underfoot conditions that fans are issued with vouchers on entering the stadium in case of abandonment. The Racecourse, obviously heavy-going today, is a huge stadium once used for international games. It is not suitable for fixtures of this nature. The pitch is vast and the

FEBRUARY

away end is a disused, covered wasteland. The 90 Rovers fans are given a corner adjacent to the home end a long way from pitchside.

The rain has eased as the teams parade. Pennock has reverted to Parkin and M-Brown up front and Racine returns to the line-up with Moore dropping to the bench. From the start Forest Green stamp their authority on proceedings. In the third minute a Frear corner is swung out to Racine whose header is nodded on by Jennings from six yards; heading for the top corner, it is deflected against the bar by a defender on the line. Any reply from Wrexham is easily dealt with by Rovers' defence.

A Frear run down the left presents Carter with a great chance to open the scoring from the cut-back but his feet are tangled and the ball passes him by. However, on 21 minutes he makes amends. Such is Rovers' dominance that a goal seems inevitable and duly arrives when an M-Brown corner on the left reaches the back post for Jennings to head back in perfectly, and then for Carter to head the ball firmly past keeper Taylor from close range.

Forest Green fans are making all the noise and the 3,000-plus Wrexham fans who have had nothing to cheer are silent. It is 35 minutes before the home side have a shot on target but Jackson's shot is easily gathered by Arnold. Wedgbury had a tremendous shot blocked by good defending but Parkin will feel he should have done better on two occasions when well placed to at least hit the target. For the remainder of the half Rovers remained in control but failed to add to their advantage.

The half-time talk among Rovers fans centred around suicidal tendencies if Forest Green did not return home with three points such was the nature of the first-half showing. Wrexham had to make a change at half time and duly replaced Vidal with Moke to try and improve their situation.

It was a slow fuse as Rovers continued to have control until the hour mark. Then in a seven-minute spell the momentum shifted. Clough conceded a soft corner in a communication breakdown with Arnold. Carrington for Wrexham struck the kick perfectly into the 'disaster' zone, where Arnold punched the air and Hudson, the giant defender for Wrexham, headed the ball past him on 62 minutes.

Did that wake the home fans up? Just a little. Seven minutes later Racine was lucky not to receive a second yellow card, conceding a free kick wide out on the left. Carrington again hit a brilliant ball into a massed defence. It fell right in front of Arnold who did well to stop it crossing the line but he could only parry it to Hudson, who swept it in from point-blank range.

Rovers fans were then treated to the full Welsh song book. Land of My Fathers, Bread of Heaven, grief you couldn't make it up. Sick bags and suicide watch were the order of the day for some Rovers followers after that debacle.

The Dragons had their tails up and began to believe they were going to win a game. Pennock had to act and brought on Moore and Guthrie for Parkin and M-Brown. On 80 minutes another accurate corner from Carrington again picked out the rampant Hudson whose powerful header was stopped on the line by Arnold. It was kitchen-sink time for Rovers and they pressed Wrexham back, but were not creating clear chances and were susceptible to the counter-attack, highlighted by Jackson who carried the ball 60 yards before forcing Arnold to make a good save diving to his left.

By then Williams was on for Carter and Rovers were playing five up front, and their resilience paid off after a red card for Wedgbury as the game entered stoppage time. Wedgbury's work rate means he is always prone to yellow cards and he was shown a second on 92 minutes to the glee of Wrexham supporters, who a minute later were kicked in the nether regions when Williams, how ironic, poked the ball into the back of the net following a game of bagatelle in the mud-filled penalty area.

On the positive side it was a point gained but fans know that the failure to defend two set-plays has cost the team what should have been a comfortable victory. Forest Green are still right in the mix but Pennock will have to find the key to scoring goals if his defence cannot deal with free kicks and corners. Given the attacking performances of late, FGR are in a good position while Guthrie remains a mystery to this scribe. Ignore the neighbours, it's on to Halifax and back to winning ways.

Saturday 13.02.16
FC Halifax Town 0 FGR 2
ROVERS CLAIM ANOTHER IMPRESSIVE AWAY WIN
Richard Joyce

Two first-half goals from Jon Parkin and Elliott Frear helped Forest Green end FC Halifax's 13-match unbeaten run with a magnificent win at The Shay. Rovers made it seven wins from their last eight games with a victory that saw Ady Pennock's men produce an effective showing in a hostile and intimidating atmosphere.

In what was the two teams' first meeting this season, Parkin's goal had given FGR an important lead, and it was added to by Frear to ensure the three points were wrapped up in the opening 45 minutes.

**F
E
B
R
U
A
R
Y**

Early opportunities from Frear and Darren Carter had done little to threaten the in-form hosts, who saw Sam Walker's left-footed free kick confidently stopped by Steve Arnold in the opening stages. On 19 minutes though FGR were offered an ideal opportunity to take the lead, as referee Ian Hussin pointed to the spot to award a penalty kick following a foul in the box. Parkin stepped up but saw his effort from 12 yards saved by Sam Johnson, although the front man was able to profit from the rebound, to guide Forest Green crucially into the lead. And it was an advantage that was doubled ten minutes later when on the half-hour mark a wonderful team goal saw Frear hit the net. The instrumental Rob Sinclair's pass into the path of Keanu Marsh-Brown was turned across the face of goal, where Frear was on hand to slam home his side's second.

Rattled, Halifax tried to get back into the tie quickly, but Walker's hit from distance was saved superbly by Arnold, while Frear was denied the chance to score a brace with a vital low save by Johnson in the home side's goal.

Halifax, managed by former Forest Green boss Jim Harvey, threw former Fulham youngster Richard Peniket on as a substitute at half time, and the front man headed a great chance over the bar early on in the second period. A rare foray forward for Aarran Racine saw his fizzing effort kept out, and Sinclair's attempt with a lob from distance dropped just over the bar. FGR did brilliantly to contain any attacking attempts from the hosts, and with gaps appearing in more regular fashion, Carter was only inches away from smashing in a third as his strike from distance slammed onto the crossbar. Kingsley James's low shot was easily dealt with by Arnold in the closing minutes as Forest Green looked the more likely to add to the scoreline. Substitute Kurtis Guthrie's strike from distance bounced wide; meanwhile, the dangerous Marsh-Brown was left frustrated that he couldn't add a final moment of celebration when his effort late on was saved terrifically by the feet of Johnson.

DESTINATION HALIFAX
Rambling Man

Another Saturday, another long haul north. My turn to drive with passengers Compo, Foggy and Deep-Throat. All strangely uncertain how things would go given the suspension earned at Wrexham by ever-present Wedge; not least of course, Halifax unbeaten in 13 and managed by former FGR favourite Jim Harvey.

Jim had spiced things up in the preceding days with interviews about his controversial sacking in 2009 and how he'd have taken us to the

Promised Land by now. That had not gone down too well in the Five Valleys. With much for Halifax to do to avoid the drop it also seemed rather early to be claiming immortality.

An early start was for once rewarded by sparse traffic. By noon, we were enjoying an open fire at the Turnpike, Rishworth Moor with views over Booth Wood Reservoir and less picturesque, the congested M62 beyond on the skyline. Apparently it's the highest section of motorway in UK. After another stop at a converted mill at Greetland, we rolled into The Shay. My fifth time at this puzzling barn of a stadium, built for 15,000, but regular home to less than 10% of that capacity.

On this day, 1,300 tykes and about 70 yeomen of Stroud would scatter among two sides of the stadium. As soon as we found our seats, it hit you like a kipper in the face: the anger of the supporters, quite unlike the warm welcome to be found at most other National League venues. It was astounding. If your team is penalized, or more often when it is not, expect near neighbours to leave their places and shout the odds in your face. Small crowds maybe, but still intimidating.

Fortunately for Rovers, the fresh-faced referee was made of the right stuff. On 20 minutes, he had the temerity to award a penalty to Rovers just because Racine and Jennings had been crudely ambushed pursuing a cross in the box. The Beast converted at the second attempt. Anger was replaced by red-hot fury for the next 75 minutes with Yorkshireman Parkin and penalty-victim Jennings the targets.

Ten minutes later, a lovely team counter settled the argument. A quick ball from defence found Sinclair, who sped it wide to Keanu Marsh-Brown. He skinned the defence before crossing to Elliott Frear to tap in. Poetry in motion cheered to the girders by the sonorous 70, ignoring the tantrums elsewhere.

From that point, the match was a relative cruise – a calm and professional win that burst Jimbo's bubble and sent the home supporters to their lairs as irate as honey badgers. I was not unhappy to depart the Theatre of Rage.

As we trooped towards the main stand exit, I noticed a blind chap to my right, led by his guide dog. I stopped, touched his arm and said for him to leave in front of me. He turned and growled, "Bloody awful ref." He might as well as punched me, I was so surprised. How would he know! My shock turned to laughter, struck by the irony of a blind person complaining to a near deaf bloke (me) and looked about in case a mute was signing his protests!

One surreal day

F
E
B
R
U
A
R
Y

ROVERS ENJOY MAXIMUM RETURN AT HALIFAX
Jokerman

Forest Green supporters were treated to free travel, courtesy of the football club, as they head north to Calderdale and a game against in-form Halifax Town. Rejuvenated by one-time FGR manager Jim Harvey, they are unbeaten in 13 since he took full charge. Rovers fans are trying not to dwell on last week's draw at Wrexham which saw the club relinquish top spot to the Cheltenham Ladies, or Laddies, take your pick.

Crossing the moors, the road drops into the valley revealing a landscape of buildings reflecting a bygone industrial era. From such, just a fly-kick from The Shay stadium rises a listed building, the Three Pigeons public house of unique interior design offering no less than eight real ales on tap. Restraint was required but kicking off with a Yorkshire Blonde 3.9% volume was the perfect start to the afternoon.

Meanwhile back at The Shay Pennock, was sticking with Parkin up front when many Rovers fans would have preferred Moore to be given a start on recent performance. Pipe starts in place of the suspended Wedgbury. Half the stadium is closed but the 1,300 crowd, including 80 FGR fans still looks sparse as the game kicks off under cloudy but dry conditions. It is a low-key start but on 13 minutes a Frear corner ends with Carter hitting a skier over the bar. In reply a Halifax free kick by Walker is easily saved by Arnold.

The game more than livened up around the 20-minute mark when Parkin won a free kick midway in the Halifax half. M-Brown struck the ball invitingly into the area. Everybody fouls everybody else at corners and free kicks before the ball arrives. Just occasionally the referee will point to the spot. Jennings up in attack went for the ball and was impeded, the referee pointed to the spot and effectively woke up the collective spitting cobra among the home fans.

The atmosphere was tainted for the duration. Rovers fans held their breath as the out-of-form Parkin stepped up to take the kick. He struck the ball with little conviction and Johnson, the Halifax keeper, blocked the shot diving to his left; fortunately for the striker the ball rebounded into his path, and he netted to put Rovers in front. Stung into action, Halifax attacked and Bolton crossed for Burrow who headed the ball narrowly wide.

On 25 minutes Racine made a terrific block on a shot from Walker, who had broken free inside the area. Bennett, Clough and Racine were taking no prisoners in snuffing out the Halifax attacks and were being catcalled by the home crowd who had branded Jennings a cheat following the penalty decision. Forest Green further imposed their superiority on 30 minutes when Sinclair hit an exquisite pass down the right-hand channel to M-Brown, who outpaced the defence and hit the ball low across the area to the back post where Frear beat the defender and slammed the ball back across Johnson inside the right-hand post.

Halifax were desperate to get back into the game and Roberts set up McDonald who struck a good drive from the edge of the box that Arnold beat clear. As the home side pressed, Rovers nearly caught them on the break when Sinclair sent M-Brown clear only to be foiled by Johnson who blocked the shot with his legs.

As the Rovers fans voiced their support, the home contingent across the divide in seating poured scorn. There appeared to be plenty of the, how they say up here 'eeee, I could ride a bike round his gob'-types among them. As half time approached Parkin fouled an opponent in front of Harvey's dug-out. The latter upped his life insurance premium by physically pushing the striker away as he went to commiserate. The officials were roundly booed off at half time.

The second half saw Halifax probably edge possession but their attack lacked anything resembling a cutting edge and never looked likely to break down Rovers' solid rearguard. Rovers were creating the better chances, and even Racine had a good shot from distance saved by Johnson while Sinclair was too heavy with an intended lob over the keeper that just cleared the crossbar.

On 70 minutes Moore replaced Parkin and soon after Guthrie came on for Frear, who faded in the second period. Moore, so much livelier than Parkin, made an impact setting up Carter who was unlucky to see his cracking shot from 30 yards crash against the bar with Johnson a spectator. Rovers were well on top and the Halifax players and fans alike were frustrated as their efforts came to nought. M-Brown began show-boating which was amusing for away fans but poured a little petrol on proceedings. A mistake by Wroe let in M-Brown but he was again denied by the legs of Johnson.

The game ended in a flare-up when Halifax substitute Hughes was tackled by Bennett inside the area. Appeals for a penalty were waved away and play continued but 'afters' between the two players concerned led to an angry exchange, which in turn led to a venomous outpouring from the home fans and much venting of spleens. Bennett, who has history at The Shay, did well to keep his cool and as the final whistle sounded, the teams were ushered off by officials down the spit-proof tunnel. An excellent performance from Forest Green Rovers, a touch of the good,

**F
E
B
R
U
A
R
Y**

the bad and the ugly for the fans. Bidding a fond farewell to The Three Pigeons, while leaving Yorkshire bitter, Rovers fans disappeared over the hill and far away with three welcome points.

Saturday 20.02.16
2 Eastleigh 1
PARKIN AT THE DOUBLE TO RECORD ANOTHER WIN
Richard Joyce

A second-half double from Jon Parkin saw Forest Green Rovers make it an incredible nine consecutive home wins in a late-show victory over Eastleigh. The experienced striker moved onto 14 goals for the campaign to help Ady Pennock's side continue their extraordinarily impressive home form this season. It was a victory dedicated by the players and the management to Garry Mitchell, the former stadium announcer at The New Lawn who sadly passed away a week ago.

And it was a hard-fought win against an Eastleigh side boasting a very talented squad of players for this level. One of their leading lights, James Constable, handed them the lead in the second half, although his side were pegged back shortly after by Parkin's brilliantly executed finish. And the experienced forward wrapped up the win with only minutes left on the clock when he stabbed home from close range.

A battling opening 45 minutes saw Eastleigh go closest first when former FGR defender Jamie Turley almost headed in at the back post from a corner. Meanwhile Keanu Marsh-Brown's run on goal ended with the former Fulham man blazing wide.

In the second half the game really began to come alive, and after Elliott Frear had forced Ross Flitney into a simple save, Dale Bennett was foiled by the Eastleigh keeper when he looked set to dash through and score. After Frear and Rob Sinclair failed to break the deadlock with further chances, Eastleigh finally took one of theirs when Constable swept home with an excellent finish to hand the visitors the lead.

The Rovers response was good, and if it wasn't for Flitney, Parkin would have claimed a goal from close range only a couple of minutes later. Instead, he did manage to net an equalizer, when only seconds later his brilliant strike flew past the former Gillingham keeper to draw his team level. Eastleigh still fancied their chance to claim a much-needed away win. However, Matt Tubbs and Ben Strevens both saw Steve Arnold deny them. Then, with only minutes left on the clock, Parkin sealed the win with the simplest of finishes from close range after Frear's corner had fallen to him in the area. It was a real dent in Eastleigh's ambitions to take something away from Nailsworth, and their afternoon was worsened when experienced midfielder Strevens was shown a straight red. The former Barnet man was sent off by referee Robert Jones for spitting at Parkin in the depths of stoppage time, to compound the visitors defeat and to wrap up an intense tie.

GREEN MACHINE-GUNS DOWN SPITFIRES
Jokerman

On a wet, windy and very murky afternoon at TNL the car-park-full signs are up an hour before kick-off for today's game against Eastleigh. There is no doubt the success the club is enjoying is attracting new supporters at home games. Over 300 have travelled from Eastleigh frustrated by postponed fixtures due to their ruined home ground playing surface. Forest Green extended their unbeaten run to eight league games with an emphatic win at Halifax last Saturday and manager Ady Pennock keeps faith with the same starting line-up this afternoon. Pipe retains his place as does Parkin who leads the line despite a strong challenge from recent signing Kieffer Moore. Prior to kick-off there is a minute's applause to mark the tragic sudden passing of Garry Mitchell as the club flags fly at half-mast. His work in the media and behind the mic endeared him not only to the football club but to the wider community across the shire.

In front of a crowd of over 2,000 the match kicked off with Rovers kicking into a strong headwind on a heavy pitch. Ex-FGR defender Turley was the first to pose a threat, hitting the side netting from a corner by Reason after 15 minutes. Constable also demonstrated his capabilities, by forcing Arnold to save at full stretch diving to his left, with a fierce shot from distance. It was a scrappy first half, littered with mistakes by both sides, certainly not helped by the conditions. Rovers had few chances and on 25 minutes Jennings on the offensive, was in collision with the Eastleigh keeper Flintley, and sustained a leg injury which he failed to run off

At half time fans reflected on an even but eminently forgettable first half. Kelly replaced the injured Jennings at the restart and from the off the game began in earnest. On 50 minutes Frear, who was giving defender Partington a nightmare afternoon, tested Flintley with an accurate shot which lacked power. Around the hour mark persistent play by Carter set up Bennett, who was through on Flintley, who dived bravely to block the ball and injured himself in the process.

Rovers were increasing the pressure on the Eastleigh defence, forcing consecutive corners but it was the visitors who broke the deadlock.

F
E
B
R
U
A
R
Y

Constable set up Reason whose shot from 15 yards was saved low down by Arnold. But it was the provider-turned-goalscorer only a couple of minutes later who, given room on the edge of the area, turned and struck a low shot past Arnold who hardly moved.

The goal galvanized Forest Green who went on the rampage, laying siege to the Eastleigh goal and within three minutes were level. A pinpoint 40-yard cross from Kelly on the left touchline fell to Parkin, who struck a volley from 15 yards that threatened to rip the roof of the net. Flintley did well to get out of the way. The Rovers Goliath had been having an indifferent run of form but this was special. His celebration right in front of the incandescent Eastleigh fans was as magnificent as the goal strike in both planning and deployment.

Rovers were in the ascendency with 23 minutes remaining. M-Brown, ably supported by Bennet, was a threat down the right, while Frear was a class act on the other flank. Eastleigh were not giving up but Rovers' defence were on their mettle. Pipe was inspired, throwing himself headlong into challenges when required, blocking everything that came his way.

The whole team were together and playing well and the visitors were visibly upset: needle was creeping into the play. Parkin had been getting the treatment all afternoon from both Eastleigh's fans and defenders alike. The pot was simmering as the game entered the final quarter.

Arnold raised the heart rate of home fans when under no pressure decided to punch a high looping ball from Strevens. It fell to substitute Cook but fortunately was blocked away for a corner. Pennock made the changes on 87 minutes, Wedgbury for Carter and Moore for Sinclair who had battled all afternoon in an unfamiliar role.

The substitutions were made while Frear was waiting to take a corner, which he promptly did, landing the ball on the six-yard line amid a mass skirmish from which emerged the boot of Parkin to force the ball into the net for the winning goal. This pleased the home fans no end but from the Eastleigh point of view the simmering pot began to boil.

Six minutes remained of which four were added time. Rovers played cat and mouse, running the clock down in the corners as the Eastleigh players lost their discipline. Partington, Frear's 'bunny', had a tantrum and was booked and Strevens became a contender for Gobber of the Month and was sent off.

This unsavoury end to the game did nothing to detract from what was a splendid all-round performance from Forest Green who came from behind yet again, showing spirit and commitment as the season enters the final third. The goal proclamations of RJ left Mitch in no doubt of the result, a fitting end to a happy/sad day.

Tuesday 23.02.16
Guiseley 0 FGR 1
FGR MAKE IT TEN UNBEATEN WITH LATE STRIKE
Richard Joyce
Substitute Brett Williams came off the bench to help Forest Green Rovers clinch a massive midweek away win at Guiseley with a thumping late strike. The former Aldershot hot shot slammed home with the clock ticking to earn Ady Pennock's team a huge three points and to continue Rovers magnificent run of results. Forest Green have now taken 28 points out of a possible 30 in their last ten games, and made the long Tuesday night trip to West Yorkshire a successful one against a Guiseley side who would have certainly felt hard done by Williams's late goal.

The hosts impressed on the night and produced a bright start. After Arnold had kept Nicky Boshell's seventh-minute effort out, they almost took the lead, only for on-loan striker Emile Sinclair's low hit to be denied the chance of hitting the net when it agonizingly struck both posts.

Gradually Rovers found their feet, and Elliott Frear almost provided the night's first goal when his fine central run saw him break through, only to see Dan Atkinson deny him with a crucial save.

The former Leeds United goalkeeper then produced an even better stop from Frear five minutes later. Dale Bennett's teasing cross to the back post was pushed towards goal by the left winger; however, Atkinson made a reactive save to keep the ball out. Once again Frear was presented with a huge opportunity on 33 minutes after another fine run. This time though he turned back into danger when in the clear and Guiseley recovered when he looked set to score. Guiseley's threat continued towards the interval, and Arnold got down well to save Sinclair's hit after he had turned well in the area.

After the break the game continued in the same vein, with Bennett's block denying Boshell and Darren Carter's excellently taken drive kept out well down the other end. Sinclair then must have thought he had finally put Guiseley in front again, only to be denied by the woodwork for a second occasion as his well-taken shot clipped the bar. The game really was end-to-end and another opportunity fell Rovers way on 72 minutes when Keanu Marsh-Brown had an effort kept out.

Both teams had their fair share of chances throughout the night, and the game was deserving of a goal, and fortunately for Rovers it fell in

F
E
B
R
U
A
R
Y

their favour. A burst forward saw a slick pass from Kieffer Moore slip Marsh-Brown into position in the box, and he lined up Williams to slam home via the underside of the bar. It was a huge blow for the hosts who will have felt hard done by after all they had put into the tie, and just one final opportunity fell their way late on in their attempts to salvage an equalizer. James Hurst couldn't profit though when his low hit from distance slipped past the post as Forest Green yet again held on to pick up a magnificent result.

DESTINATION GUISELEY
Rambling Man
If I'm honest, having made an abortive trip to Guiseley already, and still smarting from the 'hospitality' afforded by locals at The Shay, another trip to West Yorkshire did not have me slavering. How wrong can you be? Compo's problematic back forced his late withdrawal from our settled away squad. No time for substitutions so, with Foggy at the wheel, he, Clegg and I made an early start up the M5. Rush hour had passed and we made swift progress to our interim target, the Caphouse Colliery in Overton, near Wakefield, home to the National Coal Mining Museum.

How do you feel about going 450 feet down a mineshaft in something resembling a Tesco's shopping trolley? Well, it gave us food for thought and made me realize that my thick cream jumper was not the wisest choice for the headline underground tour. If you don't suffer from claustrophobia, this is a must-do experience, enhanced for us by a chatty, football-loving 'ex-miner host' (geddit?!) who'd spied the FGR badge on Foggy's jacket. To see the conditions in which ten-year-old kids were forced to work in the eighteenth and nineteenth centuries – after all, only they could squeeze into dark two-foot-high seams – was simply shocking. Then to turn off all the torches and experience utter blackness just defies description. My thoughts turned uncomfortably to guessing the weight of countless tons of soil and rock resting on a few wooden pit props. That was enough to turn bowels to liquid. But one thing became clearer for me: anyone who has made the trip to northern France and Belgium will have been mortified to observe the conditions endured by soldiers in the trenches of the Great War, and the deadly tunnels dug under enemy lines to blast them to kingdom come. The similarities to the construction of colliery tunnels at Caphouse were marked. In fact the soldier-miners would have seen more daylight and been better fed. Maybe to them, the conditions in Picardy were a blessed relief from British coal mines.

Guiseley AFC yielded welcoming Tykes and a tight little ground, at full stretch to accommodate National League football. Rather like Shortwood or Brimscombe with added Portakabins. First official I bumped into was Nigel Hughes, former Gloucester City chair who moved away a few years back and is now a Guiseley director.

The match itself was good fare on a tricky surface. In the first half, the Lions passed quickly and accurately and tormented our full backs. We rode our luck, notably when Steve Arnold thankfully grasped a shot that had cannoned off the inside of both posts. We looked a tad heavy-legged but with Pipe (my man of the match), Frear and KMB prominent, FGR still might have notched several goals.

Rovers were far tighter in the second half, and took over as the home side tired. As they say, the goal was coming – rather early by our standards, in the 83rd – and benefited from the influence of subs Moore and Kelly and the impressive Williams who crashed the winning shot off the bar. Joy was capped by Nigel telling us that the Heed had held Cheltenham 0-0 at the World of Smile. (Makes me smirk every time I write that daft name – better than York City's KitKat Stadium.)

The return journey was farcical with tedious closures for M1 roadworks on which no one appeared to be working. It will take more than a fast train to turn the chaotic motorways around Bradford and Leeds into a northern powerhouse.

Saturday 27.02.16
Barrow 2 FGR 2
FGR PICK UP A POINT ON THE ROAD AT BARROW
Richard Joyce

It's now 11 games and two months unbeaten for Forest Green Rovers after a point on a difficult visit to Barrow. Ady Pennock's FGR side have faced an outstandingly difficult month on the road, but have come through it with flying colours, although they would have liked an extra two points in Cumbria.

Kieffer Moore's first-half strike gave FGR the lead, and after Darren Carter's strike had hit the post in the second half, Keanu Marsh-Brown couldn't believe his luck when a suicidal back pass saw him double Rovers' lead. The Cumbrians turned the game on its head though when they snatched a point. Danny Livesey got one back from a corner and then Jordan Williams struck towards the finish.

Moore, handed his first attacking start for the club, set about looking to make an impact early on, and after only eight minutes he was only inches away from guiding Marsh-Brown's free kick inside the post. Rob

**F
E
B
R
U
A
R
Y**

Sinclair then tried his luck with a volley shortly after a corner had fallen to him, while Barrow's first major chance came on the midpoint of the half when Steve Arnold made a fine stop to deny Andy Parry's low hit.

Down the other end only two minutes later FGR then had their biggest chance. Moore couldn't quite shove Marsh-Brown's cross into the net, and as the ball bounced out to the edge of the box, Carter saw his well-taken shot pushed onto the post by Joel Dixon. With the end of the first half coming into sight, the deadlock was finally broken in Rovers' favour with a brilliant team move. Carter's deep cross towards the back post was hit first time back across the face of goal by Elliott Frear, and Moore was on hand to touch home his first goal for the club.

After the break Forest Green appeared eager to double their lead, and the impressive Frear twice came close to adding to the scoreline when he cut inside from the right and forced Dixon into two good stops. The second goal eventually came though when on the hour mark Marsh-Brown couldn't believe his luck. Simon Grand's horrendous back pass was picked up by the number nine who took his time to round Dixon to roll the ball home in front of the travelling supporters.

It should have been three within ten minutes. Moore nodded just wide from James Jennings's cross and Frear became the second FGR player to hit the woodwork when he weaved his way into the area and slammed a right-footed attempt onto the post. Barrow then wrestled control of the tie in an imposing period that saw them find the net twice. After Arnold had made a wonderful reactive stop from Andy Cook's header, Livesey profited from a corner to knock a goal in at the back post to get one back for the hosts. And they notched another goal when, on 83 minutes, Williams turned well on the edge of the area and blasted home into the bottom corner to frustratingly level.

DESTINATION BARROW
Rambling Man
Two jaunts in four days covering 850 miles. That is what the National League throws up these days, and Rovers still have to visit Tranmere, Gateshead and Dover. Just Foggy and yours truly for this one with me grasping the round thing on the dashboard. In passing, I told him I'd had the Passat's brakes fixed which brought an expression of panic tinged with relief. Something to do with the four-hour drive ahead of us? No worries though: like an updated miracle, the motorway traffic parted and we cruised to the dramatic backdrop of Cumbria.

Being men of culture, Foggy and I decided to bestow our presence on a deserving intermediate destination. Not so intermediate in this case – Furness Abbey, just three miles from the Furness Building Society Stadium (known to football folk as Holker Street). The abbey is a sprawling, enchanting ruin. Founded by the Normans in 1123, it was a Cistercian monastery, second in wealth and status only to Fountains in Yorkshire. It is set in a beautiful 'secret' valley, low down next to a babbling stream. The once-massive buildings are fashioned from the local red sandstone, reminiscent of that to be found in Ross-on-Wye or the Jurassic coast of Devon. They show off rounded arches rather than the soaring perpendicular style, many at drunken angles, settled into the marshy ground. Furness Abbey was laid waste by Henry VIII and Thomas Cromwell. Dissolved is the expression that covers the mid-sixteenth-century destruction, but in truth, much of the stonework was plundered by locals for houses and suchlike.

Quite a contrast to the Edwardian home of the Bluebirds. I last found myself at Holker Street, co-commentating on a defeat in the Fleetwood/Harvey era. Nothing much has changed at the old place, whose proximity to the dark waters of the Irish Sea reminds you how far you are from football heartland. The stands behind both goals have long since perished, but those flanking the length of the ground are made of sterner stuff, incorporating some of the stoutest girder uprights you will come across. Time Team would do a job on dating the different layers of peeling blue paint.

Cutting through the decay, the hospitality of the Cumbrian locals was a joy. Dreadful weather has starved them of much football this year, but they are warm people and have the loudest bellow in the League.

So to the match. Beneath the level, thinly grassed surface was rolled, hard mud that produced elaborate ball bounces. A day for tin hats as home manager Cox planned a rollicking siege.

It took Rovers half an hour to work out that the ball was better used on the ground, and then they prospered. After some near misses, Moore tapped in his first for the club after great work from Frear and Carter. Frear had a purple spell at the start of the second period, testing the home keeper and rattling a post that after a horrendous back pass had set up Keanu for the second.

But if Rovers thought a cruising win was on, Cumbrian lungs shouted otherwise. A storming comeback brought two deserved goals, the second by Williams would have graced any match. FGR, downcast at missing the chance to go top, but thankful for taking four points from two distant games.

ROVERS' BALLOON DEFLATED WITH DEFEAT AT HOME TO GRIMSBY
TOWN. Despite opportunities presented by unexpected Cheltenham
losses and stuttering form, it did not re-inflate. For many supporters, the
results of attritional play were coming home to roost. If your approach
is one dimensional, once the goals dry up, it is hard to reinstate the flow.
A single win and three draws made it Cheltenham's title to lose. The
unofficial crown of Best Manager had already been won. Ady Pennock
was under pressure, more than anyone outside the county will have
realized.

We have skilful players who cannot play together
Their synapses do not compute, on the same wavelength – NEVER
No Kelly again, even though in midfield we craved
Someone with intelligence, passing – is our manager depraved?

(Excerpt from 'Disappointment' by The Farmcotian)

Friday 04.03.16
FGR 0 Grimsby 1
ROVERS' HOME-WINNING RUN COMES TO AN END
Richard Joyce

Craig Disley's second-half header ended Forest Green Rovers' magnificent
home-winning record and 11-match unbeaten run in front of the BT
Sport cameras. The Mariners skipper headed home 20 minutes from the
finish at The New Lawn as FGR's marvellous unbeaten run saw them
lose for the first time since Boxing Day.

FGR retain their second place position in the table, still well in front of
Grimsby who still have a number of games in hand, with Ady Pennock's
side now facing nine major tests in their attempts to continue their pursuit
for Football League promotion glory.

With Jon Parkin and Sam Wedgbury restored to the starting XI, Forest
Green produced some eye-catching moves early on, but couldn't force
Grimsby goalkeeper James McKeown into any saves.

Rovers' stopper Steve Arnold though made a wonderful save from
Mariners' loan debutant Pat Hoban on 33 minutes. Grimsby's newest
addition from Oxford United smashed a long-range effort on goal that
Arnold tipped over emphatically.

Andy Monkhouse's header for Bristol Rovers last season in Nailsworth
earned the Pirates a draw. And the wide man could have put Grimsby in
front when he found room round the back of the box, only to nod his

aerial effort off target. The instrumental Rob Sinclair was catching the eye in midfield, and his excellent work just before the half-time whistle saw him set Darren Carter for a shot that almost snuck in.

After the break Rovers enjoyed an excellent spell. Carter was denied by McKeown, while Keanu Marsh-Brown also saw his low effort kept out. Then ten minutes into the half Charlie Clough's attempt from a set piece was hacked clear by a Grimsby defender before it could cross the line. However, once the away team got their goal they didn't look back, and they claimed it on 71 minutes when Disley's header was too far for Arnold to reach across his goal.

Paul Hurst's outfit looked to double their lead immediately, but were denied by a combination of Arnold and Dale Bennett, while the FGR keeper made another fantastic save from former Lincoln City man Jon Nolan's hit from the left. Padraig Amond, Grimsby's and the league's leading marksman this term, had a great chance that he skewed over in a final ten minutes that saw Forest Green produce one final opportunity in an attempt to draw level.

James Jennings's free kick was well struck by the left back, although it was straight into the arms of McKeown who managed to keep a clean sheet and to help his side return home to Lincolnshire with maximum points.

ROVERS GAFFED BY TRAWLERMEN
Jokerman
Following the disappointment of the performance at Barrow on Saturday, spirits were lifted by Eastleigh's victory over Cheltenham on Tuesday. That result gives Rovers a second opportunity to go above the league leaders if they can prevail against Grimsby tonight. Temperatures are around 4°C and falling, with wintery showers thrown in as a 2,000-plus crowd greets the teams onto a playing surface showing signs of wear.

Pennock has reinstated Parkin and Wedgbury with Moore and Pipe returning to the bench. The first half is a dull affair notable only for a Parkin skirmish with Grimsby keeper McKeown, resulting in penalty appeals being waved away, while at the other end, a screamer from 25 yards by Amond saw Arnold tip the ball over the bar, and a cross from Tait reached Monkhouse at the back post who headed wide when he might have done better.

A pattern did develop, however, in Rovers mainly relying on M-Brown free kicks to create goal chances. The highlight for the television cameras was probably the hundreds of Grimsby supporters at the away end who

M
A
R
C
H

kept up raucous chanting throughout a half that saw both teams cancel each other out.

There was a better start to the game after the break and Rovers took the initiative. On 54 minutes another well-flighted free kick from M-Brown saw Clough challenging but the ball was deflected over the bar for a corner. From which the same combination ended when Clough's shot was scrambled away with the keeper nowhere.

Grimsby, however, hit back when Hoban shot on the turn inside the area, which brought out the best in Arnold diving low to his right, to turn the ball away for a corner. After the hour mark, with Rovers failing to create a clear goal-scoring chance, the visitors came back strongly. On 71 minutes Monkhouse on the left clipped a cross into the area to Disley who guided a precise header wide of Arnold inside the right-hand post. It appeared almost in slow motion to the home supporters whereas the Grimsby fans went mildly berserk behind the goal.

Pennock switched Carter for Moore. It was, however, Grimsby who should have extended their advantage on 74 minutes when Amond set up Monkhouse in oceans of space, where only the brilliance of Arnold denied him, the ball spinning up under the bar where Bennett was on hand to clear. A couple of minutes later Nolan on a run had his shot again well saved by the Rovers keeper.

Since the goal Grimsby took charge of the game and when Pennock sent on Guthrie and Williams for Frear and Parkin it made little difference. The Rovers players worked hard with little reward, unable to create chances from wide positions and coming up against a Grimsby side well drilled in defence and with a much sharper cutting edge. Only Arnold kept the score down to a single goal.

There will be more twists and turns before the season ends but the play-offs look the more likely just now for FGR, but the obese one is some way off yet.

The supporters who experienced years of relegation fights are surely not among the despairing here: today's visiting fans have suffered years of pain re-promotion from this league, and Rovers are merely novices.

FGR V GRIMSBY TOWN
FGR Student Ambassador Wilf Doble
My name is Wilf Doble and I am the FGR ambassador for Woodchester Primary School. I've been watching Forest Green since I was less than a year old (or so my dad tells me!). Apparently, Stuart Fleetwood, in his first spell at the club, nearly knocked my head off when he shot wide –

I was behind the goal in a baby carrier on my dad's back at the time. Now that I am nine years old I remember the games much better. This season we have done a bit of touring around the country with FGR and have looked around some interesting places – Kidderminster, Chester, Wrexham, Oxford and Torquay.

Kidderminster was fun as the ground is next door to the Severn Valley Railway with its steam trains. The oldest international football stadium in the world (apparently) is the Racecourse Ground of Wrexham FC. Chester had some great city walls to walk on and Torquay took us to the pretty cold seaside on Boxing Day. My favourite stadium so far has been the Kassam Stadium in Oxford which is an unusual stadium because it only has three sides.

Match report: Grimsby (along with Tranmere Rovers and Wrexham) is one of the three best-supported clubs in the National League. Their home crowds have averaged over 4,500 this season. Forest Green crowds continue to rise – our average gate this season is over 1,600 (another increase on the previous year) and almost 2,250 people saw this game. Who knows what might happen if we get our new stadium! A good number of Grimsby fans made the long journey south for this Friday evening game. Many were armed with plastic inflatable fish; many were chanting "we only sing when we're fishing!" They were in good voice and they had reason to be – on the night they were the better side and they won by a solitary goal. It was a rare off-night for Rovers. Perhaps us FGR fans need to get ourselves a good choirmaster and some plastic inflatable vegetables for future matches?

Saturday 12.03.16
Gateshead 0 FGR 1
POINTS RECORD BROKEN WITH TOP AWAY WIN
Richard Joyce
A rocket James Jennings header helped Forest Green Rovers break their fifth-tier points total record in a superb professional performance at Gateshead. The left back continued his threat in the opposition's penalty area with a terrifically taken header from an Elliott Frear corner, as a 16th clean sheet of the campaign assisted in helping FGR to a notable away win.

The Heed are chasing a place in the play-offs, so this victory, which has seen Rovers smash their record 79 points total garnered last season, looks set to be crucial in the promotion run-in with eight huge clashes still to go.

M
A
R
C
H

Rovers' control was illustrated from as early as the first minute when the Gateshead post was rattled after a Keanu Marsh-Brown ball into the area was deflected onto the woodwork. Steve Arnold meanwhile got his gloves on the ball early on with a good save from Danny Johnson, while former FGR stopper Sam Russell made a crucial stop to keep his old club at bay. Marsh-Brown's perfect low ball across the face of goal from the right was stroked towards goal by Darren Carter, but Russell got in the way to make the save.

The Heed goalkeeper was picking the ball out of his own net two minutes later though when Jennings struck what proved to be the match-winner. Frear's superb corner in towards the near post was met by the left back whose unstoppable aerial effort slammed into the top corner. Another Jennings header just before the interval again saw the defender go close – this time ending up over the bar.

The lead belonged to FGR at the break, and Ady Pennock's side denied the home side any possibility of forcing their way back into the reckoning with a secure second-half performance.

Arnold was confidently behind a Paddy McLaughlin shot just before the hour mark, and on 69 minutes substitute Kieffer Moore's shot forced a corner that saw Charlie Clough nod over the crossbar from Marsh-Brown's delivery.

Time was running out for the hosts, and after Rob Sinclair's adventurous run had ended with the midfielder firing over, Gateshead's biggest opportunity fell the way of former Bristol City youngster Gus Mafuta five minutes from the end. His half-volley, hit after the ball had dropped to him outside the area, flew past the post to the relief of the 51 dedicated travelling supporters.

Rovers did brilliantly to limit the Heed's opportunities, although they did have one final opening at the death. Johnson managed to break through on the left-hand side of the box and his smash on goal flashed into the side netting, leaving Rovers with their clean sheet intact and with a huge three points.

DESTINATION GATESHEAD
Rambling Man

Mrs Rambling Man notched another birthday on the eve of the Heed match. So, I seduced her with tales of Tyneside, Hadrian's Wall and however many bridges arch over the Tyne these days. Even conjured up Michael Caine menacing the North East in *Get Carter!*

How could she resist a long weekend in Northumberland? Quite easily as it happens which is how I found myself 1,500 miles south of Geordieland being regaled by *la plume de ma tante* rather than *why-aye-man*. No pig's bladder in the vicinity, just planks of wood sliding over three metres depth of white stuff.

Well, I tried didn't I? All who know me understand my passion for winter sport, so either way, I couldn't lose. Thanks then to Foggy for passing on his take on our contest in the North East.

Any of you like opera? "Where the heck are you going with this R-M?" I hear club scribe Richard Joyce asking. Just bear with me Rich, I'll get there presently.

Opera is not for me, I'm afraid, cue my artistic prejudices. Too many bariatric types warbling nursery rhymes, paid whopping salaries with ticket prices to match. Which of course the Arts Council aficionados subsidise for the snooty few. It never helped me afford to see Emerson, Lake & Palmer in concert, not that I thought to ask. But the posh set have invented something useful – dainty binoculars called opera glasses.

Anyone visiting the Gateshead International Stadium could do with a pair. Sat in the side stands, even at the front, you are separated from the pitch by several verges, a long jump pit and an eight-lane running track. From that distance, the players are as recognizable as Lowry's match-stork men. Mind you, if you end up behind the goals, nothing short of the Hubble Telescope will do.

On the field of play, Rovers shrugged off their first defeat of 2016 (to Grimsby at fortress New Lawn) and dominated proceedings. Not even old FGR favourite Sam Russell could save his side and his new mates could not beat our latest custodian, Steve Arnold. Rovers' winning header put me in mind of the classic children's books by Anthony Buckeridge.

Take your choice from these volumes: *Thanks to Jennings*, *Jennings as Usual*, *Just like Jennings*, *Leave it to Jennings*, *Jennings of Course!*, *Jennings Abounding*, *Trust Jennings!*, *Typically Jennings!*, *Speaking of Jennings!* & *Jennings Again!*. And there are 15 other titles that do not work quite as well. So, guess who scored? Next up, Tranny at the Wirral. No let-up for the boys in black and green.

Saturday 19.03.16
Tranmere Rovers 1 FGR 1
PRENTON PARK POSITIVES FOR FOREST GREEN
Richard Joyce
Ten-man Forest Green Rovers moved a point closer to the top of the table with a draw on the club's first visit to Tranmere's Prenton Park. Darren

**M
A
R
C
H**

Carter both scored and saw red in the second half against a Tranmere side who, having been behind at half time, scored early in the second period to set up a tense 45 minutes of football.

A scrappy affair that lacked quality, but it was a very good point against one of the clubs relegated from League Two at the end of last season, as the National League continues its nail-biting finish.

From as early as the fifth minute FGR found the lead thanks to Carter's shot which set up a perfect early platform. Steve Arnold's long kick forward was touched on by Jon Parkin, and Carter sprinted through to snatch an early goal. Tranmere immediately threatened to get back on level terms. Experienced defender Steve McNulty, however, couldn't keep two headed efforts down after good deliveries into the box from Adam Mekki. Apart from a poor finish from ex-Blackpool man Gary Taylor-Fletcher, there was little action heading for the interval as the game struggled to get going with referee John Busby busy with his whistle.

The hosts got off to the perfect start in the second half when they slammed home a 48th-minute equalizer. Jay Harris was the beneficiary, as the former Wrexham midfielder latched on to a wonderful defence-splitting pass, and smashed in to draw parity. With several Forest Green players on yellow cards, the number of fouls being totted up eventually told when Carter was given his marching orders for a tangle in the middle of the park.

The goalscorer's early exit left FGR with ten men for the final half hour, but within minutes Keanu Marsh-Brown forced Tranmere keeper Scott Davies into an excellent fingertip stop with a free kick from deep that almost crept in under the bar.

Ady Pennock's charges adapted well to their one-man disadvantage, making life difficult for the hosts, who could only muster a Taylor-Fletcher header towards the finish. Meanwhile down the other end FGR almost nicked victory at the start of stoppage time, only for the impressive Charlie Clough to nod narrowly over from substitute Marcus Kelly's corner. Harris's late drive, which rolled well wide, was Tranmere's final effort, and the last kick of the game, as FGR returned to Gloucestershire continuing the hunt for promotion with what was another very good point.

DESTINATION TRANMERE
Rambling Man

The fixture on the Wirral had long been earmarked in my calendar. It was always going to be a big game at the business end of the season and an area (let alone a stadium) that I'd never visited. Weeks ago, I'd made tentative plans for a long weekend involving visits to the famous Liverpool Museums and Docks, National Trust's Speke Hall and other gems. I had even asked whether Mrs Rambling Man might come along. Sadly, all my plans crashed and burned. Midweek before the match, I was felled by a mega-dose of man-flu.

Now I am not one to indulge illness, unless of course I am the patient. Mrs R-M pretty much feels that the female gender has drawn the short straw where malady and afflictions are concerned. But she has never suffered the debilitating and sport-deprivational effects of man-flu. True, childbirth and suchlike must smart a bit, but when I retire poorly to my bedchamber the grim reaper is sharpening his blade.

Though I was wracked by delirium, Compo, Foggy and Deep-Throat were in rude health and ventured north in the former's silver Beamer. The Black and White attractions of Chester made a worthy pit-stop en route to the Wirral and impressive Prenton Park.

Tranmere Rovers have been based at the stadium for over a century. Yet it is smart, modern place, with an all-seater capacity of nearly 17,000. That makes it the biggest ground in the National League. Three seasons ago their regular gate was in five figures as the hosts did battle in the Championship, so their fall has been meteoric, enough to traumatize most loyal supporters. Nonetheless, I am told that the welcome and hospitality afforded was heartwarming and greatly appreciated by FGR supporters.

After an up-and-down campaign, with a regular influx of players to an already large squad, Tranmere's season is looking up, albeit nervously. One defeat in nine, hovering just outside the play-offs. Their 2-0 win at The New Lawn in the autumn marked FGR's lowest ebb of a fine season and crowned a triumphant return for James Norwood, late of our parish. Yet, with the sides around them improving and having games in hand, Nors' Tranmere were desperate to make it a double.

Predictably, the game was tension-packed, disjointed and made worse by a fussy referee who was clearly not a fan of West Country types.

Darren Carter's fifth-minute goal silenced the 5,000-strong home crowd as 100-plus travellers made merry. The 'home Rovers' did not recover until the second period but quickly levelled.

Carter then received a contentious second yellow but that only served to spur the visitors. Under the cosh for most of the half, they still created the better goalscoring chances and held out for a valuable point, character in abundance. Yet again, man of the match Charlie Clough was the fulcrum. With Cheltenham losing again, the pressure cooker is hissing.

M
A
R
C
H

KICKS-FOR-FREE REFEREE WHISTLING IN THE DARK
Jokerman

Bouncing back from a home defeat against Grimsby, Forest Green secured a fine win away at Gateshead last Saturday to keep the pressure on Cheltenham Town at the top of The National League. It was a real confidence booster ahead of today's daunting task away at Tranmere Rovers who are desperately seeking a play-off place after a disappointing campaign.

The Kendo roadrunner glides north with a full crew. Sweeping past the industrialized south bank of the River Mersey, with its oil refineries and car plant, fans arrive at Wirral and the impressive Prenton Park, home to Tranmere Rovers FC. A huge marquee has been erected in the car park to provide a bar for supporters. One may liken it to a big top which is apt to the circus that is about to follow.

The stadium is superb in complete contrast to the unfit-for-purpose Gateshead affair. The seats are steeply banked and fans are on top of the action. There was little consideration for visiting vegan personnel who were housed in the Cowshed. A crowd of over 5,000 greeted the teams of which there were a 100-plus to support Forest Green.

Ady Pennock kept faith with the same line-up, the main talking point was of Guthrie who was conspicuous by his absence, even from the bench, but that's another story. Under a grey, cloud-covered sky Tranmere were soon on the offensive, winning an early corner and making their intentions clear.

On five minutes Arnold tried to balance things up by going route one and ballooned a kick downfield. The ball bounced once between Parkin, Carter and a defender, Carter reacted best and turned and knocked the ball past keeper Davies, low inside the right-hand post. A dream start for Forest Green and the Cowshed brigade.

Tranmere fans were silenced and remained so for the rest of the half. Their team immediately tried to hit back and ex-FGR player Norwood cut in from the left and forced Arnold to save a fierce shot at his near post on eight minutes.

Two corners saw Mekki, the Tranmere winger, twice pick out McNulty at the back post, but both headers cleared the bar. Tranmere continued to dominate possession which forced Rovers to snap at their heels in efforts to regain the ball, which in turn did not endear themselves to the referee.

This led to endless free kicks and tempers became frayed among players on both sides and incensed the home supporters. The half ended with Tranmere on top but there was no way through the Rovers defence and

Arnold remained untroubled. The half-time talk among FGR fans was whether the team could hang on to their lead as there was no sign of a further threat from Parkin who hadn't won a header against McNultey. Frear and M-Brown were not making any impression on a good Tranmere defence.

The home side continued where they left off and were level within three minutes of the restart. Probably the best footballing move of the game led to the goal. A sweeping half-dozen passes starting inside their own half saw Tranmere slice through Rovers' defence, with Taylor-Fletcher providing the killer ball through to Harris goalside of Jennings; he smashed the ball low past Arnold and the home fans woke up big time.

It was a backs to the wall job for Rovers now and the underlying current of needle crept more and more into the game. The referee clearly did not like Forest Green's attitude and favoured the home side massively. Under siege Rovers broke away upfield on the hour and with a promising ball forward, the referee pulled play back as Carter on the charge collided with Harris and was deemed to have fouled the player and was given a second yellow, followed by the inevitable red card.

It would be 20 minutes before Pennock made a change. Around 65 minutes M-Brown swung in a free kick that had Davies tipping the ball over his crossbar. From the corner a Clough header was cleared away. It was a rare attack for Rovers but Tranmere, for all their possession, were not troubling Arnold who was well protected by his defenders. Norwood did not help his side's cause by wasting two minutes remonstrating with the linesman which eventually led to the referee becoming involved but he took no action against the player. It was that sort of game.

Another flashpoint occurred when Bennett was in a 50-50 collision with Kirby, with both going for the ball. The Tranmere player came off second best, and the home fans went berserk. Their player was laid out for several minutes with the casualty department in attendance.

Stating that Maggie Thatcher was the prime minister, in answer to a lucidity question, he arose, looking like a milkshake after the embalmers had finished with him, to huge applause while Bennett was vilified as both players stood on the touchline.

On 80 minutes Williams replaced M-Brown and soon after Kelly came on for Frear. The game was played out with Forest Green on the back foot but Arnold was never called on to make anything other than routine saves. Rovers' defence worked extremely hard but with the players at their disposal, Tranmere Rovers, apart from their excellent goal, fell

M
A
R
C
H

woefully short and illustrated why they are not in contention for the title. Indeed, Clough's late header could have stolen the game for Forest Green that probably would have called for a police escort off the Wirral.

Forest Green fans left the Cowshed scratching their heads over their team's performance. Was Rovers' defence that good or was Tranmere's attack that poor?

The attack was almost non-existent but Pennock persevered. He is clearly from the Tony Pulis school of management but the table does not lie and FGR supporters will be hoping he can lift the club into the Football League.

Friday 25.03.16
FGR 0 Aldershot Town 0
ROVERS ARE HELD AT HOME BY THE SHOTS
Richard Joyce

An Aldershot Town side set up to secure a much-needed away clean sheet denied Forest Green the winning start to Easter they strongly savoured at The New Lawn. A crowd of over 2,300 were inside to witness Rovers' first goalless draw of the season, as the Easter sun shone on Nailsworth, but couldn't inspire Ady Pennock's men to what would have been an ideal start to the weekend.

Attentions will now turn to Monday's trip to Bromley, as the sensational promotion race continues at a rapid pace.

Throughout the afternoon FGR dominated proceedings against the Shots, and just before the quarter-of-an-hour mark James Jennings came agonizingly close to finding the opener, although he couldn't touch in Elliott Frear's pull-back from a Jon Parkin ball into the box. Former Welling United forward Ross Lafayette did a good job in a solitary striker's role for the Shots, and in the 19th minute he did well to turn inside the FGR area. However he couldn't keep his attempt on goal down. Charlie Clough's header from a Keanu Marsh-Brown corner was held by Aldershot's Phil Smith, while Steve Arnold made the first of two good saves to deny Sam Hatton's low hit midway through the half. His second stop saw him prevent Jim Stevenson from netting, who had broken through the middle to fire off an effort.

The half ended with Kieffer Moore heading a touch from Jennings wide, and the second half began with the athletic front man again in action in front of goal. Frear did well to put a good ball into the area but Moore couldn't find the back of the net. Following efforts from Parkin and another one from Moore that still couldn't break the deadlock, the final 30 minutes brought about a frustrating half-hour as FGR struggled to break down a Shots side with a mass of bodies being kept behind the ball.

Brett Williams was introduced as a substitute against his old club. He had a great chance with a header from a well-delivered Marsh-Brown free kick, although he couldn't keep it down and it flew just over the crossbar. Rovers' best route to goal seemed to be to bombard balls into the area from out wide, and Kurtis Guthrie couldn't follow up his goal for England C in the week with a stretching header from a Jennings delivery. Meanwhile, Williams had another opportunity in front of goal as the clock ticked towards 90 minutes. He was denied however by Smith who saw his attempt slam right into his arms.

It looked as though Aldershot had managed to successfully pick up a much-needed clean sheet on the road when Marsh-Brown's stoppage-time corner came to nothing. The New Lawn crowd had witnessed their first goalless draw of the season. Rovers head to Bromley next on Easter Monday for a huge clash against the Kent side, with the dream of earning automatic promotion to the Football League for the first ever time, well and truly on.

ARNOLD STARS AS ROVERS FIRE BLANKS
Jokerman

Two games in four days will test Forest Green's resolve regarding their league title aspirations.

Today's visitors Aldershot Town have hit a poor run of form and are at long odds to cause a surprise.

The only question for Rovers fans is will the strikers do themselves justice. Against 'top sides' Grimsby and Tranmere recently, apart from a route one goal, it is hard to recall a 'should have scored' opportunity. If one considers Braintree and Dover 'top sides' then only a minimum of five victories will suffice against the 'lesser' opposition over the remaining fixtures. An obvious supposition but football has a habit of confounding the best of forecasters.

On a fine sunny afternoon an excellent crowd in excess of 2,000 greets the teams to kick off the bank holiday weekend. A one minute's silence is held to remember the victims of the recent terror attack in Brussels. Ady Pennock has recalled Kieffer Moore to the side to replace the suspended Carter.

Forest Green start the game in the ascendancy. An early M-Brown free kick from halfway nearly finds its way straight through a crowded penalty area but Aldershot keeper Smith is alert. On 15 minutes good work by

M
A
R
C
H

Parkin sees a cross to the back post that Frear knocks back to Jennings but he can only direct his shot wide. Despite looking the more likely side, it's Aldershot who go close when Lafayette collects a pass inside the area and holds off both Racine and Clough to shoot across Arnold, but just wide of the left-hand post. Rovers reply with a Clough header from a Frear cross but his effort lacks enough power to trouble Smith.

Aldershot skipper Hatton then exchanges passes with Rasulo on the right and forces Arnold to make a fine save diving to his right to concede a corner. Half an hour in and Sinclair loses possession in midfield and a quick pass through the centre gives Stevenson a sight of goal, and he hits a brutal shot that Arnold does well to beat away. For Rovers Frear meets an M-Brown cross at the back post but his connection is poor and Smith saves comfortably. A first half that saw Rovers in possession but the visitors came far closer to scoring.

No changes at half time and Forest Green started brightly again with Frear making a good run down the left but Moore was offside in meeting the cross. Aldershot's attacking threat all but dried up during the second period and Rovers' creativity was non-existent. There was no lack of effort but as the late Johan Cruyff said the game is played with the mind, the work is done by the legs. Pennock made the changes with Guthrie, Williams and Jeffrey replacing Moore, Parkin and Frear but it was to no avail. Am M-Brown free kick picked out Williams who put his header over the crossbar, and the same player brought the only save of the second half of note by either keeper, when an over-the-shoulder effort from six yards was directed straight at Smith. There was to be no added-time drama and the game ended in anti-climax for the 2,000 home fans. Six fixtures remain but Forest Green must find their goalscoring touch to have any chance of avoiding the dreaded lottery of the play-offs.

Monday 28.03.16
Bromley 2 FGR 2
LATE SUCKER PUNCH DENIES FOREST GREEN
Richard Joyce

Stoppage-time heartbreak saw Forest Green Rovers end their Easter Monday trip to Bromley with a draw having held a two-goal lead at the break. Kurtis Guthrie's double put Rovers into a great position at half time at Hayes Lane; however, goals from Pierre Joseph-Dubois and a last-gasp Jack Holland goal from a set piece stopped FGR from claiming what would have been the ideal end to the Easter double header.

There were four changes made to the FGR line-up that started Good

Friday's home stalemate with Aldershot Town. And Rovers started on the front foot in impressive fashion, with Aarran Racine's long-range hit that went out for a corner, followed by Ady Pennock's side taking the lead. Positive build-up play brought with it a little bit of fortune. A Brett Williams shot smashed into the leg of Guthrie, which wrong-footed Alan Julian, to install some early daylight between the teams.

Bromley struggled to put together a response, although they did have a shot on goal on 20 minutes that was easily gathered by Steve Arnold from the foot of the prolific Moses Emmanuel. A couple of minutes later Darren Carter blasted a shot on the Bromley goal that was well watched by Julian. And the ex-Stevenage keeper made a stunning double-save just past the half-hour mark to ensure it was only a goal difference between the two sides.

He twice stopped Williams from finding the net inside the area, with the second save a particularly outstanding effort. However, he couldn't stop Guthrie from adding his second right on the stroke of half time. Marcus Kelly's superb ball into the danger zone fell to England C man Guthrie, who slammed home to double the advantage before the break.

Guthrie almost netted a third with a header from a James Jennings cross early in the second period, although it would be the hosts who would score next, as Joseph-Dubois tucked in from close range from Adam Cunnington's knock-down. Bromley's goal understandably added extra nerves, but FGR dealt with them well, and on 69 minutes Keanu Marsh-Brown's corner was very nearly headed home at the far post by Carter.

The contest gradually edged towards the finish. With victory in sight, Rovers cause was bettered when with less than five minutes to go a dangerous Paul Rodgers tackle saw the hosts go down to ten men. But they would win a corner deep into stoppage time that would make all the difference. Holland got up through a sea of bodies to direct the ball past a helpless Arnold, to deny Forest Green a winning end to Easter, and to keep Rovers second in the table.

DESTINATION BROMLEY
Rambling Man
In the parlance of George W, I greatly misunderestimated the severity of my man-flu. Thinking it was on the wane, I put in an appearance on the Western Terrace v Aldershot on Good Friday. My reward for enduring an inexplicably inept 0-0 was a sudden decline into quadruple pneumonia.

By now, Mrs Rambling Man was infected too, albeit she was making

MARCH

a big deal out of it, unable to display my *sang-froid*. Rovers' fixture at Bromley on Easter Monday was collateral damage, an unprecedented third straight absence at an away game. My eyes and ears would be Compo and Foggy who were travelling separately with their families, along with 130 or so from the Five Valleys.

It was frustrating to miss the game. As with Tranmere a week or so back, I'd been looking forward to the trip to another club I'd not previously visited. At the fifth tier for its first time, Bromley has acquitted itself well.

A topsy-turvy season sees the club sat in mid-table, unbothered by relegation or play-off contention. I guess their chirpy supporters would have happily accepted that position if offered in August 2015.

Similar to Welling, Bromley is North Kent, long since lassoed by the M25 and taken prisoner by Greater London. By all accounts, it's a smart, compact ground mixing the old and new. It also plays home to Cray Wanderers.

Improbably, my research dug up that the record attendance stands at 10,798 for a game against Nigeria in September 1949. Don't ask me why.

Ady's reaction to the Aldershot bore-draw was unusually sweeping. Parkin, Moore and Frear were appointed to the bench, replaced by Marcus Kelly, Kurtis Guthrie and the unsuspended Darren Carter.

A dominant first half suggested that the changes were well conceived as Rovers reached half time two goals to the good, both by Kurtis. However, the second period turned the game on its head as Rovers did a Barrow, the equalizer coming in the 93rd minute (thought a late goal was our trick?).

Back in Stroud, man-flu felt all the worse for the apparent surrender. But recovery began later that evening when the cocky Robins fluffed the advantage they'd been gifted and conceded a 93rd-minute goal too, to lose at Wrexham.

That sets up Rovers' next home game against the same North Wales outfit, whose play-off hopes have been rekindled. Never a dull moment.

ROVERS MUGGED BUT GUTHRIE MAKES POINT
Jokerman

Bromley, the first of the three remaining fixtures on the road, all of which are in an easterly direction. Full of eastern promise they will need to be, if Forest Green Rovers are to steal the title away from the neighbours. Following the more than disappointing draw against Aldershot at TNL, manager Ady Pennock will have to galvanize his players who appear to be faltering as the finishing end is at hand.

The overnight storm *Katie* threatened the fixture but all is well as Kendo flogs the revs around the M25 in bright sunshine. A full contingent disembark in the stadium car park separated from the main road by a farmyard.

Rovers fans, beer monsters, one-agerboys and winos alike are welcomed into the club bar and spend a convivial hour enjoying excellent Cornish pasties to boot. The team news filters through and Pennock has shaken things up. Carter returns and there are starting places for Guthrie, Williams and Kelly.

The playing surface is rough but not heavy. Rovers start quickly and Williams draws a foul on the edge of the box. Kelly's free kick is blocked out to Racine whose goalbound shot is deflected for a corner. It is taken short, forced out to Kelly who picks out Racine at the back post. His shot is blocked away left to Williams who hits the ball low towards goal, where it strikes a defender and deflects to Guthrie, who smacks the ball into the net from six yards past the helpless Bromley keeper Julian. Four minutes and 150 Rovers supporters are very happy.

Rovers remain in charge with Kelly and Carter showing up well and the defence having few problems from Bromley's strikers.

Julian is by far the busier keeper and gathers a Carter free kick and, on 30 minutes has to slap away an in swinging M-Brown corner from under the crossbar. Kelly is prominent forcing an attack where the ball breaks to Williams, who smashes a shot from an acute angle that Julian blocks brilliantly at his near post, and makes it a double save as the rebound gives the striker a second chance.

In time-added-on Rovers double their advantage when Guthrie wins a free kick near the right touchline.

Kelly drops the ball into the danger zone where a hesitant Bromley defence allows Jennings to arrive in behind and stab the ball goalward. Blocked only to Guthrie, the frustrated striker gleefully pokes it past Julian from close range.

Rovers fans are a happy bunch at the interval. Whether Bromley players had been shown the four corners by their manager or not, they came out with a purpose at the start of the second half.

The home side took away the initiative from Forest Green and looked the better side the more the game progressed. Sinclair damaged a hamstring courageously making a block and was replaced by Wedgbury.

Around the hour mark when Rovers were finding it hard to pass wind, Bromley put themselves back in the game.

A hurried clearance to the halfway line was hoisted back to the right-hand edge of the penalty area, where Cunnington struck the ball first time, catching Rovers' defence flat-footed. The ball beat all but Joseph-Dobois arriving at the back post to sweep the ball home. This was not good and anxiety set in for Rovers' players and fans alike.

Pennock made changes, Frear for M-Brown and Moore for Williams. Rovers did then appear to steady the ship and when Rodgers was shown a straight red card for a late lunge on Jennings inside the last five minutes, hopes were raised. Five minutes of added time were lit up on the board which caused a murmur.

After three of them Bromley won a corner on the right. Substitute Gordon hit an outswinger, Bromley captain Swaine headed the ball across goal and Holland racing in crashed an unstoppable header past Arnold. This action almost triggered a synchronized vomit of Cornish pasties from the away end.

Rovers raced to the other end in a desperate attempt to rescue the situation. Following a penalty-area scramble, they won a corner from which Frear picked out Jennings at the near post, but his header was blocked away and the referee blew his whistle.

The echoes of 'two nil and you gave it up' or similar resounded. All aboard and heading for the M25, Rovers fans listened to Pennock spitting feathers into Bob's microphone.

Driving towards a spectacular sunset and somewhere around junction 15 on the M4, the Monty Python Foot fell heavily, spilling Robins blood all over The Racecourse. Forest Green fans didn't know whether to laugh or cry at missed opportunities.

However, by the time Kendo was bypassing Swindon, his vehicle was Rockin'. After all, one way or another life is but a joke.

SADLY, ROVERS FURROW OF FUNK CONTINUED. Two more bore-draws and two dismal home defeats brought Ady Pennock's tenure to a close. An astonishing fall in the context of the season as a whole. Dale Vince has acquired a reputation as a loyal, untypical football club chairman who plans for the long term. But he determined that Rovers had little or no chance to negotiate the play-offs with their tactic and form of the previous few months. No one crowed over the likeable Ady's departure. Equally, the vast majority of Rovers supporters understood how catastrophic Rovers' spring has been. Results, tactics, player selections and behind-the-scenes tantrums – all seemed to contribute to the nose-dive. Few disagreed with The Electric Chair's decision. To popular acclaim, Academy Manager 'Scotty' Bartlett took over the reins. He brought a two-match 100% winning streak from his first caretaker role after David Hockaday's departure, and promptly ended the regular season on a high with victory at Dover. Three in three!

And so it became clear as the play-offs beckoned
Dale realized the slide was scary – not good enough second
Many thought Ady had lost the dressing room
The last nine matches (an early season parallel) increased the gloom

(Excerpt from 'The Leaving' by The Farmcotian)

Saturday 02.04.16
FGR 0 Wrexham 0
ROVERS DENIED BY TENACIOUS WREXHAM
Richard Joyce
There are four massive matches remaining in Forest Green Rovers' National League season after one-time Football League outfit Wrexham held Ady Pennock's side to a goalless draw at The New Lawn. A relentless final half-hour of FGR attacking football, against a Gary Mills side who were down to nine men following red cards shown to Blaine Hudson and Connor Jennings, just couldn't see Rovers find a breakthrough against a team desperate to fight their way into the play-offs. The result now means Forest Green are four points behind leaders Cheltenham Town with meetings against Braintree, Woking, FC Halifax and Dover Athletic still to come.

From the start Rovers were bright in the April sun in front of a good home crowd, and Marcus Kelly had the game's first effort on nine minutes, although he couldn't keep his strike down. James Jennings meanwhile

A
P
R
I
L

came agonizingly close to breaking the deadlock when his header from a corner was cleared off the line midway through a half, where at the break, FGR would have felt their early dominance had been deserving of a couple more clearer opportunities.

A rare attacking glimpse from the away side early in the second 45 minutes saw man of the match Charlie Clough forced to defend well to deny Connor Jennings, who had broken clear in the box. From that point onwards though it was Forest Green who huffed and puffed in a frustrating half that saw the match officials fail to let the game flow.

Wrexham keeper Rhys Taylor was well alert to keep his side level, and produced the first of several good stops on 67 minutes when he reacted well to Elliott Frear's stretching effort. Then came the first of the North Wales team's two reds. The sluggish Hudson got the wrong side of Kurtis Guthrie who had broken through, and was given his marching orders. And only three minutes later Wrexham's trip to Gloucestershire became an even harder task when skipper Jennings was shown a second yellow card and an early trip to the changing rooms.

Down to nine, Pennock's troops continued to fight their way through to a much needed goal, but former Chelsea youngster Taylor again made a great stop to prevent Frear from hitting the net.

After Jennings had volleyed over a Darren Carter cross, Guthrie powered wide with a big chance as the tie entered stoppage time. He couldn't slam home when the ball dropped to him in a busy Wrexham area. Another Guthrie header in five minutes of additional time flew over, while substitute Kieffer Moore's header zipped just off target in a dramatic late FGR onslaught. One final opportunity fell to Jon Parkin. But the experienced hit man couldn't again find a way past Taylor, who made one final crucial save to earn the travelling fans a massive point at The New Lawn.

HARD ROAD TO RAGS OR RICHES DRAWS CLOSER FOR FGR
Jokerman

Saturday morning finds Forest Green Rovers five points adrift in their quest for the title with five fixtures remaining. Five wins is a tall order and still would not guarantee success but would lift morale in view of recent disappointments. One Forum thread understandably pushed Footieman over the edge. One of the lessons of history is that nothing is often a good thing to do and always a clever thing to say.

Today's visitors, Wrexham have brought an impressive 500-plus contingent of supporters, sheep lovers to the core. Shaun and his mates have studied the fixture list and duly fled from the adjacent field. In view of the pre-match appetiser, Rovers will be looking to slaughter the opposition this afternoon, in the virtual sense of course. Under blue skies with temperatures in the mid-teens the teams take the field. Manager Pennock has kept faith with Guthrie and Kelly while Frear and Wedgbury return to the starting line-up.

Wrexham kicked off but it was Forest Green that took the initiative, winning a couple of early corners before Guthrie, Kelly and Frear combined to set up Jennings on the overlap, but he could only hit the ball into the side netting. Wrexham's first corner was on 20 minutes and easily cleared to the other end, where Rovers won two more and from the second came close to opening the scoring. Frear picked out Jennings who directed his header inside the left-hand post, only to see Wrexham defender Evans clear the ball off the line. Racine was booked for an innocuous foul which was to become significant and referee Treleaven's starter for nine. The first half ended with Rovers having dominated but neither keeper had made a save. Indeed, Wrexham were showing no ambition to mount any worthwhile pressure on the Rovers defence.

The second half started in the same vein with Arnold in the Rovers goal all but redundant. However, on 53minutes, Wrexham came their closest to scoring when Connor Jennings for the visitors, brother to James of Rovers, was dispossessed well inside the area by a terrific tackle by Clough.

Five minutes later Rovers should have been in front when Frear broke through the centre with Kelly in close support. A simple pass would have sufficed but indecision and the chance was lost.

On the hour the bookings took an upturn when Wrexham's Smith was in an altercation with a linesman that also saw M-Brown booked. Guthrie's name was added when he was jumped into by keeper Taylor after being first to a cross from Bennett. On 70 minutes Parkin replaced the ineffective M-Brown. Wrexham then proceeded to make it easy for Treleaven to become the highest-profile man on the pitch. In a three-minute spell Hudson was shown a straight red for preventing Guthrie from breaking through, and his teammate Jennings joined him in the shower when he completed a set of three that he won't be bragging about, for a deliberate trip on Carter in an off-the-ball incident.

Cue siege mentality from Wrexham, all-out assault from Rovers. A 30-yard drive from Frear had Taylor diving low to his left to turn the ball round the post. The same player was again on target from an acute angle but Taylor was equal to the task. The clock was ticking and Pennock replaced Frear with Moore. Frear was not amused. As the game entered five minutes of added-time, Rovers missed their best chances of victory. The first fell to Guthrie who under no pressure fired the ball wide from 12 yards. The second came when Clough headed across goal to Parkin who shanked his effort from close range and Taylor gathered.

The game was up and the referee went off to write his memoirs. Four consecutive drawn matches have done immeasurable damage to Forest Green's title hopes. Failure to hold two-goal advantages twice, score goals at home against Aldershot and nine-man Wrexham, have underlined the team's frailties as the season entered its defining period. Four matches remain but the title looks a forlorn hope unless the neighbours implode. The squeaky bum competition looks imminent. On current form you have to ask yourself, 'Are you sitting comfortably?'

Saturday 09.04.16
Braintree Town 1 FGR 1
CARTER EARNS ROVERS A POINT AT THE AVANTI
Richard Joyce
Darren Carter's first-half equalizer earned Forest Green Rovers a fifth consecutive draw, at the Avanti Stadium against play-off-chasing Braintree Town. The midfielder capped a fine first-half showing with a goal towards the latter end of the opening 45 minutes after Braintree captain Kenny Davis had put the Essex side ahead from the penalty spot. Ady Pennock's side travelled desperate for three points, but they couldn't quite manage to break down an Irons outfit who in the second half had a series of chances themselves.

A bright opening saw Kurtis Guthrie come inches away from opening the scoring after only five minutes. He flicked a terrific Keanu Marsh-Brown cross towards goal and Braintree goalkeeper Tom King was relieved to watch the ball zoom past his back post. Sam Habergham's crucial block on 20 minutes denied a fantastic FGR breakaway that saw Elliott Frear do well to set up the onrushing Carter whose strike was deflected away. Braintree had failed to register a shot on Rovers' goal; however, they would be the first team to find the net, and they did so via the penalty spot just after the half-hour mark. James Jennings got caught the wrong side of Chez Isaac and brought the former Watford man down, which allowed midfied man Davis the chance to send Steve Arnold the wrong way from the spot.

The response from Forest Green was swift as Carter levelled proceedings three minutes later. He seized upon Jon Parkin's good knock-down and slammed home past Millwall loanee King. Jennings almost came close to turning the match completely into Rovers' favour, but he saw his header from a Carter cross just before half time narrowly go over.

Frear marked a positive start to the second half with a long-range attempt that went wide, and Parkin's hooked effort from an Arnold long ball failed to test King. Braintree then forced Arnold into his first save of the game on the hour mark when Isaac was allowed the room to blast a shot off on goal that was gathered at the second attempt. Following Guthrie's excellent weaving run that ended with a tame shot on goal, the home side enjoyed a bright spell that started with Mitch Brundle's long-range free kick that was well saved by Arnold after Charlie Clough had upended the tricky Akinola. And the Rovers goalkeeper produced the save of the game minutes later from Akinola when he got down low to turn his low hit away.

A vital Clough clearance at the final moment then denied Braintree substitute Michael Cheek from rolling in after he'd beaten Arnold to a long ball. And it was the crossbar that would next deny the hosts when Brundle saw his header on goal pelt against the woodwork from Isaac's lifted free kick.

Pennock made three substitutions to freshen up some attacking energy for the final quarter of an hour, which included Marcus Kelly being introduced for his hundredth league appearance. However, they couldn't make the difference needed to find a winning goal, and Rovers returned home to Gloucestershire with a fifth consecutive point.

DESTINATION BRAINTREE
Rambling Man

Restored to health, I was looking forward to the last-chance-saloon fixture at Cressing Road, Braintree. Sorry, the Avanti Stadium. Both teams needed a win – Rovers to nurture fading homes of the Championship pennant, The Iron to revive play-off hopes after three losses. Should be a cracker?

My turn to take the wheel. The rendezvous at 0930 hours at The Glider Café saw Foggy and Deep-Throat climb aboard. Traffic on the M4, M25 and M11 was mercifully fluid and after a pit-stop at South Mimms Services, we arrived at our intermediate destination of culture – Paycocke's House at Coggeshall, ten minutes east of Braintree.

Paycocke's maintains the noble tradition of Tudor mansions near National League stadia. Shows how far sighted the heavy-hitters were in those days, choosing to build near future centres of the beautiful game.

A
P
R
I
L

Thomas Paycocke was a wealthy, self-made man, the son of a butcher. He had the house built in 1509, the year in which Henry VII died, to be succeeded by his son, the flamboyant Henry VIII. The house is the usual half-timbered recipe and features elaborately carved ceiling beams and linen-fold oak wall panelling, characteristic of the time. It is cosily wonky and comes over as a comfortable family home rather than a mansion. Well worth our fleeting visit.

The Avanti is less picturesque but makes up for that in its unique character. The ground and the immediate area owe their existence to Crittall Windows – those cold, condensation-prone metal-framed jobs we seniors remember only too well. You arrive via a tortuous route through a post-war social housing estate. A main seated stand on one side is flanked by a covered standing terrace on the other. Chunky steel girders are in profusion. The ends have narrow uncovered terraces. The pitch itself is a constant problem to the home team, good drainage thwarted by underlying London clay. Oh, and such fans' separation as exists is demarcated by yellow cones courtesy of the North Essex Parking Partnership!

2016 marked my third or fourth visit to Cressing Road. Foggy and I were entertained by familiar and friendly faces in the Directors' Portakabin. Last time they'd had me rocking with the tales of a run-in with the National League over a match cancellation: stated reason, a squadron of ducks swimming through midfield. This time, their proud boast was to have drunk themselves through the Macclesfield Directors' Suite's stock of hospitality alcohol. Believe me, they are full value.

The resultant 1-1 suited neither side. Rovers dominated the first half but as has happened too often lately, guilt-edged chances were spurned. A rare foray by the home team brought a penalty and a scarcely deserved lead, quickly rubbed out by Carter seizing on a loose ball with some venom. The second half did not threaten a glut of goals and the frustrating parity was unbroken. So ended a pleasant day. But realistically, Rovers must now gear themselves for the play-offs while Braintree need snookers.

Saturday 16.04.16
FGR 1 Woking 2
FOREST GREEN PUNISHED LATE ON BY THE CARDS
Richard Joyce

A stoppage-time winner from Woking's on-loan Norwich City defender Cameron Norman condemned Forest Green Rovers to defeat in the club's penultimate home fixture of the season. The centre back slammed home in the dying moments at The New Lawn to steal the points in a clash that Rovers will have felt they should have had wrapped up and finished by half time. Kieffer Moore's early goal had put Ady Pennock's charges in the lead, but after failing to capitalize on a whole host of chances, the away side equalized in the second half from the penalty spot, and then saw Norman smash in late on.

Looking to get back to winning ways, FGR were thankful for a crucial save from Steve Arnold after only three minutes early on when the dangerous Bruno Andrade broke clear in the game's first major opening. An open first ten minutes then saw Forest Green strike first blood as Moore finished well to put his team into the lead. Sam Wedgbury's wonderful through ball was latched onto by Moore's run into space, and he dispatched a classy finish past the on rushing Jake Cole to break the deadlock.

The rest of the half saw Rovers take control, and they were denied on several occasions by Cole or the offside flag. Aaron Racine's free header didn't have enough power behind it from Wedgbury's free kick on 16 minutes, while Elliott Frear couldn't direct his right-footed effort on target after Moore's cross into the box had fallen to the winger. Frear then turned provider for Kurtis Guthrie who saw his header settle on the roof of the Woking net. Then two big chances just before half time proved crucial in terms of keeping the away outfit in touch. Firstly Cole made a fantastic stop to prevent Guthrie from firing in, and then the front man was denied a goal by the linesman's flag for offside after Keanu Marsh-Brown had teed him up.

FGR started the second half appearing to be in a similar mood when, after only two minutes into the second 45 minutes, Guthrie slammed another attempt just over. Although after a period of inactivity Woking would get back into it from the penalty spot when David Pipe brought down the pacey Andrade who had burst clear. On-loan Dagenham & Redbridge forward Dan Carr saw his spot kick almost kept out by Arnold who couldn't get a strong enough hand on the ball and the Surrey side was level.

A flood of openings in the final ten minutes couldn't see FGR regain the lead, despite a good chance from Frear, and a heading opportunity at the back post for Darren Carter. Moore then had two massive opportunities at the death. His header was firstly clawed away from goal by Cole, while another aerial attempt seconds later slammed against the crossbar. Within a minute Rovers' failure to find the target again was punished. Norman was the beneficiary as he latched onto a free ball in the box from a set piece, and drove home through a sea of bodies to clinch the away side victory.

A
P
R
I
L

ROVERS COMMIT CARDINAL SIN AT THE DEATH
Jokerman

Five games unbeaten, five games without winning and the title has all but gone. Forest Green Rovers need just three points from three remaining fixtures to guarantee runner-up spot in the National League, the highest in the club's history. It is unfortunate that this league is the only one offering just a single automatic promotion place. A second is gained by negotiating the best-of-three competition that should be sponsored by 'Andrex' and carry a health warning.

After six years at the helm Dale Vince will be hoping the club can succeed this year, an achievement that could possibly accelerate the club moving to sea level. Today's visitors Woking are already 'on the beach' and Rovers manager Ady Pennock must use these three games to give his side a cutting edge in time for the nerve shredder.

Both Parkin and Bennett are sidelined and are replaced by Pipe and Moore. Plenty of sunshine but Rovers are kicking into a bitter wind in the first half. An early warning for the home side comes after only three minutes when Woking winger Andrade beats Pipe for pace and fires a shot across Arnold, who saves diving low to his left. It was Rovers, however, who were looking more likely and on ten minutes they took the lead. Carter linked well with Wedgbury and it was the latter who slipped a pass inside to Moore, running diagonally across the area. The striker hit the ball first time, back across the Woking keeper Cole and inside the left-hand post.

Rovers then proceeded to create several goalscoring chances. Jennings sent Moore down the left and he pulled the ball back to Frear whose low shot went narrowly wide. Frear then linked with M-Brown who crossed for Guthrie but his header put the ball on the top netting. Probably the best move of the half saw Moore draw the defence, which enabled Wedgbury to thread an exquisite pass through to M-Brown into the area. Opting to ensure a certain goal, he slipped a pass to Guthrie who frustratingly was offside. It had been a very open first half with both sides seeing plenty of possession but Forest Green were by far the more creative.

The second half carried on in the same vein with Rovers pressing for a second goal. A great flowing move ended with Guthrie putting Moore through with a clear sight of goal but his shot was weak and Cole saved easily. At the other end Andrade had a free kick from the edge of the area comfortably saved by Arnold. On 69 minutes the same player hit Rovers on the break, again outrunning Pipe down the left, cutting into the area where the Rovers skipper made a desperate tackle and the referee pointed to the spot. Carr stepped up and struck the ball low to the left. Arnold anticipated correctly but the ball went in off his arm and the post.

Pennock made changes: Williams for Guthrie and Jeffrey for M-Brown. Woking followed up with a couple of corners but it was Rovers who did all the pressing. Frear had a powerful shot on the turn well saved by Cole and a Jennings header was deflected inches wide by Carter at the back post. Kelly replaced Carter for the final minutes and Rovers won several corners. On 89 minutes Moore was very unlucky not to score. Jeffrey picked the tall striker out with a cross from the right only to see his header cleared from under the bar by Norman. The ball found its way back to Jeffrey who again crossed to Moore but this time his header struck the crossbar and went over.

The game went in to four minutes of added-time and Woking won a corner on the right. Arnold punched the ball clear only as far as Andrade who hit his cross to the back post, where Arnold and Clough impeded each other, and the ball dropped to Norman who hit a low shot inside the left-hand post. For the 60 travelling Woking fans it was momentous and for FGR fans it was calamitous. It was a disappointing outcome for Rovers who created enough chances to win several games. The brickbats are out, of course, and social media with its million tons of baggage. Expectation is the factor that unbalances the football supporters mind to reasonable thinking. One may not agree with Mr Vince and his way of running the football club, but is the venture unsuccessful? Ask a Tranmere fan. Chairman? Ask a Newcastle fan. Hope. Do not become a no-hoper or all is lost. The play-offs beckon. Keep the faith or take up gardening.

FGR V WOKING
FGR Student Ambassador Isabelle Arris
Hi, I'm Isabelle Arris and I've almost finished my first year representing Forest Green as an ambassador. To promote the club at my school, I have a noticeboard with the upcoming matches, league table and previous results. I also email about upcoming games and vouchers that are available. I have come to most home games with my family and have even been with Sofia, my Spanish exchange partner! After joining the Prediction League when Mr Butterworth suggested it to the ambassadors, I won my first month predicting and this week I predicted a 3-0 win for the Rovers against Woking.

Today, FGR go up against Woking who are 15th in the table. A win in this match would secure second place and reduce the gap from Cheltenham if they don't win. Woking, who have drawn three times in their last four games, have only got three points in their last eight games.

Within the first few minutes of kick-off, both teams had already had shots, with Moore having his deflected off the line. In the tenth minute, Moore managed to place the ball in the bottom left corner of the net to put FGR ahead. Play was even after the goal, with the ball switching ends and both teams having shots. Woking even managed to kick the ball over the stand! Another chance was lost in the 31st minute when Marsh-Brown's shot on target was saved by the goalie. Throughout the first half, the physio came on twice, both for FGR players, Pipe and Racine. The first half ended with Forest Green in the lead after Arnold managed to catch Woking's free kick shot in the 47th minute.

Throughout this season, sometimes I have had a meal with my dad in the Carole Embrey Suite before kick-off but today we decided to have some chips at half time – which were delicious as always!

The second half started off quite slowly. However, seven minutes in, Pipe had to clear a Woking shot off the line after a great run by Murtagh. Woking came out with more purpose from their half-time team talk; in my opinion Forest Green always seems to take a while to get going. In the 67th minute, Woking won a penalty after Pipe pulled Andrade, one of Woking's fastest players, down at the edge of the goal. Woking's number 23 took the penalty and scored in the bottom left, bringing the score to 1-1. FGR tried to win back the lead but Frear's shot was saved by the goalkeeper and Moore hit the crossbar.

Then in the 91st minute, after a fumble in the box where Clough got in Arnold's way, Woking managed to score, putting them in the lead. The final score was 2-1 to The Cards, ending their 14-match run of no wins and meaning that we still have not secured second place in the table. I am looking forward to the play-offs and, if we win, the chance to go to Wembley for the first time. I would just like to thank Mr Butterworth for introducing me to the Ambassador Scheme and for all of his hard work this season.

Saturday 23.04.16
FGR 0 FC Halifax Town 1
RECORD-BREAKING FINISH DESPITE DEFEAT
Richard Joyce

A second half Shaquille McDonald goal helped FC Halifax Town to a vital win at The New Lawn in Forest Green Rovers' final home match ahead of the play-offs. The on-loan Derby County youngster came off the bench and helped drag the Shaymen out of the bottom four with a major three points, as FGR suffered three worrying injuries ahead of next month's play-off semi-finals. Sam Wedgbury was stretchered off just before half time with a bad knee injury, while Dale Bennett limped off with a hamstring problem, and Anthony Jeffrey's ankle saw him become the third Rovers player forced off.

It was an unwanted end to FGR's final home game of the league campaign, although Grimsby Town's defeat elsewhere confirmed a second place finish for Ady Pennock's side – a second consecutive year the Rovers boss has led the club to a highest league finish.

Halifax, managed by former Forest Green manager Jim Harvey, started positively. Kingsley James saw an early attempt go over, while Richard Peniket forced Steve Arnold into a good stop. Gradually though, Rovers came into the game, and a delightful touch from Brett Williams set the forward free, only for him to drag his shot wide when he had got into a shooting position. Then came a bizarre five-minute spell at the end of the half. Wedgbury went down with a likely season-ending injury, while Bennett and Jeffrey also limped off, and at the same time the away side saw Hamza Bencherif and Peniket go off injured as well.

The injuries disrupted what had been an entertaining affair that at times lacked quality, but it again picked up once the second half began, and Jon Parkin went close with a volley on the turn early on.

And just three minutes later FGR had the ball in the back of the net. However, the linesman's flag denied Marcus Kelly, whose free kick from a wide area had nestled in Sam Johnson's goal, with an offside decision. Substitute Elliott Frear teed Parkin for another hit that went narrowly over, but then on 70 minutes McDonald whipped the ball home from close range after a set piece had fallen to him, to break the deadlock.

An urgent FGR comeback began, but they struggled to test Halifax's glove-man Johnson, despite a header from Kieffer Moore and a long-range hit from James Jennings. Kurtis Guthrie had a great chance in the final ten minutes after he had done well to break through; however, he couldn't apply the much-needed finish, as he powered over the bar. At the full-time whistle results elsewhere had confirmed Forest Green's record second-place finish, but significant injuries put a dampener on proceedings, ahead of next weekend's final trip of the season to Dover.

THE MISERABLE HAVE NO OTHER MEDICINE – BUT ONLY HOPE
Jokerman

The penultimate home game of the season requires Forest Green Rovers to gain a point to secure second place in the National League. Rovers

A
P
R
I
L

fans, however, will be hoping for a return to form from their side to whom winning is but a distant memory. Confidence is a prerequisite going into the play-offs and FGR have ten days to find some. Today's visitors, Halifax Town, are in the 'drop zone', desperate for points and will make it difficult for Rovers.

Manager Ady Pennock has hinted at making changes to his starting line-up and so it proves. Racine and Carter do not feature and there are starts for both Jeffrey and Jefford. Parkin leads the attack supported by Williams. Frear and Jennings are benched. The odds on an FGR win are noticeably lengthened prior to kick-off to nearly even money. The sun is shining but it is a nipping and an eager air that greets the teams as they parade.

Halifax start the brighter and carry the first threat on 14 minutes when Peniket drives into the area and hits a fierce shot straight at Arnold who clears. Rovers' line-up looks unbalanced and for 30 minutes the defence does a containing job on the more lively attack of Halifax. On 34 minutes a long ball from Moore down the right flank is expertly controlled by Williams as it drops over his shoulder. He cuts inside but drags his shot wide of the right-hand post. A minute later Wedgbury goes down off the ball in agony and it is plain to see he has a serious injury. Stretchered off after lengthy treatment, he is replaced by Pipe. Halifax continue to press and James tests Arnold from distance which the Rovers keeper is equal to. Arnold's distribution is slow, making Rovers' attacks ponderous.

In added time in the first half Bennett pulls up lame and is replaced by Jennings. At the other end of the pitch Halifax player Peniket is a victim of injury which sees him also stretchered off. Added time continues and Wroe, the Halifax skipper, hits a curling shot that beats Arnold but rattles the top netting, deceiving the visiting fans who think he has scored. Forest Green then lost Jeffrey who limped off to be replaced by Frear, thus exhausting the subs' bench for Rovers. When sorrows come, they come not in single spies ... but in battalions.

The home fans were not impressed by the first-half display and it is fair to say there was some discontent amid the mutterings during the break. The second half started better for Rovers and they were showing more purpose in attack. Frear was raiding down the left and cut the ball back to Parkin whose excellent shot on the turn was deflected wide. On 52 minutes Johnson, the Halifax keeper, did well to pluck a Kelly corner off the head of Moore. Soon after, Kelly hit a terrific free kick from the right-hand touchline that ended up in the net but was ruled out for offside against the converging attackers. Minutes later Jennings made a goal-saving block from Halifax substitute Hughes who latched on to a cross from MacDonald.

Rovers were enjoying a good spell and around the hour their best move materialized down the left, where Frear exchanged passes with Jefford and the ball was pulled back to Parkin, who was so unlucky to see his chipped effort beat Johnson but drop just over the crossbar. MacDonald was replaced by the six-foot-plus Hattersley on 69 minutes for Halifax and a minute later they took the lead. A corner on the right by Wroe fell on the edge of the box where Burrow stooped low to head goalward. Sub Shaq McDonald was first to react and he blasted the ball low into the right-hand corner of the goal. The travelling Halifax fans were ecstatic; Rovers fans were gutted.

With 20 minutes left there was still time but the goal seemed to knock Rovers and they began to moan at each other as passes went astray. On 83 minutes Hattersley headed narrowly wide from a corner that saw Rovers launch a quick attack, which ended with Guthrie holding off two defenders but with a clear shot at goal, he blazed the ball over the bar. After that Rovers ran out of ideas and Halifax ran the clock down and kept their National League status hopes alive. Results elsewhere helped Forest Green to secure second place with a game remaining.

What hath this day deserved? What hath it done
That in golden letters should be set
Among the high tides in the calender?
For Halifax no doubt for FGR I think not.
It is required
You do awake your faith.

Saturday 30.04.16
Dover Athletic 0 FGR 1
BARTLETT GETS OFF TO A WINNING FGR START
Richard Joyce

New caretaker manager Scott Bartlett began his temporary managerial spell in impressive fashion with a well-deserved victory at Dover Athletic, who will now be his side's play-off semi-final opponents. Appointed to the role late on Wednesday, in only a few days Bartlett managed to engineer Forest Green's first win in over six weeks, as the squad picked up a morale-boosting victory at a ground where the two teams will do battle all over again on Wednesday night.

Brett Williams's strike early in the second half was enough to seal a

A P R I L

welcome three points, as a strong defensive showing saw goalkeeper Steve Arnold keep a welcome clean sheet.

A number of selection decisions saw Bartlett make a number of changes to his new side. He included FGR Academy second-year midfielder Joe Stokes in his starting XI. The Wotton-under-Edge 18-year-old shone in midfield on his debut, as Rovers showed plenty of ambition and excitement throughout the tie.

Elliott Frear's low hit on 20 minutes was the afternoon's first notable opportunity, and the winger's strike was pushed onto the post by Dover keeper Andy Rafferty. Minutes later Tom Murphy headed wide inside the FGR box, while the hosts also saw Tyrone Marsh screw a shot off target when he was through on goal. Then, for the second time in the half, James Jennings's threat from a set piece once again saw him go close, as he hit the woodwork from Marcus Kelly's fine delivery.

Immediately after the break Rovers started brightly, and they were rewarded when Williams burst through to open the scoring. Great work by Aaron Racine saw him slip the ball into the path of Williams, who drove from deep and buried a shot despite Rafferty's best efforts to keep it out.

Racine then had a go himself with a header that Rafferty saved just before the hour mark, while only a minute later his central defensive partner, Charlie Clough, saw a scooped effort kept away from goal. A vital Aswad Thomas block on the line for the hosts denied Racine again with another header.

With both team's play-off involvement already secured before the game, a number of changes through substitutions disrupted the flow of the tie. However, FGR continued to create chances, and replacement Keanu Marsh-Brown punched an effort towards goal, and Stokes was close to finding the perfect ball for Ben Jefford who couldn't quite force home from close range. One final opportunity for the hosts to salvage a draw saw Connor Essam head wide late on, as the final result, combined with scorelines elsewhere, confirmed that Forest Green and Dover will now go head-to-head in the play-offs to fight it out for a place at Wembley. Bartlett will take his squad back to The Crabble on Wednesday night in the play-off semi-finals first leg, and will then host Dover on Saturday night in what promises to be two huge games.

DESTINATION DOVER
Rambling Man
As things were to transpire, the contest at Dover would be the second in

a season's quartet. More on that later. It had been a momentous week at The New Lawn. Successive home defeats to Woking and Halifax were more evidence of two months' crumbling form and morale, the depth of which was probably not understood outside the Five Valleys. Suffice to say that The Electric Chair's decision for change was universally popular, as was Scotty Bartlett's second stint as *numero uno*. Certainly, it put a spring into the pedal of those of us who drive thousands of miles in support of our team.

So with spring-like optimism breaking out all over, I collected Foggy and Deep-Throat from the Glider and chugged eastward in the venerable Passat. Our rendezvous had been 9.30 a.m. despite the late 5.30 p.m. kick-off, as we were determined to explore one of the famous castles of Kent.

By noon, we were rolling up the drive of Hever Castle, around ten miles south of the half past six position on the M25 clock. Founded in the thirteenth century, Hever is most famous for being the ancestral seat of the Boleyns and childhood home of the ill-fated Anne, second bride of Henry VIII.

From the outside, it has all the credentials. Its white stone elevations have the requisite towers, battlements and draw-bridge, surrounded by a carp-infested moat. The lovely formal gardens and lake owe more to comfort than defence, and that is the tale inside too – more a fortified manor house than a draughty old castle.

We have the fabulously wealthy Astor family to thank for saving the castle and estate from rack and ruin. They bought in at the start of the twentieth century and restored the place in just five years. The carved panelled and beamed and moulded ceilings of the interior are staggering, matched by wonderful period paintings and furnishings featuring the Boleyns, Henrys VII and VIII, Thomas Cranmer and a host of famous Tudor courtiers. And the displays and collections take you through the centuries to the Jacobite period and the Astor family. Highly recommended.

Some four hours later, we arrived at the characterful Crabble, ancestral home of Dover AFC. It felt good to be back on a hill, albeit cut in halfway up a chalk one, rather than atop a Cotswold. Smiles aplenty and warm greetings smacked of genuine local supporters, not just end-of-term atmosphere.

Both teams were understrength, Dover the more so. But star billing went to Rovers' 18-year-old Academy teenager Joe Stokes making his debut, standing in for cruelly injured Wedge. Rovers were dominant

A P R I L

throughout and took a welcome win through a well-taken goal by Brett Williams. It meant Dover dropped two places to fifth due to Braintree's demolition of Altrincham, and that Rovers and Dover would meet in the play-offs starting back in Kent on 4 May. As we headed home well after 8 p.m., Joe was still in his FGR kit on the pitch, grin wider than the Dartford crossing.

Rambling Man at Wembley before kick-off.

The *Gloucester Citizen*'s take on Rambling Man's delayed trip to The Balkans. (*With kind permission of* Stroud Life)

PRIDE AND PASSION RESTORED, Scotty so nearly secured dreamland and immortality! A second win at Dover Athletic in four days, and a draw at home at a 'rocking' New Lawn three days later meant Rovers had reached the deciding hurdle – The Play-Off Final at Wembley v perennial bridesmaids, Grimsby Town. Ultimately though, cruel injuries to Wedgbury, Sinclair and Kelly had left a 65-year-old midfield pairing that could not compete with Grimsby's energy. The joyful hordes from The Theatre of Fish deserved the win, with an impressive display. Moreover, Grimsby's manager Paul Hurst had showed great dignity and strength of character to guide his side back into the Football League, after their unfair defeat by the Gas 12 months earlier. Yet it was a glorious effort and a fine finale to Rovers' season that could or should have been. Optimism was resurgent replacing April's despair.

I wandered lonely as a fan
Who sits on high o'er Cotswold hills,
Across the valley I scan
A host of lime green shirts – chills, spills and thrills;
A new season starts, beneath Forest Green trees,
Hopefully not stuttering or guttering but performing please.
Continuous are ours stars that must shine
and twinkle on The New Lawn sward,
They stretched in 4-4-2 line
Put opposition to the sword:
Two thousand fans saw I at a glance,
Tossing their heads, singing Rovers chants

(Excerpt from 'Words for what they are Worth' by The Farmcotian (and 'The Bard'), a reflective view of the season as a whole)

Wednesday 04.05.16
Dover Athletic 0 FGR 1 (National League play-off semi-final 1st leg)
WILLIAMS STRIKES FOR KEY FIRST-LEG VICTORY
Richard Joyce
A stunning Brett Williams strike has given Forest Green Rovers a one-goal advantage heading into the second leg of the play-off semi-finals. For the third time this season Rovers registered a victory over play-off opponents Dover Athletic, as Scott Bartlett's impressive spell in caretaker charge continued with a significant first-leg away success. Dover will now travel to Nailsworth on Saturday where the two sides do battle again, in what's

**M
A
Y**

sure to be another hotly contested and tight battle for a place at Wembley.

Early on-goal efforts on the night from the hosts' Stefan Payne and Nicky Deverdics did little to unsettle Rovers, who then forced Mitch Walker into two much-needed saves – first to deny Kurtis Guthrie, and then Keanu Marsh-Brown. A blow on the quarter-of-the-hour mark then forced FGR into a set-up change. Marcus Kelly was sadly forced to hobble off with a hamstring problem, and was replaced by Williams. The former Reading forward scored the winning goal at The Crabble at the weekend, and he would prove to be the man who would break the deadlock.

A catalogue of errors from the home side saw Marsh-Brown keep the ball in play and deliver the ball into the box, where it eventually found its way to Williams on the outside of the area, who curled a wonderful finish in to the top corner. It was a goal that knocked the home side, although to their credit they fought back with two major chances that were brilliantly defended by FGR. Charlie Clough produced an outstanding tackle to deny Ricky Miller, and then Dale Bennett's crucial block prevented Payne from slamming in what looked sure to be a goal.

A speculative Elliott Frear volley from a pinpoint Marsh-Brown cross early in the second half almost made it an early second-half double, while Dover spurned two good chances as they tried to find a way to draw level. Aswad Thomas headed wide from a corner, and Miller powered off target after he had let fly in a central area. Dover stopper Walker was then forced into producing another great save on 71 minutes. He tipped over Aarran Racine's header from a driven Marsh-Brown corner. A superb defensive showing ensured it was another clean sheet for Scott Bartlett's men, although the hosts did come close in the final minutes. Payne picked up the ball and found a bit of room outside the FGR box, but his right-footed hit flew the wrong way past Steve Arnold's post.

DESTINATION DOVER[2]

Rambling Man

Another day, another Dover! Just four days after completing a League win double over The Whites, came a second trip to Kent for match number three in a series of four. As usual, we met at The Glider Café, Foggy being at the helm in the Astra. Compo joined us along with a new travelling companion, Morse. The 11.45 a.m. rendezvous was early enough to allow for a forensic examination of Dover Castle, with an interim stop at a small town on the M25 called Cobham Services.

As per the previous match, the spring sun had put his hat on. So much so that the Astra's climate control was unable to cope as Foggy's passengers sweated off the pounds. It was like a mobile spa. Arrival at Dover Castle at 3 p.m. was a blessed relief. Never having ventured to this commanding fortification, I had not realized how much there was to see, nor the depth of history right back to the Iron Age. It is truly astonishing and deserved more than the two and a half hours we could afford. The crystal-clear skies maximized the breathtaking views over Dover harbour and Calais beyond. I have not been impressed by the quality of experience served up by English Heritage at other prime venues, but at Dover they have pulled out all the stops – helpful and friendly guides at every turn, clever exhibitions and film shows (in the awe-inspiring tunnels) and furnishing that really showcases the amazing castle itself. With their help, you can wonder at the Roman Pharos, Saxon church, miles of tunnels dug into the chalk hill dating from the Napoleonic wars, Dover's role and bombardment in the Second World War and of course the wonderfully complete inner castle and battlements that were founded in the twelfth century. Next time you head for the Ferries or La Manche, give the castle a chance – you'll love it.

All of which put us in a great frame of mind to renew our relationship with the peerless hosts at The Crabble. Sure, the match was highly important to both clubs, and BT was out in force with live coverage. But that did not get in the way of good, old-fashioned hospitality whether from the marshals, supporters or club officials. Make no mistake, Dover AFC is set up on the right lines and has been a joy to visit. Their number will be well received at The New Lawn.

When hostilities got underway, Rovers showed that Scotty's revolution had good foundations. The eleven snapped into action and did not let the hosts settle. Even injuries to Kelly and Jennings did not interrupt their dominance as Steve Arnold was not called upon to save a shot all match. At the other end, Frear, Marsh-Brown, Guthrie and Carter were a constant threat along with Kelly's substitute Brett Williams. After Kelly's early departure, Rovers switched from 4-3-3 to 4-3-2-1 (I think!) with Williams relishing the opportunity to lead the line. Marsh-Brown's chasing down a lost cause ten minutes before half time, led to the ball landing at Williams's feet, outside the penalty area. One touch then a curled effort into the top corner. His second cracking strike in four days, and another worthy winner.

Thus, advantage FGR and growing confidence among a happily united squad, management and support. All know that this is just half time in the tie and that the job must be completed at The New Lawn before dreams of Wembley and beyond can be realized. Bring it on.

GROUNDHOG DAY

Jokerman

Wednesday, 4 May 2016. Gearing up for two, possibly three, games that will define Forest Green Rovers' league status. Around Easter time the manager and players were crushed under the pressure of keeping up with Cheltenham Town at the top of the National League. Affable Ady, maybe that was his problem, Mr Nice Guy. The title lost, Chairman Vince made a decision. Alas poor Pennock, his head did roll. The Axminster soaked up the crimson and the back room staff fled the bean field. Once again Scott Bartlett was called upon to steady the ship. Done at this evening's venue last Saturday by a Williams goal to nil, albeit both managers played mind games with team selection ahead of this more vital fixture.

To be brutal the team have collapsed in a heap, have injury problems, a toothless attack and a vacancy for a manager heading into this play-off semi-final first leg at Dover. One could be forgiven if expectations are guarded. However, as the supporters' coaches begin the long haul east, it begs the question: Will this be the road to glory ... or perdition? The latter is out of the question so Forest Green Rovers have no choice. The fans on board go in search of heroes.

Kendo's route splits the country from the Severn to the South East coast. Perfect weather, blue skies, sun soaking the oil fields of rape flower and raptors gliding effortlessly above 40 shades of green. Spring at last. An ale or three in the beer garden of The Cricketers' Arms provided a tranquil setting prior to the hill walk to the away end. (The slope of the playing surface from side to side can be a worry for heavy drinkers.)

Just over a hundred Rovers supporters are gathered behind the goal. Outnumbered 20 to one, the home support is drowned out, no bother. Manager Bartlett recalls Bennett and Sinclair to the starting line-up with M-Brown and Guthrie leading the attack. Dover field almost an entire new eleven from Saturday's fixture.

Dover provides the first threat when Modeste crosses to Millar but Arnold catches his flicked shot comfortably. Deverdics then fired a free kick over the bar before Rovers replied at the other end with a Guthrie shot on the turn which Walker, the Dover custodian, pushed round the post. This was quickly followed by an M-Brown shot from distance that had Walker at full stretch to tip over the bar. Forest Green's injury woes increased on 15 minutes when Kelly, visibly upset, was helped off with a hamstring problem and replaced by Williams. Undaunted, Rovers pressed with a couple of corners that culminated with a Bennett shot that just cleared the crossbar.

Dover replied in kind but it was Williams for Forest Green who set the game alight on 35 minutes. M-Brown chased a clearance down to the corner flag and hit a cross into the centre where the ball was scrambled away only as far as Williams on the left-hand corner of the area. The striker took a touch and struck the ball perfectly over Walker and inside the right-hand post. The Rovers contingent at the other end went mildly berserk. Dover hit back and on 43 minutes: a misjudgement by Racine put Miller clean through on Arnold 12 yards out. About to score, Clough threw himself in front to block away the danger. Breathtaking. Seconds later it was even closer to being level. Modeste, always a threat, reached the by-line and hit a low cross inside the six-yard box where Payne, about to side-foot the ball past Arnold, was denied by Bennett who somehow contrived to put his foot in and the ball looped up over the bar. Heart-stopping. As the half ended M-Brown went close but his shot was deflected narrowly over the bar. The Rovers faithful gave their team a rousing send-off as the half-time whistle sounded.

The second half was a scrappy affair and never reached the excitement levels of the first period. Neither keeper was really troubled and Forest Green were dealt yet another blow when Jennings hobbled off on 68 minutes with an ankle injury following a tackle. Pipe was more than an able replacement and the Rovers defence dealt well with the threat from Modeste and Deverdics. The best chance of the half fell to Payne when he was set up on the edge of the box with a clear shot at goal but screwed the ball wide of the upright. In added time a Deverdics free kick from the D gave Payne a shot that was blocked and Rovers headed home with a well-earned though narrow victory.

The players came and returned the plaudits with the Rovers fans at the final whistle. The supporters' long journey in search of heroes had not been in vain. The job is half done; focus and application will be key at TNL on Saturday evening. Williams is on a hat-trick. Set that wake-up call. Sonny and Cher are warming up.

Saturday 07.05.16
FGR 1 Dover Athletic 1 (National League play-off semi-final 2nd leg)
FGR ARE WEMBLEY-BOUND FOR PLAY-OFF FINAL
Richard Joyce
Forest Green Rovers will go to Wembley to contest the National League promotion final after Keanu Marsh-Brown's stunning goal sealed a 2-1 aggregate victory over Dover Athletic in the play-off semi-final second leg at The New Lawn. Already leading by one goal heading into the tie after

**M
A
Y**

Wednesday's narrow victory down at Dover, Marsh-Brown's delicious finish was enough to earn a draw against an improved Dover side, who can hold their heads high after a tremendous season.

Ricky Miller's deflected goal had drawn the Kent side level early in the second half, although Rovers bounced back almost immediately to seal the goal that will see the club return to Wembley for the first time since 1998. Just one match now stands in the way of FGR and caretaker manager Scott Bartlett whose outstanding run of results in charge of Forest Green continue at a highly impressive pace.

From the start the away side were keen to get back on level terms. They dominated the early proceedings with both Nick Deverdics and Miller punching chances towards goal. Brett Williams was the goalscoring hero in midweek, and it appeared the front man should have had a penalty on 12 minutes after he had been brought down, but referee Michael Salisbury ignored his protests.

He bounced back by forcing Dover keeper Mitch Walker into a good save after excellent footwork to find room to get a shot away. A massive chance then fell the way of the visitors ten minutes before the break. Former Luton man Miller couldn't capitalize, blasting wide from close range.

The opening ten minutes of the second half would decide the night as Dover again started brightly. Firstly Steve Arnold saved well from a Ricky Modeste effort, and then they took the lead to draw level on aggregate. Ben Jefford was the unfortunate party as Miller's hit deflected cruelly off him to wrong-foot Arnold, and to send the away fans into raptures. Their joy was, however, short-lived as Rovers hit back almost straight away through Marsh-Brown. The England C man, pushed out to the left-hand side after an injury to Elliott Frear, picked out the top corner with a fabulous curving effort, almost reminiscent of Williams's midweek goal at The Crabble.

It was a blow for Dover who almost hit back just after the hour mark when Sam Magri's powerful strike slammed onto the bar, and they again went close when Chris Kinnear's dipping volley edged just wide. A nervy final ten minutes saw Rovers do everything to keep the ball away from goal, and it was target achieved on the full-time whistle, as the supporters streamed onto the pitch to celebrate with the players, and to start dreaming of watching Forest Green do battle on the hallowed turf at Wembley.

GREAT SCOTT! THE BOYS ARE HEADING FOR TOWN
Jokerman
This evening Forest Green Rovers are looking to move a step closer to

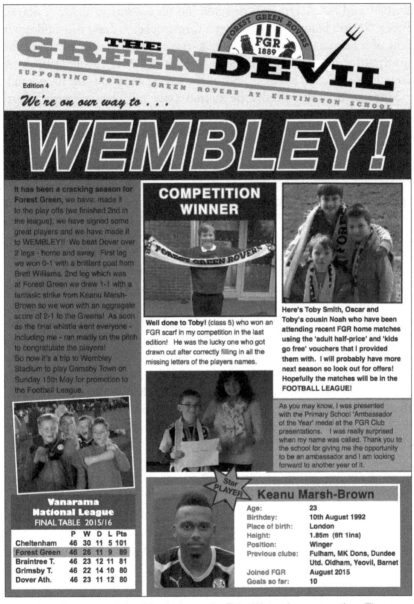

Take a bow Eastington School for Ambassador Tyler Watson's own creation, *The Green Devil* bulletin.

Football League status in the second leg of their play-off semi-final. Holding a one-goal lead after a tenacious performance at The Crabble on Wednesday night, they are favourites to progress. Stand-in manager Scott

**M
A
Y**

Bartlett and his players will be under no illusions as to the task ahead. Forest Green's home form has been a catastrophe. A draw will suffice but fans of a nervous disposition would prefer a home win not achieved for nearly three months. This fact alone will give Dover encouragement. A crowd of over 2,500 is inside TNL as the setting sun floods the East Stand.

Manager Bartlett replaces the injured Kelly and Jennings with Jefford and Williams in his starting line-up. A goal behind, it was no surprise that Dover took the initiative and for 15 minutes Rovers did a containing job. Dover striker Miller had the first shot at goal but was too high. On 15 minutes Guthrie's was the first shot on target as he forced Walker to save low down at his near post. A turn and shot from Payne on 20 minutes had Arnold merely a spectator but to the relief of Rovers fans the shot went narrowly wide of the upright. Williams replied for Rovers when he worked hard to create an opening and stuck a terrific shot across Walker, who just managed to turn the ball away for a corner.

The visitors kept pressing and Clough was booked for stopping Miller breaking through the line. It was Miller who nearly took advantage of a rare mix-up in defence by Rovers. Arnold hesitated over a loose ball but the striker lacked composure and lashed the ball wide from an acute angle. On balance Forest Green were soaking up the pressure, the defence so capable and Arnold dealing confidently with crosses this evening. In added time in the first half it was Rovers who came closest to scoring. A Frear corner from the right was met by Clough who powered a header that skimmed the bar. Half time was a welcome respite for players and fans alike from what had been a game played at a frantic pace with little time given to dwell on the ball.

Nothing changed at the restart. Dover took up where they had left off, pushing for the vital first goal. On 49 minutes they had their reward and for the Rovers defence it was the cruellest of blows. Miller cut in from the left and hit a shot across Arnold who moved to his left to cover. The ball struck Jefford and entered the net to his right. This triggered mass celebrations among the 300-plus Dover fans. Given the pattern of the game, Rovers fans began suffering from nervous tension. Frear was down and was replaced by Moore immediately after the goal.

Forest Green battled on and Jefford, showing no ill effects from his misfortune, continued to win his headers and put his foot in. For five minutes Dover sensed they were the more likely side to score again. On 54 minutes, M-Brown, the will o' the wisp with quick feet, took the ball down the left wing and cut back inside and stopped. The whole Dover defence was facing him. He jinked inside again and stopped. The anxious

Rovers fans were hurling advice. He ignored them. He jinked again and bang! There was no gap: Walker in the Dover goal knew it was covered, that the ball was going wide of the right-hand post. But M-Brown knew he had hit the sweet spot. Like an air-to-air missile, the ball curved wickedly, and for FGR fans it was delicious. Walker watched in horror as the ball not so much screamed but whistled – probably 'Dixie' – as it went past him into the net. It was hard to tell as it was drowned by the roar as 2,500 rose to acknowledge this magical goal. RJ on the mic naturally lost the plot and went all South American.

It was far from over and the visitors again stepped up a gear and kept Rovers on the back foot. They came very close to an equalizer on 62 minutes when a dangerous cross from the left had Arnold punching away from under his bar. The ball fell only as far as Magri who hit a powerful shot against the underside of the crossbar. It was a real let-off for Rovers. The game became ever more frenetic. M-Brown made a brilliant run down the left and his cross along the six-yard line was agonizingly just out of reach of Guthrie. Players on both sides were giving everything. The football may not have been technically brilliant but it was breathtaking to watch. Kinnear shot narrowly wide with Arnold beaten but FGR were holding out well as the game entered the final minutes. Parkin replaced Williams and Kamdjo came on for Carter to see the game out.

The superlatives have run out for Clough; he was literally head and shoulders above the rest and deserved MoM. However, he will not be singled out as every Forest Green player gave it their all as did the worthy Dover side. In the end, yeah, the nerves were jangling but it was Forest Green who found the Heart of Saturday Night.

Sunday 15.05.16
FGR 1 Grimsby Town 3 (National League play-off final)
PROMOTION DREAMS ARE ENDED AT WEMBLEY
Richard Joyce

Forest Green Rovers will compete again in the National League next season after Grimsby Town came out on top in the play-off final at Wembley Stadium. Two conceded goals in three first-half minutes just before half time proved significant on the biggest day in FGR's 127-year history, as the Mariners sealed their return to the Football League, making up for their penalty shoot-out loss to Bristol Rovers in last season's final.

Led by caretaker boss Scott Bartlett, Rovers did force their way back into the match thanks to Keanu Marsh-Brown's memorable long-distance strike, however they couldn't draw level, although they did see a number of good chances fall their way. Despite finishing second in the table Rovers will have to do it all over again in the fifth tier for a 19th consecutive season next term; however, they will wonder whether things could have been different were key men Rob Sinclair, Marcus Kelly and Sam Wedgbury not ruled out through injuries.

Bartlett's men started very brightly, but an end-to-end start to the occasion saw Grimsby come close a number of times early on. Steve Arnold made a good save to deny Craig Disley, and after he had comfortably gathered Omar Bogle's free kick, the goalkeeper again made a tremendous stop to keep out Bogle's attempted finish inside the six-yard box.

The influential Marsh-Brown then crossed for Kurtis Guthrie in a major FGR opening at the other end that the forward couldn't quite get on the end of. Marsh-Brown then exhibited his outstanding ability when shooting from distance as he made Grimsby's James McKeown produce an uncomfortable save from his long-range drive.

Both teams were offering a threat in front of goal, and it took another terrific Arnold push onto the post from the Mariners' nimble wide man Nathan Arnold to keep the scoreline untouched. However, that would very quickly change in a mad two minutes that saw Bogle score twice in quick succession to change the look of the game. He firstly nodded in a free kick, and then made the most of an error in the FGR box to slam home his own and Grimsby's second.

A formation change at the start of the second half was positive from Rovers and Grimsby were put under early pressure, although Jon Parkin and Charlie Clough spurned two great opportunities when through on goal. On the hour mark FGR's positive response saw them hit back. Marsh-Brown was the man responsible as his formidable smash from 30 yards flew past McKeown to edge his side back into proceedings.

From that point on though, when Rovers needed chances most, they struggled to find a way through, and apart from a couple of Darren Carter openings, it was Grimsby's Arnold who forced a good save from his namesake in the FGR goal with a low shot on 75 minutes.

A Parkin effort that flew over the bar in stoppage time appeared to be Forest Green's last chance, and Grimsby wrapped up their promotion with a goal in the dying moments. Substitute Pat Hoban's blocked shot fell kindly to Nathan Arnold who rounded the onrushing Steve Arnold to slip the ball into the back of the net in front of the travelling Mariners faithful. It was the end of FGR's promotion dreams for the season, as caretaker boss Bartlett saw his inspiring temporary spell as manager finish on one of the biggest stages of all, ahead of a new era next season under the guidance of newly appointed manager, Mark Cooper.

DESTINATION WEMBLEY
Rambling Man

Let's start at the end for a change. The line between the success you crave and relative failure is a thin one. But it should not be allowed to eradicate unprecedented landmarks over nine foregoing months. Still, it hurts. Rovers had been propelled into their first National League play-off final at the expense of Dover Athletic. Their passport comprised two goals of high quality. The winner in the first (away) leg came courtesy of resurgent striker Brett Williams, while mercurial Keanu Marsh-Brown curled the all-important equalizer in the home leg.

Rovers second-place league finish was a distant nine points ahead of their final opponents, fourth-placed Grimsby Town, so often the fall guys in the League's brutal contest for the second promotion spot. The date for the Wembley final was long set for 15 May, and that posed a giant-size problem for me: months back, Mrs Rambling Man had been pressing me to agree a trip to Montenegro. A family friend had suffered bereavement in 2015. The widow and her late husband had purchased a property in that country and she sought advice on evolving plans for its improvement. Holiday and bricks and mortar – not a bad combination in my book. I gladly agreed to help, dusting down my moribund qualifications of Chartered Surveyor (retired). As for a date, I had procrastinated through the autumn, given that Rovers' record-breaking season was in full swing. Impatient for a decision, Mrs R-B arranged that we would fly out on 15 May. Vaguely, I recall thinking, "That's fine – early summer and no football to fret about." How wrong is it possible to be? Nanoseconds after the Manchester flights were booked, The Robins deposed Rovers at the top of the table. Subsequently, our season arrowed towards the play-offs like a loosed pointy thing at an ever-looming target. With reluctance, time and again, I told everyone that I would fly to Montenegro, irrespective. At every telling, I sounded less convincing least of all to myself.

Several factors tipped the balance. Top man Scotty Bartlett stepped into the breech vacated by Ady Pennock and brought renewed sweetness and light. Flowers bloomed, birds tweeted and the players danced over the turf once more. As the Wembley final was secured, friends and fellow supporters mocked the horlicks I'd got myself into. Then, our local newshounds asked to write about my dilemma. That was it: I could stand the pretence no longer! So it was that a litany of expense and re-

**M
A
Y**

arrangement began. Mrs R-B would make the trip to Manchester alone; that was the easy bit (I'd sew the sleeves back on my shirts and unshrink my jumpers another time). Predictably, EasyJet was neither sympathetic nor accommodating: a three-figure flight cost blown.

Next challenge: how to get to Tivat, the airport at Montenegro, as soon as possible after the final whistle? Answer: impossible the same day, and difficult a day later. After much surfing, the best bet was a Monarch flight from Gatwick to Dubrovnik in Croatia, at 6.15 a.m. on Monday 16th. As the Balkan crow flies, Dubrovnik is around 25 miles north of Tivat. I booked, waving goodbye to another three-figure sum. That just left the simple obstacles of getting from Dubrovnik to the Montenegro border, getting across country to a ferry point at the Bay of Tivat, crossing the straits and reaching my destination in the hills above Tivat. Simple.

For good measure, the family threw a few more spanners into the works. Second-born, Phil, decided he'd like to come to Wembley, so chalk up two tickets and the coach and train fares from his flat in Oxford. Then, France-residing first-born arrived *chez nous* for a long weekend on 13 May and would need a lift to Stroud bus station for her return journey at 7 a.m. on the morning of the Wembley final. Oh joy. Hours of top management work by yours truly were needed before the following timetable of events emerged:

Sunday 15 May
6.45 a.m. Drive first-born to bus station. Return home to fill a backpack with FGR paraphernalia, overnight stuff and passport
9.30 a.m. Walk the two miles back to the bus station with fully stocked backpack to catch FGR special coach 13. Chew frantically to keep inevitable coach travel nausea at bay
1.00 p.m. Arrive at Wembley and find way to The Green Man PH to meet second-born
2.00 p.m. Walk to stadium to soak up atmosphere then watch our agonizing defeat
7.02 p.m. Fond goodbyes to second-born, then catch Southern Train at Wembley Stadium station to Gatwick (via Marylebone, tube to Victoria and Gatwick Express)
8.30 p.m. Exhausted and famished, check in at Hilton, South Terminal, queuing for half an hour at reception. Buy hot dog, watch The Toon thrash Spurs on Sky 1's game of the day then try to sleep.
Monday 16 May
3.30 a.m. After a wakeful night decide to get up and trudge to departures.

Security unusually free so settle down with laptop in lounge. Post my mournful account on FGR Fans Forum

6.15 a.m. Flight leaves on time and arrives at 10 a.m. local time

10.15 a.m. As arranged through contacts of friends, meet taxi driver Goran at Dubrovnik. He drives me across Croatia–Montenegro border and to the ferry at the Bay of Tivat. Long delay while he chats to the Montenegrin border guard – they belong to the same card school! Dropped at the ferry in teeming rain, wave farewell 50 euros lighter

11.00 a.m. Catch ferry to Tivat port on the south side of the bay, across the narrow straits. Telephone Mrs R-B and friend to meet me in their hire car

12 noon. Collapse into car, cold and soaking wet. Football season finally over, start of holiday in prospe.ct

In the words of David Coleman, I must now interrupt myself. On two counts: Firstly, despite angst, there had been a terrific match at Wembley even though FGR came second. Significantly, Sinclair had been added to the wounded list, joining Kelly, Wedgbury and Jennings (substitute). Yet Rovers competed well, fluffed good chances, conceded twice minutes before half time then scored the match's best goal (Keanu Marsh-Brown) with half an hour left. But with Grimsby rocking, our energy and luck expired. The third goal at the death was the coup de grace. A valiant effort but Grimsby deserved its victory and overdue return to the Football League, and secondly, it had been one amazing season: several records smashed, record support achieved, wonderful places visited and many new friends made both at home and at opponents' clubs.

That, is sport. Unpredictable, exciting, frustrating and much else besides. When the disappointment subsides, all FGR supporters should take pride from a remarkable season of unprecedented achievement on and off the pitch. Until next season, thanks for tolerating my rants and enjoy the brief respite from hostilities.

THE MARINERS CONSIGN ROVERS TO THE DEEP
Jokerman
Sunday, 15 May 2016. A date that could well resound in the history of Forest Green Rovers.

Despite a collapse in form and managerial change, the club defeated Dover Athletic in the National League play-off semi-final under interim manager Scott Bartlett. Chairman Dale Vince wasted no time appointing next season's manager to support Scott through the short build-up, and

**M
A
Y**

on a day where the stakes are extremely high. Mark Cooper is the chosen one. All fans would agree he was an inspirational captain of FGR during their Conference struggles. Did he ever miss a penalty?

The play-offs are always crammed at the end of the league programme and give little time for players and fans alike to prepare for this most important of games. Undaunted, the Forest Green Rovers fans join the convoy of coaches while others use rail and road to head up town. London Town. The city that sees you coming, where money is a leading player and Mammon is the star striker.

It is the home of the rebuilt Wembley Stadium, the mortgage of which fans will be paying for the next 500 years. Forest Green supporters will not be dwelling on that; they have more important fish to fry all the way from Grimsby Town. The fishmongers are hot favourites to win the final. The positive thinkers among Forest Green fans are hoping the rekindled spirit in the team will be enough to cause an upset.

It was a gloriously sunny day as Kendo slipped the clutch and set Rovers rollin' to Wembley. Over a beer or two on Olympic Way it was plain to see Grimsby fans were out in force. Inside the stadium over 17,000 gathered with between 4,000 and 5,000 supporting the village side. Forest Green management team of Bartlett and Cooper preferred Jefford over Jennings and Pipe over Sinclair. The team's failings of late have been in attack. Today Williams and Guthrie lead the line.

From the kick-off Forest Green hold their own for the first half-hour of the contest as both sides probe for an opening. The first alarm for Rovers came on ten minutes when a Nolan free kick picked out Bogle whose downward header from six yards was well saved by Arnold, falling low to his left. Rovers replied in kind when M-Brown from wide on the right created a marvellous chance for Guthrie, who was unable to make contact with the ball as it fizzed across the six-yard box. It encouraged Rovers and on 32 minutes M-Brown fired in a shot from distance that was fumbled by Grimsby keeper McKeown, who was rescued by his defence who slammed the ball away for a corner.

This seemed to wake Grimsby up and in the final ten minutes of the half they took the game by the throat. The Grimsby midfield, already a dominant factor, stepped up a gear, forcing Rovers to concede free kicks and went closest to scoring on 40 minutes when Nathan Arnold hit a superb shot from 20 yards that Arnold at full stretch fingertipped against the right-hand post. It was only a brief respite as the pressure was applied.

Winning another free kick out on the right, Nolan swung in a cross to the back post. Arnold hesitated and was in no-man's land when Bogle won the header via Carter, and the ball was past him inside the right-hand post. Grimsby fans took off.

It was time for calm from Rovers. Anything but. Within a minute it was two nil. A raid down the left saw Robertson cross; Jefford cleared to Frear on the edge of the area but he only hit the ball straight to Nathan Arnold, who hit a fierce shot that his namesake spilled at the feet of Bogle, who gleefully smashed the ball past him and Forest Green were reeling. Gone in 60 seconds springs to mind as the half-time whistle sounded.

Rovers fans had that hollow feeling inside as they spent their life savings trying to fill it with beer and hot dogs during the interval. With Moore absent from the bench, Bartlett had little option but to introduce Parkin for the second half. He could have taken off the ineffective Guthrie or Williams but chose the latter. Five minutes in and M-Brown was again the provider as Forest Green pressed forward in an effort to gain a foothold in the match. His wicked low cross from the right beat the defence and landed at Parkin's feet. From a yard out he somehow contrived to screw the ball wide. FGR fans were bereft.

They kept up the momentum and caused the Grimsby defence some anxious moments. McKeown in goal looking decidedly shaky as on more than one occasion they had to scramble the ball clear.

It was left to Forest Green's most talented player to give his team hope. From 30 yards out on the right he struck an awesome shot into the top corner inside the right-hand post and for the only time in the game the Grimsby choked on their fish pies. A goal fitting for the stage it was on but it was not to be for Rovers as their opponents regained their poise and soaked up what little pressure was applied.

On 75 minutes Nathan Arnold forced a good save from Steve Arnold. Bartlett made the changes – Jennings for Jefford and Jeffrey for Guthrie – but it made no difference. Rovers tired towards the end and in added time Grimsby hit back, and when the ball was only blocked to Nathan Arnold, the striker rounded the keeper and sent his side into the Football League.

Rovers' attack is a real problem. Frear has been out of form; his only highlight today was appearing on the front of the programme and Guthrie looked out of his depth. Parkin will not watch the replay either. It's easy to pick fault but the team gave it their best shot and had to concede to the better side. riumph is built on the disappointment of others. It has been a season where Forest Green Rovers probably flattered to deceive but supporters should not despair. The Mark Cooper Factor will kick in. The 2016/17 season awaits.

MAY

MY FGR EXPERIENCE AT WEMBLEY

FGR Student Ambassador Elsie Heslop

On Sunday the 15 May, over 4,000 Forest Green Rovers fans came along to watch FGR play against Grimsby in the play-off final at Wembley. The winner would then get promoted to League 2 along with Cheltenham, who automatically went through as they won the League.

My family and I got to Wembley early and had a look around the area, but as we were exploring all we could see were Grimsby supporters who were everywhere. They must have had a pretty long journey to Wembley to see their team. However, we knew that Grimsby would play their best as this was their fourth time in a play-off final so they knew the ground well.

FGR had recently made their youth team coach caretaker manager: Scott Bartlett, who has been coaching the team for the last couple of games for FGR. Even though Grimsby were the favourites to win, we still tried our best not to make it easy for them. It was a hard-fought first half and just on half time Grimsby scored a lucky goal from a deflection which upset the way Forest Green played. Grimsby were clever and used this to their advantage and immediately scored another lucky goal after our goalkeeper dropped the ball. So far things weren't going to plan.

Second half and Grimsby got a little bit worried when Keanu Marsh-Brown scored a brilliant goal right into the top corner of the net, easily the best goal of the game. We were all up on our feet cheering as loud as we could which also kept the Grimsby fans quiet. After that, we had another couple of shots which could have put us level but unfortunately we couldn't finish them off, meaning that the score was still 2-1.

It was nearing the end of the game when Grimsby had to be really cruel and score another goal, again, another lucky goal. My head was in my hands as I realized that League 2 was not in our reach, but I wasn't annoyed or disappointed. Little old FGR went to Wembley, scored at Wembley, and scored the best goal of the game. That's something to be proud of. The players tried their best and you can't ask for much more.

In the end the score was 3-1, meaning we remain in the National League. But there are still high hopes to beat our record season next year and win the league to get automatic promotion or to play again at Wembley Stadium in next season's play-off final. So, Grimsby and Cheltenham are going through into League 2 but that means two teams from League 2 have to be relegated and those teams are Dagenham & Redbridge and York. They will be joining us next season in the National League. Look forward to next season, and I'll see you there!

COME ON YOU ROVERS!

Poets' Corner

This concluding chapter sets out the best poetic verse to appear on the FGR Fans Forum's Poets' Corner as judged by me (!) with the guiding hand of the Bard himself, The Farmcotian. The poems are set out chronologically with a line or two explaining their context. Some posters found poetry difficult to reconcile with a football forum. For me though, it is the diversity of expression that makes the Forum such a tonic to visit

Evidently Nailsworthtown
The Farmcotian

(Written in the style of John Cooper Clark – at the beginning of the season after the friendly victory v Cardiff City)

Many on this forum have a flipping mope
They'd tell you we had no flipping hope
The season might as well flipping end here
It'll be a year with no flipping cheer

But at the flipping TNL tonight
The new lads were a flipping delight
No flipping lump ball today
On the flipping ground the new lads played

An unknown keeper flipping arrived
'Cause none of our keepers had flipping survived
From flipping Hartlepool he had flipping driven
Played like a flipping hero, MoM given

The season looks full of flipping hope
The new lads will be no flipping joke
So let us cheer them to the flipping rafters
Promo flipping beckons, these lads are flipping grafters

A difference of opinions
The Farmcotian

(This poem was inspired by spats on the Fans Forum over the extent of free expression)

A difference of opinions just means you and I
On different subjects do not see eye to eye
And who is wrong or right is not for me to say
Since we do look at life in a different way.

On any one subject all will not agree
And what's right to you may not be right to me
If we all thought the same how boring we would be
Though 'tis said what we dislike in others in ourselves we do see.

'Tis our individuality from others that place us apart
But what does matter most is you be kind of heart
And you do not find joy in another's downfall
And you embrace the truth in a fair go for all.

We are all individuals for want of a better name
And even those with similar views not exactly the same
Despite a common ancestry and similar DNA
We all look at life in a different way.

Of similar things many of us may dream
But we all are quite different or so it does seem
Though we can be judged by the company we keep
The karma we sow is the karma we reap.

It is our differing views on forums such as this
Which shows our love of club – such bliss
So let us ensure there is room for all views
To share FGR stories – spread the news

Let's hope we can agree to disagree.

Unattributed home game
Chris Gump

There's a breathless hush at The New Lawn tonight
All to play for and the match to win
A pristine pitch and a blinding light,
Minutes to play and the last sub in.
And it's not for the sake of a ribboned coat,
Or the selfish hope of a season's fame,
But his captain's hand on his shoulder smote
"Play up! play up! and play the game!"

Welling
Pitchfork

(With reference to Leonard Cohen's 'Suzanne', and her tea and oranges)

Now Ady takes your hand
And he leads you to The New Lawn
His team are wearing their colours
From Ecotricity's best designers
And the sunset is so beautiful
On the hillside in the distance
And Dale shows you where to look
Among the vegan food and wildflowers
There are heroes on Matt's green grass
There are cheering fans on the terrace
They are shouting for more goals
Will it be 1-0 forever?
While Ady brings on new players
And you want the game to finish
And you want three points collected
Now we know that we can trust them

(For she's touched your perfect body with her mind.)

Barrow boys come south
The Farmcotian

Barrow newly promoted to the National League
Visit the TNL for the first time

It's early in the season so no fatigue
We hope they'll not disturb our starting paradigm

Custodians they have two
Dixon currently is number one
But five conceded – quite a few
For only two played – we should break through

At the back the current four
Are Ashton, Cowperthwaite but two
Livesey and Grand have yet to shut the door
We should three or four accrue

A midfield that a coach and horses have run through
Fofana, Mellor, Harvey and Cook
Frear, Sincs, Wedge and Kurtis should turn the thumbscrew
Our midfield should easily run the playbook

Up front Symington and Hayworth have led the line
But their forum is critical of the formation being played
Say manager Edo is suspect, is tactically blind
With skill and panache this team should be flayed

Our strikers must be more on the mark
More shots on target should be our desire
Aim for three or four should be in our ballpark
As Grimsby did – it'll be what Ady requires

We were all impressed with the new style of play
It's far too early in the season to see whether it will last
But playing from the back I hope is here to stay
Maxted's quick distribution has caught on fast

Frear's got belief and takes defenders on as though they don't exist
And his crossing has been superb
O'Connor for me is the link we have missed
With Parkin or Guthrie many a centre half will perturb

So as far as I can see the future is very bright
With so many good players on the bench
In Ady and Jamie we trust to get it right
Against the 'might' of Barrow our thirst should we quench
The mighty Rovers will the Bluebirds smite.

(After the match another verse was added, prompted by the regrettable behaviour of
a minority of Barrow fans)

But what would Barrow's fathers and mothers of yesteryear make of how
Their descendants represent a proud history and heritage now
They'd be ashamed to call them sons and daughters who disgrace
Traditions forged in northern climes at industry's white hot furnace

Untitled
Pitchfork

New players have been added
To put us in with a shout
Are we better for it?

Today we found out
Fourteen of our players took to the field
We saw, we heard, all was revealed
Forest Green are now top of the league

Rework of Jimmi Hendrix song
Voodoobluesman

(Wah wah pedal at the ready!)

Well we're not quite next to a mountain
But we stand at the top of a hill.
Yes we're not quite next to a mountain
but we stand at the top of a hill.

We pick up all the players and make a team
Who raise a noise in the stand.
Cause we are Forest Green, Forest Green
Lord knows we are Forest Green.

(air guitars out, gents and ladies)

We will play for all the sweet time
And put it right in the back of the net.
Oh we'll play for all of the sweet time
And put it right in the back of the net.

If we don't see you in this league
We'll meet ya in the next
And don't be late, don't be late.
Cause we are Forest Green, Forest Green
Lord knows we are Forest Green.

New words to 'Wild Thing'
The Farmcotian

'Wild Wing' – Come on South Standers, sing it with me!

Right wing, you make my heart sing
Oh
You beat your full back – it's groovy
Right wing
Left wing Elliot I think you move me
But I want a goal for sure
Come on and cross it to Kurtis one more time
We're winning
Right wing, Keanu makes my heart sing

Oh
He makes like a movie
Cross it again
Rovers swing
Yeah
Rovers swing you know you move us
It's promotion for sure
Come on and sock it to Lincoln one more time
Oh yes we love ya
FGR swings, and makes our hearts sing

You make scoring and winning, groovy
Yeah Keanu on right wing
Yeah Elliot on left wing
Yeah yeah Keanu pulls strings
Yeah yeah yeah on the right wing
Oh sock it to me
Wild wingers

Barrow, Boreham Wood, Lincoln precis
The Operator

'Tis no wonder we are perched on top of the league
With 14 players pitchbound we were bound to succeed
Barrow had ten then nine
What a pantomime

Boreham Wood was similar though better
Only one got a red letter
So will it be eleven, ten or nine
to struggle against our team so sublime?

We can take on Lincoln's men
Even if we are down to ten
With Parkin's shots from halfway
We will see another winning day

The Warrior
The Farmcotian, after Bromley & Chester

He's leading us to heights anew,
Leading the team to an Olympian view
A hundred and twenty-five years of history
Our Pipey could lead us on a magical Odyssey.

At The New Lawn, we gathered there,
Expectant that Bromley we would ensnare.
But they had a belief of their own
Newly promoted, pace and grit would be shown.

(Chant)
Pipey is a warrior,
A slave he'll never be
A soldier and a conqueror
A hero to thee and me

We started with vim and vigour
But could we pull that scoring trigger
No sooner had Aaron answered the call
Than Bromley made the score one all

From then on it was squeaky bum time
No fluency, harried defenders holding the line
Blurred of vision, injured and scarred
But one showed the courage, stood guard, battle hard

Pipey is a warrior,
A slave he'll never be
A soldier and a conqueror
A hero to thee and me

To win it would not be easy
Some of our misplaced passes made us queasy
But luck was on our side once more
As Delano scrambled, poked and scored

With Super Ted our custodian sublime
He repelled the invaders time after time
And with captain courageous – body on the line
He declared "Victory will be mine!"

Pipey is a warrior,
A slave he'll never be
A soldier and a conqueror
A hero to thee and me

Before the Cheltenham Town home match
Bill Wagstaff

If we are mark'd to lose, we are enow
To do our team's loss; and if to win,
The fewer men, the greater share of honour.
God's will! I pray thee, wish not one man more.
By Jove, I am not covetous for promotion,
Nor care I who doth feed upon my cost;
It yearns me not if men my strip wear;
Such outward things dwell not in my desires.

But if it be a sin to covet honour,
I am the most offending soul alive.
No, faith, my coz, wish not a man from Forest Green.
God's peace! I would not lose so great an honour
As one man more methinks would share from me
For the best hope I have. O, do not wish one more!

Rather proclaim it, Vince, through my host,
That he which hath no stomach to this game,
Let him depart; his passport shall be made,
And crowns for convoy put into his purse;
We would not lose in that man's company
That fears his fellowship to lose with us.

This day is call'd the feast of Pennock.
He that outlives this day, and comes safe home,
Will stand a tip-toe when this day is nam'd,
And rouse him at the name of Pennock.
He that shall live this day, and see old age,
Will yearly on the vigil feast his neighbours,
And say, "To-morrow is Saint Pennock."
Then will he strip his sleeve and show his scars,
And say, "These wounds I had on Pennock's day."

Old men forget; yet all shall be forgot,
But he'll remember, with advantages,
What feats he did that day. Then shall our names,
Familiar in his mouth as household words-
Pipey the King, Parkin and O'Connor,
Guthrie and Frear, Racine and Maxted –
Be in their flowing cups freshly remem'bred.

This story shall the good man teach his son;
And Pennock shall ne'er go by,
From this day to the ending of the world,
But we in it shall be remembered –
We few, we happy few, we band of brothers;
For he to-ay that passes his ball with me
Shall be my brother; be he ne'er so vile,
This day shall gentle his condition;
And gentlemen in Nailsworth now-a-bed
Shall think themselves accurs'd they were not here,
And hold their manhoods cheap whiles any speaks
That played with us upon Saint Pennock's day.

No more the little team upon the hill
Crispin Thomas

(This composition was received from Crispin by FGR's press office)

there are llamas in a field beside the entrance
and they're posing for the passing crowd who stare
there's a big red bus that's serving drinks and nibbles
and a festival-like feeling in the air

you can say that we've no right to even be here
you can smirk and mock and there are some that will
but something's stirring here that's quite amazing
no more the little team upon the hill

we've seen club cars running on electric
and roof top solar panels on the stand
there are green flags flying sending out the message
and they're reaching out to every football fan

you can marvel at our solar robot mower
as it navigates its way in Satnav style
it's a futuristic vision of sustaining
and Forest Green lead by a country mile

there's a tasty vegan pie and mash on offer
organic as the pitch that sets the scene
there are plumbers, artists, plasterers and poets
and families with children dressed in green

and we're not in some great teeming football city
we have sheep and hills and meadows flanked by trees
we're respecting our environment and planet
we're the Rovers, come and join us if you please.

War or peace?
The Farmcotian

(Before the Guiseley home match, this came as a result of a warlike exchange of views
on the forum where, anger, passion and so on were becoming mixed. Written to point
out what passion meant to the author)

Insidiously the crepuscular, fetid thought of battle
Lodges in the minds of the forest confederates, know thine enemy.
Shall we wage war and conflict upon our adversaries
Or spread harmony, accord and good will to our foes

Is it a matter that is more momentous than 'life or death'
Or are we just dogged in our determination to conquer the field
To vanquish those that are laid bare before us
But to honour those who fall on our hallowed turf

Passion can be confused with anger, rage, conflict and even hatred
But we are stronger than that and support with emotion
Not dullness, indifference or lethargy, so if a warlike tone invades
Do not confuse with loathing, destruction or malevolence.

They are after all only words not deeds

Farmcotian's shorts
The Operator

(The Farmcotian refused to change from his shorts during our early season winning streak. It prompted a short verse from The Operator, before the Eastleigh away game which was lost!)

Farmcotian's shorts are magic
They brings us such great luck
But when Guiseley's goalie wore them
They looked like they'd got stuck

he saved them to the left of him
he saved them to his right
but when he pulled them up a bit
he lost a little height

Ohhhhhhh ...

Farmcotian's superstition
The Farmcotian, with apologies to Stevie Wonder

Ady's superstitious, the boys are on the ball,
Farmcotian's superstitious, lucky shorts say it all,
Eleven times worn we win - at least they cover his aspidistra!
Promotion is a cert, no bad luck, this run is gonna last

When you believe in things that you don't understand,
Then you suffer,
Superstition – it's bloody cold!

Ady's superstitious, and so are many fans,
Don't rid me of the problem, do all that you can,
Keep me in a daydream, keep the shorts goin' strong,
You don't wanna save me, at least it's not a thong

When you believe in things that you don't understand,
Then you suffer,
Superstition is the only way, yeah, yeah

Ady's superstitious, nothin' more to say,
'Cotian's superstitious, promotion's on its way,
Eleven matches on the bounce, hairy legs not class,
Tonight's the test – will both team and man land on their aspidistra

When you believe in things that you don't understand,

Then you suffer,
Superstitions the only way, yeah, yeah, yeah

Rock on!

Far from a Chester-draws
The Farmcotian

(A different take on a narrow win)

I rarely disagree with my esteemed colleague Mr Gump
I witnessed a game that was great and didn't give me the hump,
But what we do about the first ten minutes, I don't know
We're limp, lifeless, under power, no passion, no flow

It seems to take a goal or mishap to release them from a trance
But this is an area that Ady's team talk must lance
'Cause in the last twenty-five minutes of the half the team
Played the ball on the ground, and Parkin played like a dream

Keanu pleases and infuriates in equal measure, his work rate is poor,
the goal was sublime but his passing to use an analogy is manure
As to man of the match it was a close-run thing
The Beast means so much but to me for the day Cloughie was king

We were lucky they were poor in the air
And I still worry we put the ball up there
Once we play those passing moves on the floor
It is a style we appreciate, cheer and adore

I have never seen Ady so up for the fight
He cajoled, shouted, pleaded with all his might
And don't ever say again how comatose the East Stand are
We were the most vocal we have been in the season so far

Was the person who gave JJ man of the match actually at the game?
His performance in the first twenty minutes was shaky, edgy, tame
Sincs and Wedge put in their usual effort and Carter came up to muster
Elliot had poor service from JJ, flat passing caused him to stutter

Finally, I wanted to say how much I enjoyed the game
It was feisty, end to end, absorbing, never tame
Better finishing could have made it even more exciting
But with games like that the casual fan FGR will be enticing.

El Glosico
Voodoobluesman

(Cheltenham Town supporter Red Robin chirped away on the FGR Fans Forum throughout the season. Always good natured and welcomed, his playful barbs drew some excellent verses from Voodoobluesman and The Farmcotian. Deservedly, The Robins had the last laugh, overhauling FGR to win the National League emphatically)

Who killed off Cocky Redrobin?
I, said Jon Parkin,
As I shot the goal in,
I killed off Cocky Redrobin.
Who saw him cry?

I, said Lady Magpie
with my little eye,
I saw him cry.

Who made his bad mood?
I, said Keanu
with my little one-two,
I made his bad mood.

Who'll please the crowd?
I, said Sinclair
with my beard and hair,
I'll please the crowd.

Who'll dig his grave?
I, said Pitchfork,
With a little hard work,
I'll dig his grave.

Who'll be the parson?
I, said Richard Atkins,
I'll give satisfactions,
I'll be the parson.

Who'll be the clerk
I, said michael,
if I can put in some capitals
I'll be the clerk.

Who'll buy the drinks?
I, said Ausie Stu
I'll fetch it in a minute or two,
I'll buy the drinks.

Who'll be chief mourner?
I, said Dreat Dane,
If it doesn't rain.
I'll be chief mourner.

Who'll carry on coughin'?
I, said John Lite
if it's not through the night,
I'll carry on coughin'

Who'll bear the pall?
We, said FGR-RJS,
both Greeners & Junior,
We'll bear the pall.

Who'll write a psalm?
I, said Farmcotian
I'll write yet another one
I'll write a psalm.

Who'll toll the bell?
I, said Joycie
In my loud FGR voice(y)
I'll toll the bell.

All the CTFC forum
fell a-sighing and a-sobbing,
when they heard the bell toll
for poor Cocky Redrobin

When the red red robin comes sob sob sobbing along
The Farmcotian

(This verse proved how wrong one can be)

When old red red robin comes sob, sob, sobbing along along
He'll be regretting his decision to support the Robins all nightlong
Wake up, wake up you dunderhead get promotion out of 'yer head
Cheer up, cheer up, the league is dead, pray, lose, cry, be unhappy

In our Dale we trust
The Farmcotian

(In November 2015 there seemed to be some anti-Dale Vince and -Ady Pennock
stirrings and this poem was written to address some of those views)

It's in our Chairman Dale Vince we must trust
From what I see and read he has saved Forest Green
To get behind his aims and policies is a must
We must realize that without him we'd be has-beens

Dale seems to think our Ady's doing a good job
But a few seem to disagree with that point of view
Despite us being top of the league, he will allegedly rob
FGR of outright promotion – not enough points we'll accrue

But it is vegan food that is on most fans' minds
But as our Dale says he is not ramming it down our throat
But you can bring your own food – it takes all kinds
But for me the vegan food on sale will always get my vote

It seems our Chair is in it for the long haul and that we should applaud
The investment, publicity, sustainability he has brought to FGR
The sheer energy and innovation cannot be ignored
In my honest opinion he's Dale Vince, the Forest Green Rovers star

The Charge of the Green Brigade
The Lord Farmcotian

(A reworking of Lord Tennyson's poem in tribute to our hard-working team and
management)

Top of the league, top of the league
Top of the league, nearly
Forest in the Vale of the Green
They thundered and they plundered
Forward my brave bonny boys
Strike at their defence, our general said
Forest in the Vale of the Green
They plundered and they thundered.

Forward the Green Brigade
Was there a man afraid

Not that our captain knew
Sometimes they stumbl'd
No goals, but several in reply
No one knew the reason why
Points lost; forwards goal shy
Into the heat of the battle
They thundered but blundered

Robins on the top of them
Whites immediately below them
Robins again confront them
Rovers tore them asunder
Storm'd them with shots, gave them hell
Under the Greens' onslaught every team fell
The bell tolled the death knell,
Into the heart of the fight
We all raised the decibels
Our mighty team thundered

Rovers' glory can never fade
All the great matches that we've played
All league teams shuddered
Honour the fight that they've made
Honour our Green Brigade
As they plunder and thunder.

A Christmas song
Voodoobluesman

(A fairytale of Forest Green, with apologies to the mighty Shane McGowan)

It was Christmas Eve, Dale
In the East Stand
An old man said to me, "Won't win another one"
And then he sang a song
"Come on you Rovers"
I turned my face away
And dreamed about league two

Got on a lucky one
Came in at ten to one
I've got a feeling
This year's for me and you
So happy Christmas
I love you FGR
I can see a better time
When all our dreams come true

They've got cars plugged 'on charge'
They've got rivers of green
But the wind goes right through you
It's no place for the team
When you first took my eye
On a cold pre-season game
You promised me
League 2 was waiting for me
You were handsome
But not pretty

Lords of Nailsworth City
When the team finished playing
They mumbled for more
The Green Man was swinging,
All the South Stand were singing
We scored from a corner
Then charged through their half

The boys of the Famous South Stand choir
Were singing, "Rovers come on"
And the bells were ringing out
For promotion

You're a bum
You're a punk
You're an old ref on junk
Standing there almost blind on a bribe from the other side
We've got Parkin, O'Connor
Elliot and Guthrie
Happy Conference your aspidistra
I pray God it's our last

The boys of the Famous South Stand choir
Were singing, "Rovers come on"
And the bells were ringing out
For promotion
We could all be someone
We're better than anyone
I took my dreams of you
When I first found you
I kept them with me, Ady
I put them with my own
Can't make it on our own
I've built my dreams around you

The boys of the Famous South Stand choir
Were singing, "Rovers come on"
And the bells were ringing out
For promotion

Christmas ABC
The Farmcotian

A
Brilliant
Christmas
Day
Enervates
FGR's
Gay
HOME
Interplay
Just
Keep
Lasting
Midway
Never
Offer

Passageway
Qualify
Rightaway
So
Teams
Underplay
Victoriously
Wish
Xmas Day
Zion

Christmas Day
Pitchfork

I
wrote
a poem
in the shape
of a Christmas tree
Borehamwood threatened
but Kurtis chopped them down
3 more valuable points to our
FGR
team
Enjoy your presents
HAPPY XMAS

The Boring Wood match (or Happy Christmas to all)
The Farmcotian

Have you ever been expectant at a match
And left wondering how you won?
Players playing as individuals but still snatched
Points three from a shabby show
Yet Boring Wood were summarily dispatched

Clough was towering in defence once more
He gets better with every game
Racine is sheer class so much in his game to adore
In Eliott Frear we have the fastest winger in the League
So they with The Beast are really top drawer
Today it really didn't come together, I'm afraid
Management and tactics not there, often a bore
Although substitution brought results and Kurtis scores
So Happy Christmas to all FGR fans and to you and yours

Disappointment
The Farmcotian

(Having being absent for a while, the author vented his frustration after the goalless
Aldershot match)

A beautiful day for a game to win easy
But the performance was terrible, made me feel queasy
What on earth was going on
Players were strangers, paying for that was clearly a con

Yet again our MoM was a defender
We waved the white flag, total surrender

I cannot recall their goalie needing to stop a shot,
Williams the goal yawning headed over – what a clot

We have skilful players who cannot play together
Their synapses do not compute, on the same wavelength – NEVER
No Kelly again, even though in midfield we craved
Someone with intelligence, passing – is our manager depraved?

Marsh-Brown had a reasonable game today
But he hardly passes precisely, takes too many touches – ball goes astray
Wedge and Sinclair worked very hard – but played across the pitch
They need to pass forward - clearly a glitch

It cried out for a Kelly to get Frear in the game
The tactics did not change – at home most weeks it's always the same
We've got the most points ever in our history
But that's down to the oppo's quality – how we're up there – to me a complete mystery
We still have a chance to go up by right
But the play-offs loom large, unlikely to give Grimsby a fright
So let us hope that Monday produces better fare
Or I'll tear out what's left of my receding hair!

Why
The Farmcotian

(After the surrender of a two-goal lead at Bromley, with apologies to Mr Kipling who does make exceedingly good cakes)

If you can't keep your head when all about you
Are keeping theirs and the manager takes no view
If you can't trust your team and most fans doubt you,
And you make no allowance for your players doubting too;
If you can sit on a lead, and not be swayed by experience,
Of so sitting before, don't deal in acquiescence
Or being afraid, don't give way to being afraid,
And yet learn, nor be scared to learn:

If we can dream – and not make dreams our master;
If we can believe – and not express our thoughts in vain;
If we can meet with Triumph and not too much Disaster
And treat those two goal leads with joy;
If our leader can bear to hear the truth we've spoken
Twisted by tactics and make a trap for our dreams,
Or watch the dreams we gave our passion to, broken,
And stoop and build 'em up again with naive stratagems:

If you can make one heap of a mess of winning
And risk it on an irrational turn of safety – we're at a loss
And draw, so we have to start again at the beginning
And never admit that it's your fault – we're still at a loss;
If you could inspire your side to strain every nerve and sinew
To serve your will long after they are bemused,
And ending up holding on when there is no reason to
Except your will which inexplicably says to them: "Hold on!"

If you can talk with your supporters and keep their aims in view,
Or take advice – and not lose a proper practical touch,
If neither foes nor allies can understand you,
If all men wish you well, but not too much;

215

If you can learn the art of tactics and eschew the quest for a draw
With only sixty minutes' worth of distance run,
Ours would have been the Championship and everything it brings with it,
And – what is more – you could even become a manager one day, my son!

Shakepeare reworked
The Farmcotian

(These verses followed the watching of Shakespeare's anniversary with automatic promotion a fast escaping dream the Bard was called upon for his intervention and *divine* inspiration!)

Is this the play-offs I see before me.
The hope of promotion in my head? Come, let me dream here
We have it not and yet I believe in thee still
This may be my fatal vision and not sensible
But just a mirage, it is perhaps not in sight
A dagger in the heart, our early season form a false creation
An apparition, a dream in my fevered brain?

I see thee yet but thy form is a tale of woe
And it is on hope that I must draw
Who marshall'st us and has failed in that duty?
Battle tactics askew and passion low
Mine eyes see the detritus which passes for our play
From bad to worse, yet the Holy Grail I see thee still
But we must perform again, stir the sinews and the blood
Which was so before – failure – there must be no such thing.

The badgers strike back
The Farmcotian

(A verse by FGR's own Richard Joyce moved The Farmcotian to suggest restoration of the Badger mascot)

We lost our badger mascot a few seasons back
But now the real badgers have gone on the attack
"That ridiculous gargoyle that replaced our race,
Was a heinous crime – a disgrace"

Now they have to creep in at the dead of night
Grubbing for morsels in row H – a desperate plight
"We yearn for our black and white icon to return – it's been too long
"Bring our badger cousin back" – you know we can't be wrong!

Positivity
The Farmcotian

(A one-verse hope for the play-offs)

When all about you are doubting your attitude, fight, grit
Prove them all wrong, play hard for your badge and club
Our opponents into the pitch, their noses rub
'Cause if we win at Wembley – who gives a s**t

The leaving
The Farmcotian

(A celebration of the life and times of Ady Pennock, bidding him a fond farewell. He
was sacked just before potentially the most important games in the club's history.
However, few supporters mourned his passing)
It has been an interesting and rollercoaster ride
When Ady was appointed as the manager of our side
Maintaining in his first season the status quo
When it became clear Hockaday had to go

Then fifth, our highest, and a play-off place
It became clear, a better team, now firmly in the race
Some still had reservations but who could ignore
The next season would be a cracker a team to adore

Wow – what a start we had to the 15/16 season
Undefeated, Champions – other thoughts, well treason
But the first signs of discord started to appear
Results were suffering but surely nothing to fear

Fans favorites being left out, even sold to our rivals,
Good forwards sold, given away, the inferior arrivals
We couldn't score to save our lives, fans began to question
Attitude, management, favoured players' selection

And so it became clear as the play-offs beckoned
Dale realized the slide was scary – not good enough second
Many thought Ady had lost the dressing room
The last nine matches (an early season parallel) increased the gloom

And so we must look to the immediate task in hand
Promotion to the League with our Scott in charge – dreamland
We thank Ady for our progress but not our style
And wish him well, find a new club, not long in exile

But we need a new manager who must be in place close season
Experience, man-management skills, list high in the reasons
Much to do, new contracts, a playing style with panache
New groundsmen, a pitch worthy of players cutting a dash

So to Ady Pennock we say goodbye and a good new job you'll pluck
But beware of teams like Leeds who recruit men down on their luck
I'm sad to say that Rovers future is better with you leaving
Thanks for getting us halfway up the mountain and in the dream believing

To the play-offs
Greeners

On a hill in Gloucestershire
Lived a man who loved the earth
And he told us of a life
In the land of wind machines

So he bought the club that we love
And he changed the kit to green
Now we'll march to Wember-ley
To cheer on Forest Green

We all follow the mighty Forest Green,
The mighty Forest Green, the mighty Forest Green
We all follow the mighty Forest Green,
The mighty Forest Green, the mighty Forest Green!

And our friends in the eesi end,
Many more of them in the main stand
And the band begins to play

(full speed ahead Mr Parkin, full speed ahead!
full speed over here sir,
action stations! action stations!
aye, aye sir, goal!
Heaven, Heaven!)

As we live a life of ease (life of ease)
Everyone of us (everyone of us)
Has all we need (has all we need)
Sky is blue (sky is blue)
Shirts are Green (shirts are Green)
We're the mighty (we are the mighty)
Forest Green (Forest Green)
We all follow the mighty Forest Green,
The mighty Forest Green, the mighty Forest Green
We all follow the mighty Forest Green,
The mighty Forest Green, the mighty Forest Green!

We all follow the mighty Forest Green,
The mighty Forest Green, the mighty Forest Green
We all follow the mighty Forest Green,
The mighty Forest Green, the mighty Forest Green!

Exhaustion, disbelief and emotion
The Farmcotian

(After the momentous play-off second leg match that saw Rovers win through to the play-off final)

That emotion this morning is still raw
Did I really witness what I thought I saw
Have we really reached that hallowed ground
North, South and East fans, ne'er heard such a sound

Exhaustion of the players may be naught to the fan
Watching this match between the fingers of both hands
Our lads could do something about the match
They could play, fight, and the opposition dispatch

But we the observers sat, stood and squirmed
Until the blessed relief of the whistle, Wembley confirmed
Exhausted, tired, happy, enervated, but still disbelief
Dover were best, but we prevailed, overwhelmed with relief

It's the spirit that players, management and fans showed
The transcended the game, senses set to overload
The outpouring of joy at the final whistle
Led to the tone and the feeling behind this epistle

So as I sit here with smile, exhaustion but above all jubilation
Still in shock that last night was not an hallucination
We are really are Wembley-bound and we go with the expectation
Of Football League, exhaustion, tears, joy but above all celebration

Come on you Rovers!

Words for what they are worth
The Farmcotian (and 'the Bard')

(Tribute to FGR's record-breaking season)

I wandered lonely as a fan
Who sits on high o'er Cotswold hills,
Across the valley I scan
A host of lime green shirts – chills, spills and thrills;
A new season starts, beneath Forest Green trees,
Hopefully not stuttering or guttering but performing please.
Continuous are ours stars that must shine
and twinkle on The New Lawn sward,
They stretched in 4-4-2 line
Put opposition to the sword:
Two thousand fans saw I at a glance,
Tossing their heads, singing Rovers chants

The east stand tried their best; but they
Ne'er out-did the south stand singing in glee:
A poet could not but be gay,
In such a companionable company:
I gazed – and gazed – but little thought
what joy the Rovers show to me had brought:

For oft, when on my couch I lie
In usually vacant or contemplative mood,
The lime green and black flashes upon that inward eye
The bliss of three points gained, loyalty renewed;
And then my heart with pleasure fills,
And rejoices once again o'er those Cotswold Hills.

2015/16 Statistics

VANARAMA NATIONAL LEAGUE TABLE

Pos	Club	P	W	D	L	F	A	W	D	L	F	A	GD	Pts
1	Cheltenham Town	46	17	5	1	49	13	13	6	4	38	17	57	101
2	**Forest Green Rovers**	46	15	3	5	37	17	11	8	4	32	25	27	89
3	Braintree Town	46	13	6	4	24	12	10	6	7	32	26	18	81
4	Grimsby Town	46	13	6	4	44	17	9	8	6	38	28	37	80
5	Dover Athletic	46	13	5	5	43	22	10	6	7	32	31	22	80
6	Tranmere Rovers	46	12	2	9	31	23	10	10	3	30	21	17	78
7	Eastleigh	46	13	5	5	32	23	8	7	8	32	30	11	75
8	Wrexham	46	13	4	6	48	27	7	5	11	23	29	15	69
9	Gateshead	46	9	4	10	33	39	10	6	7	26	31	-11	67
10	Macclesfield Town	46	10	5	8	28	21	9	4	10	32	27	12	66
11	Barrow	46	11	8	4	38	26	6	6	11	26	45	-7	65
12	Woking	46	9	7	7	36	29	8	3	12	35	39	3	61
13	Lincoln City	46	10	7	6	37	25	6	6	11	32	43	1	61
14	Bromley	46	11	4	8	38	26	6	5	12	29	46	-5	60
15	Aldershot Town	46	7	4	12	23	31	9	4	10	31	41	-18	56
16	Southport	46	6	7	10	34	44	8	6	9	18	21	-13	55
17	Chester	46	9	8	6	43	29	5	4	14	24	42	-4	54
18	Torquay United	46	7	5	11	26	33	6	7	10	28	43	-22	51
19	Boreham Wood	46	5	7	11	18	24	7	7	9	26	25	-5	50
20	Guiseley	46	8	7	8	33	38	3	9	11	14	32	-23	49
21	Halifax Town	46	6	10	7	35	43	6	2	15	20	39	-27	48
22	Altrincham	46	8	9	6	34	30	2	5	16	14	43	-25	44
23	Kidderminster Harriers	46	5	7	11	21	29	4	6	13	28	42	-22	40
24	Welling United	46	5	6	12	21	33	3	5	15	14	40	-38	35

CLUB STATISTICS

Date	Opponents	Atten	Result	Goals	MoM	Pos
08/08/15	Altrincham	975	Won 1-0	Parkin	Sinclair	7
Tues 11 Aug 15	**Welling United**	**1076**	**Won 1-0**	**O'Connor**	**Wedgbury**	**4**
Sat 15 Aug 15	**Barrow**	**1217**	**Won 4-0**	**O'Connor (2), Guthrie, Racine**	**Racine**	**1**
Tues 18 Aug 15	Boreham Wood	464	Won 1-0	Guthrie,	Guthrie	1
Sat 22 Aug 15	**Lincoln City**	**1385**	**Won 3-1**	**Jennings, O'Connor, Parkin**	**Sinclair**	**1**
Sat 29 Aug 15	Kidderminster Harriers	1905	Won 2-0	Marsh-Brown, Parkin	Pipe	1
Mon 31 Aug 15	**Bromley**	**1764**	**Won 2-1**	**Jennings (2)**	**Maxted**	**1**
Sat 5 Sep 15	Chester	2163	Won 2-1	Frear, O'Connor	Frear	1
Sat 12 Sep 15	**Southport**	**1535**	**Won 2-1**	**Marsh-Brown, O'Connor**	**Bennett**	**1**
Tues 15 Sep 15	Woking	1775	Lost 1-2	Guthrie	Maxted	1
Sat 19 Sep 15	Macclesfield Town	1311	Lost 1-4	Parkin	Maxted	1
Tues 22 Sep 15	Cheltenham Town	3127	Drew 2-2	Pipe, Guthrie	Pipe	1
Sat 26 Sep 15	Gateshead	1256	Lost 0-1		**Sinclair**	1
Sat 3 Oct 15	Grimsby Town	5034	Drew 1-1	Parkin	Frear	1
Tues 6 Oct 15	Aldershot Town	1353	Won 3-0	Guthrie, Carter, O'Connor	Carter	1
Sat 10 Oct 15	**Guiseley**	**1749**	**Won 3-0**	**Frear, Parkin, O'Connor**	**Parkin**	**1**
Tues 13 Oct 15	Eastleigh	2884	Lost 2-3	O'Connor, Frear	O'Connor	1
Sat 17 Oct 15	Tranmere Rovers	2133	Lost 0-2		**Racine**	1
Sat 24 Oct 15	Margate (FAC 4Q)	1302	Won 2-1	Marsh-Brown, Guthrie	Marsh-Brown	-
Sat 31 Oct 15	**Chester**	**1561**	**Won 2-1**	**Parkin, Marsh-Brown**	**Jennings**	**1**
Sat 7 Nov 15	AFC Wimbledon (FAC 1)	2465	Won 2-1	Carter, Frear	Clough	
Tues 10 Nov 15	Welling United	660	Drew 1-1	Guthrie	Frear	2
Sat 14 Nov 15	**Dover Athletic**	**1661**	**Won 3-1**	**Jennings, Frear, Carter**	**Frear**	**2**
Sat 21 Nov 15	Cheltenham Town	5449	Drew 1-1	Carter	Carter	2
Mon 23 Nov 15	Bristol City (GSC 1)	127	Won 2-1	O'Connor, OG	Marsh-Brown	-
Sat 28 Nov 15	**Altrincham**	**1292**	**Won 2-0**	**Parkin (2)**	**Parkin**	**2**
Sun 6 Dec 15	Oxford Utd (FAC 1)	4618	Lost 0-1		Arnold	-
Sat 12 Dec 15	Havant & Water'ville (FAT 1)	266	Lost 0-2		Clough	-
Sat 19 Dec 15	**Boreham Wood**	**1356**	**Won 1-0**	**Guthrie**	**Frear**	**2**

Date	Opponents	Atten	Result	Goals	MoM	Pos
Sat 26 Dec 15	Torquay United	2051	Lost 1-4	Marsh-Brown	Frear	2
Mon 28 Dec 15	Kidderminster Harriers	2110	Won 3-0	Parkin, Williams, Guthrie	Wedgbury	2
Fri 1 Jan 16	Torquay United	1907	Won 3-1	OG, Marsh-Brown, Carter	Marsh-Brown	2
Sat 16 Jan 16	Lincoln City	1975	Won 1-0	Marsh-Brown	Marsh-Brown	2
Sat 23 Jan 16	Braintree Town	1507	Won 1-0	Parkin	Moore	1
Tues 26 Jan 16	Southport	707	Won 1-0	Guthrie	Clough	1
Sat 30 Jan 16	Macclesfield Town	1617	Won 2-1	Jennings, Clough	Jennings	1
Sat 6 Feb 16	Wrexham	3891	Drew 2-2	Carter, Williams	Jennings	2
Sat 13 Feb 16	FC Halifax Town	1329	Won 2-0	Parkin, Frear	Sinclair	2
Sat 20 Feb 16	Eastleigh	2221	Won 2-1	Parkin (2)	Parkin	2
Tues 23 Feb 16	Guiseley	550	Won 1-0	Williams	Pipe	2
Sat 27 Feb 16	Barrow	1233	Drew 2-2	Moore, Marsh-Brown	Frear	2
Fri 4 Mar 16	Grimsby Town	2242	Lost 0-1		Racine	2
Sat 12 Mar 16	Gateshead	887	Won 1-0	Jennings	Jennings	2
Mon 14 Mar 16	Shortwood United (GCC Q-F)	319	Won pens	Guthrie	Kelly	-
Sat 19 Mar 16	Tranmere Rovers	5073	Drew 1-1	Carter	Clough	2
Sat 26 Mar 16	Aldershot Town	2272	Drew 0-0		Clough	2
Mon 28 Mar 16	Bromley	1455	Drew 2-2	Guthrie (2)	Kelly	2
Sat 2 April 16	Wrexham	2246	Drew 0-0		Clough	2
Sat 9 April 16	Braintree Town	740	Drew 1-1	Carter	Clough	2
Tues 12 April 16	Bristol Rovers (GSC S-F)	-	Won 4-3	Moore (2), Williams (2)	Williams	-
Sat 16 April 16	Woking	1605	Lost 1-2	Moore	Moore	2
Sat 23 April 16	FC Halifax Town	1942	Lost 0-1		Kelly	2
Sat 30 April 16	Dover Athletic	1651	Won 1-0	Williams	Racine	2
Wed 4 May 16	Dover Athletic (NL Play-Off 1st leg)	2071	Won 1-0	Williams	Clough	-
Sat 7 May 16	Dover Athletic (NL Play-Off 2nd leg)	2755	Drew 1-1	Marsh-Brown	Clough	-
Mon 9 May 16	Bishop's Cleeve (GSC Final)	264	Won 1-0	Jeffrey	Holmes	-
Sun 15 May 16	Grimsby Town (NL Promotion Final)	17,198	Lost 1-3	Marsh-Brown	Marsh-Brown	-

Acknowledgements

Even a publication as inferior as this comes on the back of much hard work and help by a cast of thousands. In no particular order, I owe much to the following:

Forest Green Rovers FC, the 'Little Club on the Hill'. My inspiration. With the backing of The Electric Chair, FGR is no longer the tiny David of old. Yet it still has the same values which snare the casual supporter and lock them in an unbreakable embrace. Supporters argue long and hard whether Forest Green is a village or hamlet or whether neighbouring Nailsworth is a village or town! Either way, there is something special that has propelled this community of less than 6,000 souls to the brink of The Football League, easily the lowest population to so aspire.

Dale Vince and his directors and team at Ecotricity and FGR. Dale is a game-changer. A genuine football man, Stroud local and possessor of a strong moral compass. On assuming control of FGR, he moved quickly to assert his personal values, including veganism, support to ecological causes and charities, sustainable policies in a number of operational areas and customer-first initiatives. Anyone who spends time with him will know that he 'does not do short term'. It has taken a while for many to come round to his way of thinking, some never will. Yet in half a dozen years, many of his 'shocking' initiatives now seem mainstream for other clubs. He has my sincere gratitude for policies that I value and for supporting charities dear to my heart, not least Gloucestershire Deaf Association of which I am honoured to be chair. Thanks too for the foreword, Dale

Jilly Cooper OBE. It has been sheer delight to get to know one of FGR's newest and most famous supporters. On finding out I was writing this book, she determined to be as helpful as possible, offered a foreword and insisted on reading the entire manuscript. Her help, tips and encouragement have been invaluable. Truly, Jilly has melted all our hearts. I'm certain the folk of the Five Valleys will be soaking up the contents of her latest blockbuster, *Mount!* Of course, many of us are in trepidation lest we crop up as characters in Jilly's latest project based on the Beautiful Game. Already, I've warned Compo, Foggy and Deep-Throat that future pre-match jaunts may have to be spiced up, so bulk orders of Viagra will be mandatory!

Peter Whitbread & David Kerry: Both have kindly volunteered many of their finest works to fill these pages under their pseudonyms The Farmcotian & Jokerman, or is it vice versa? They are the mainstay of a lively Fans Forum and true supporters in the best sense of the words

David Drew & Phil Butterworth, Foggy and Compo, not necessarily in that order. Long-time friends and constant travelling companions. David lives and breathes FGR, is Dale's club vice-chair and chair of the Advisory Board. Even in his busy past political life, David has spearheaded numerous initiatives to support and promote FGR. Phil is a clubman supreme, known to many as Pitchfork. He has had a huge part to play in FGR's community activities and has promoted the FGR Student Ambassador programme that now includes 30-odd primary, secondary & tertiary schools and colleges in Gloucestershire. His work has done more than any other in raising average attendances from 800–900 ten years back to 1,800 in 2015/16.

Richard Joyce, Tim Barnard & Heather Cook: 'Young Joycey' has been a constant source of help and is the editor of FGR's *Match Day* magazine, stadium announcer and much else besides. His match reports are the *straightest* contributions to this volume plus a welter of statistics. Tim Barnard's 'Something to Shout About' has been an invaluable reference when my memory has failed, and club statistician Heather Cook is his and Richard's guru.

Our local media moguls: Bob Hunt, John Light, Paul Furley, Ashley Loveridge, Pete Orchard and Rob Iles. One of them is Deep-Throat. We are lucky indeed to have such fine radio and newspaper journalists following our every move. All have helped me in one way or another

FGR Fans Forum. I may be biased, but a funnier more erudite football forum does not exist. I salute you my friends

The local **schools and colleges** involved in FGR's Student Ambassador programme and the peerless **ambassadors** themselves who have so helped to expand FGR as a family-friendly club.

And **everyone else** named in the book and many who are not. They know who they are even if I forget or overlook them.

Sincere thanks to you all. I hope the book does you justice